The Hindu Way of Awakening:

Its Revelation, Its Symbols

The Hindu Way of Awakening:

Its Revelation, Its Symbols

An Essential View of Religion
Swami Kriyananda (J. Donald Walters)

Crystal Clarity Publishers

Cover and book design by Christine Starner Schuppe
Original cover photo of Nataraj statue by Wayne Green
Photo of author by Christine Starner Schuppe

Printed in USA

ISBN: 1-56589-745-5

3 5 7 9 10 8 6 4 2

Crystal

Clarity

Crystal Clarity Publishers
14618 Tyler-Foote Road
Nevada City, CA 95959-8599

Phone: 800-424-1055
530-478-7600
E-mail: clarity@crystalclarity.com
Website: www.crystalclarity.com

*This book is dedicated
with gratitude, and with love:*

to "Indu" Inder Jit and Rani Bhan,
for awakening me to the need for it;

to India,
for deepening my appreciation
of the universality of truth;

to my Guru, Paramhansa Yogananda,
for awakening me to an awareness
of my higher Self;

and
to *Sanatan Dharma,*
for the eternal verities it offers to all humankind.

Table of Contents

Introduction

Hinduism is often omitted from rosters of the world's great religions. Everyone knows, of course, that Hinduism exists. Even so, it is confused in many people's minds with what they think of as Buddhism. For Buddhism fits into their concepts of what a religion ought to be. For one thing, it was founded by one individual, Gautama Buddha, who was a historic personage like Moses, Jesus, Lao Tse, Mohammed, and Zoroaster. Buddhism, moreover, like most other religions, has an organized structure (divided, like the others, into a number of sects), a set of specific dogmas, and an officially recognized Way. Moreover, like the other religions, it has its own set of clearly defined, "noble" principles for better living.

Hinduism, by contrast, seems to have merely "happened." Foreigners see in it such a bewildering array of gods and goddesses, of complex and seemingly incomprehensible ceremonies, and of confusing "explanations" for everything that most students of the subject end up merely bewildered.

A friend of mine years ago, a long-time devotee of yoga meditation practices, was able upon retirement to fulfill a lifelong dream by traveling to India. On arrival in Calcutta, he enthusiastically asked a guide to show him the spiritual sights. The man took him first to Kalighat Temple, where he was shown a goat being sacrificed to the "Divine Mother." So great was his shock that he returned immediately to his hotel, and expressed no further interest in seeing any further "spiritual" sights. When I encountered him a week later, I found him completely disillusioned with Hinduism, although still faithful to his meditation practices.

Even if the Westerner holds good intentions toward India—and my friend was certainly one such person— he may see Hinduism as containing some of the worst examples of paganism. Small wonder, then, that many people look upon Buddhism as the noblest representative of India's religion, and turn to it when wanting an Indian religion to place among the great religions of the world. For not only did Buddha found a religion: He was a religious reformer. Moreover, he offered a common-sense approach to self-betterment to which the modern mind can relate easily.

While Buddhism is relatively simple, Hinduism is complex. Hinduism recommends the worship of countless deities, many-armed, many-headed, with animal bodies or animal heads, dancing, playing on a variety of musical instruments. What, the foreigner asks, is going on? When he sees a goat being sacrificed in bloody ritual, is it any wonder he dismisses the whole show as idolatry in its most debased aspects?

By contrast, Buddhism seems, to Westerners especially, to offer a benign and palatable form of the Indian religious experience. Most students of religion know that Buddha tried to reform some of the ancient practices; they think of him as having brought order and sophistication to primitive chaos. When they prepare lists of the great world religions, they think of themselves as demonstrating respect for the religion of India by calling it Buddhism. Most of them are not even conscious of their mistake.

Buddha's position relative to Hinduism is similar, in a sense, to Martin Luther's relative to the Roman Catholic Church.* Both men were reformers, and the structure reformed by each was not supplanted by his teachings. The Catholic Church survives to this day, and has in many ways been strengthened by Luther's reforms. Hinduism, similarly, was purified and strengthened by the teachings of Buddha, and was in no way replaced by them. Most Hindus today look upon Buddha as one of their own *avataras*, or divine incarnations.

There are two aspects to Hinduism, as there are to every religion. One is outward and concerns ritual worship, traditions, and patterns of social behavior. The other is inward. This other is *essential* in both senses of the word: It contains the essence of that religion; it is, moreover, essential that this essence be understood for Hinduism really to be understood at all. This second, this essential aspect of the Hindu religion concerns the individual's relationship to God, and to higher truth.

In their inner aspect, the ancient teachings of India are so broad-based that it seems almost a contradiction of the vastness of their vision to identify it uniquely

---

*A better comparison might be the example of Jesus Christ, who was a great master. Jesus, however, unlike the others, never founded anything, but remained throughout his life a loyal Jew. Many commentators have claimed that the first actual Christian was St. Paul of Tarsus.

with any specific religion. Hinduism, in its plethora of symbols and images, is endlessly complex and therefore endlessly misunderstood, but its true mission is both simple and universal: soul-enlightenment. The way to understand this mission is to realize that it is goal-oriented, not *way*-oriented. In other words, its focus is the ultimate attainment, Self-realization in God. It is not focused on the outer rituals, which are intended merely to remind one of God. The outer teaching of Hinduism, which I call the Hindu Way of Belief, developed out of an inner vision of this universal goal of all life. To understand the outer way is not possible without first probing the inner.

The purpose of this book, then, is primarily to clarify certain deep teachings that lie, like the ocean, beneath the bewildering profusion of surface waves.

The secondary purpose of this book is to analyze a few of the symbols people commonly encounter from their very first exposure to Hinduism. I don't propose to explain those symbols in exhaustive detail, but rather to give an over-view of them that foreigners and "modernized" Indians alike may come to appreciate the Hindu Way of Belief, also, for the deep truths it contains.

For even today, thousands of years since they were first expounded by the ancient *rishi*s (spiritual sages), the religious teachings of India nourish what continues to be the most spiritually grounded civilization in the world.

Prefatory Note

This book contains, inevitably, a number of Sanskrit terms for which there are no satisfactory English equivalents. Though I have translated these terms into English, the book would, in my opinion, appear too pedantic were its pages heavily strewn with italics. What I have done, therefore, is introduce these terms conventionally in italicized form, but thereafter, at my discretion, treat them as though they existed already in English as indeed they deserve to do. For it is a genius of the English language that it welcomes foreign words so accommodatingly. Indeed, English in its antecedents isn't really a language at all; It is a synthesis of German, French, Scandinavian, Latin, Greek, and Italian, and has its own roots, besides, in Celtic, Pict, Scots, and God knows how many other indigenous languages of the English Isles. English has, more recently, been enriched by countless languages from around the world—from Indian to Eskimo, from Russian and Hungarian to Zulu.

Most of the Sanskrit words in this book have not yet been accepted officially into modern English. My alternative, which I hope is a happy one, to burdening these pages with italics has been simply to treat them as though they'd been already accepted into the family. Why not? The tradition exists already, and millions of English-speaking people the world over are already familiar with them, and use them freely without either a blush or a stammer.

Murti is an example of such a word. It is the Sanskrit for a religious or spiritual image. I tried to use it in this book, but the text at that point demanded movement with a minimum of digressive explanation. Yet in truth, *murti* serves better for describing spiritual images than its English quasi-equivalents: "image," "likeness," "statue," or "icon." I'm putting in my vote for including *murti* in our language. Should it become so, the distinction I draw between "idol" and "image" might no longer be so necessary.

Other words—"yoga," for example, and "karma"— are already in fairly common English usage, so I've omitted putting them in italics from the start.

Part One

The Revelation

Chapter One

What Is Revelation?

Revelation is a sudden and complete knowing—usually of some spiritual truth, though not always so. The certainty that revelation suggests comes not from any process of reasoning, but as a direct inspiration from the superconscious, or, more exactly, in a state of superconsciousness.

Revelation may also be less purely spiritual in nature. Composers, for example, have spoken of receiving their inspiration from higher realms: from God, as some of them have put it. Scientists, too, have sometimes had sudden glimpses into the nature of material reality for which they could not account in rational terms. The physicist Albert Einstein stated that the Law of Relativity came to him in a flash. After that experience, he labored for ten years to present it understandably to his fellow scientists.

Mahatma Gandhi's uncanny knowledge of just the right tactics to follow in the crises he faced during his struggle to free India from English rule cannot have been due to political astuteness alone. His decisions were more than intelligent: They were *intuitive;* as such, they were, at least to some degree, born of revelation.

Paramhansa Yogananda, a born leader of men, was approached in Calcutta when he was young by persons who wanted him to lead a revolution against the British. Demurring, he replied, "India will be freed during my lifetime, by peaceful means." His inner certainty in this prediction may also be classed as a kind of revelation.

Any flash of certainty that enters the mind with sudden clarity, and that is neither clouded by imagination nor merely formulated as a reasonable hypothesis, is, in its own way, a revelation.

Revelations must be in some way verifiable. That is, they must be able to withstand the test of objective reality. If they really are soul-intuitions, they will be superconscious and as such will belong to a higher, not a lower (such as subconscious), level of reality. The products of fantasy or of wishful thinking have a different quality. They might be described as tentative. Revelation doesn't merely "make sense." The deep inner certainty it conveys is absolute. It comes not as a "conclusion" to some process of thinking or reasoning, but fully developed, like the goddess Athena from the brow of Zeus.

There are, as I said, many levels of intuitive insight. By intuition one may gain access even to trivial knowledge—solutions, for example, to every-day problems. Normally, however, revelation refers to the highest order of intuition, and concerns especially the soul's relationship to God, the Absolute. Indeed, the more clearly a superconscious inspiration reveals the Divine Will, the more it deserves to be classed as revelation.

An important feature of revelation is that it is always personal; it is not public. A genuine revelation may be declared in scripture and accepted as the truth by millions, but what those millions understand of it is not *their* revelation. It is only what they have read about someone else's experience. Scripture itself can only echo revealed truth.

Words are but symbols. They do not present: They *represent*. Even when multitudes receive a revelation directly, as has in fact happened occasionally, it remains personal for each member of the crowd. If an entire nation were born blind, then suddenly given the gift of sight, the experience would be personal for each citizen. Sensory in nature, the thrill would of course diminish in time as novelties always do, but even accepting that this experience was a "revelation" of a sort to each of them, it would still be personal, and would depend on each person's ability to see.

Einstein's intuitive recognition of the Law of Relativity was a revelation in a more valid sense of the word, for it was (indeed, it could only have been) inspired by the superconscious. For us, the beneficiaries of his discovery, his revelation is not our own. Nor does it extend to those few scientists who have been able to understand it intellectually. It is a revelation only for that rare person, if such a one exists, who has been uplifted in awareness to the same degree as Einstein was during his moment of discovery.

Revelation is not static. It brings an outwardly expanding awareness, which bestows more and ever deeper insights. Einstein, after that first revelation, continued throughout his life to receive further, often amazing, insights into cosmic reality. It wasn't intellect alone that brought him those perceptions: It was the fact that he had, even if only once, touched the hem of Infinity. As he was to write many years later, the essence of scientific discovery is a sense of mystical awe before the wonders of the universe.

Meanwhile, others have been left with the mere *effects* of his revelation. Indeed, all he could give them was, in a sense, its *symbols*. The revelation was his alone.

Revelation is wisdom as distinct from intellectual knowledge. The intellect analyzes and separates, then painstakingly reassembles the parts in the hope of making them fit together again. The intellect is like a child who, after taking apart a watch, tries to put the pieces back again as they were. The intellect, though gifted at analysis, lacks the understanding necessary for anything more thereafter than synthesis. But revelation transcends reason; it perceives the essential truth of a thing in its entirety, and in a flash.

St. Teresa of Avila, in Spain, wrote, "The soul in its ecstatic state grasps in an instant more truth than can be arrived at by months, or even years, of painstaking thought and study."

Superconscious revelation perceives an underlying unity, whereas the intellect perceives only diversity. Superconscious revelation may come in an instant, whereas the intellect must plod slowly over muddy fields, its boots gathering heavy clods of definitions. Superconsciousness is solution-oriented; ordinary consciousness is problem-oriented. Theology, for example, reaches learned conclusions by careful deliberation, sometimes by heated debate, and always by a process of laborious intellectual refinement.

Revelation is ever new and ever dynamic. Intellectual definitions of revelation, on the other hand, are formulated to remain forever fixed and immutable. Revelation is expansive: theology's definitions are contractive, in the sense that they deliberately exclude other points of view but that one. The authoritative pronouncements of theologians are designed to resist challenge. Revelation is the source of all true religious inspiration. Dogma, though purporting to derive from revelation, does its best to discourage any more revelations lest they upset its carefully erected structure of reasoning.

Not every writing accepted as scripture has been founded on revelation. Friedrich Nietzsche would have been a good example of a false prophet, had anyone thought to accord him the dignity of prophet in the first place. His book, *Thus Spake Zarathustra,* has some of the ring of authentic scripture, at least in its portentous self-assurance. But although it is good literature, and is even impressive to read in brief segments, it soon betrays itself as lacking in the one essential ingredient of all scripture: consistency with the oft-stated truths of the ages. It is, rather, the raving of an ego-maniac whose life ended in madness because his human brain was not equal to the strain of his presumption.

Nietzsche's greatest fallacy was his belief that the function of philosophy is not to interpret and appraise values, but to create them. "The real philosophers," he wrote, "are commanders and lawgivers; they say: 'Thus *shall* it be!' . . . Their 'knowing' is *creating,* their creating is a lawgiving, their will to truth is *Will to Power.*" This, clearly, is not revelation but, as I said, presumption. Revelation cannot be invented. The truth itself, as Paramhansa Yogananda wrote in *Autobiography of a Yogi,* can only be perceived.

One of the hallmarks of true revelation is *consistency.* I don't mean a rubber-stamp sameness, for revelation is always, in its own way, fresh and new. Yet revelations never contradict one another.

If two travelers were to describe a city in exactly the same terms, it might be fairly safely assumed that one of them was echoing the other. Again, if they flatly contradicted each other—one of them perhaps describing the city as being surrounded by a high wall, and the other insisting that it was open on all sides to the surrounding countryside—we would assume that one of them, at least, was wrong. In either case, until we went there and saw the city for ourselves we could do no more than guess which of them had really seen the city. Only if their descriptions, though different, were not inconsistent might we assume that both of them had been there.

Some writers are adept at describing things that "eye hath not seen nor ear heard." A profane, rather than scriptural, example is the story, *Anna and the King of Siam,* about an English governess in the king's court in

Thailand during the Nineteenth Century. Westerners, lacking good reason to doubt its veracity, found the story delightful. The Thais, however, familiar with their own country and knowing a fair amount about their former king, are outraged by the book's innumerable outright inventions.

Who is to know the truth of any report, including reports of mystical revelation, if he lacks direct personal knowledge? One way of knowing at least inferentially would be if everyone writing on the subject agreed on certain essentials. Hence the importance of consistency

Where divine teachings are concerned, however, consistency with other high teachings is not enough to prove that their inspiration came from revelation. For one thing, people sometimes base their writings on the reading they have done. A well-written account of mystical experiences, such as one might encounter in a novel on the subject, might be consistent with the truth and yet not in itself be born of personal experience. The reader who lacks experience himself would need guidance to be sure whether it was really born of revelation.

There is a saying, "It takes one to know one." Usually meant derogatorily (it takes a thief, for instance, to know a thief), this saying can be applied equally well to spiritual experiences. The higher a person's own spiritual realization, the more instantly he will recognize true spiritual experience in others.

There are also objective criteria, which can be applied by everyone. And there is a *direction* of spiritual development that is relatively easy to discern: increasing inner peace, expanding awareness and sympathy, growingly impersonal love, deep soul-joy. Many are the signs—too many, indeed, to list them all here. Someone standing on a low mound would find it impossible to estimate the relative heights of Mt. Everest and Mt. Kanchenjunga, the highest and the third highest mountains in the world. From that little mound, indeed, the distinction would not even matter. Where the purpose is to rise higher, what matters is to find any hillock that is higher than the mound on which one is standing.

Considering the scriptures from this point of view, even a false scripture or one that is not born of true revelation should not be condemned, provided people draw inspiration from it. The important thing is that the inspiration they feel doesn't lower their present state of consciousness, and thereby diminish their degree of awareness. Many so-called spokespersons for spirituality delude others into imagining that some new "truth" has been discovered, one unavailable earlier during less enlightened times. Consistency through the ages is one of the surest guidelines for avoiding this error.

For if anyone should be so bold as to challenge the time-honored wisdom of the ages, as Friedrich Nietzsche did with his flash-in-the-pan philosophy, he should be ignored as a charlatan. No spiritual master has ever contradicted timeless wisdom.

Only in the spiritual field, indeed, do we encounter a fundamental consistency. Nowhere else. Where abstract principles are concerned, especially, who is there in any other field to speak for them authoritatively? Whom have innumerable "schools" of art produced to determine authoritatively the nature of good art? Whom, in business? In the field of science, "breakthroughs" are made every few years, many of which contradict tenets that long seemed firmly established. Only in the field of deep spiritual revelation is consistency the norm. Indeed, it is from superconscious insights gained into Divine Law that lesser laws have been discovered also—in art, business, science, and the humanities.

In revelation there are no surprises: There is only confirmation. Divine truths, though ever new in the sense of ever-newly inspiring, are at the same time changeless and eternal. Their *expressions* may change, but their central essence remains ever the same.

Consistency, then, is one of the hallmarks of true revelation. As waves are united by the ocean underneath them, so underneath all our restless ideas and beliefs there lies a deep stillness. And within that stillness lie soul-perceptions that have been experienced since time immemorial by the great mystics of all religions: divine love, bliss, wisdom, light, cosmic sound, and an extraordinarily heightened awareness known as ecstasy. Great saints everywhere have attained these states, regardless of their own systems of belief. In the realm of spirituality, unanimity transcends time, space, and every merely human perception of reality.

Christian writers have emphasized the progressive manifestation of God's will through history. Their view is focused on a very limited time span, culminating in events that transpired 2,000 years ago. It ignores altogether the histories of Europe, Asia, Africa, and of North and South America, as well as of other parts of the world, and is narrowed to a very small portion of the Near East.

Their focus may have a certain validity for all that, for God does also participate in human affairs, especially through the instrumentality of divinely awakened saints. There is no reason, then, to assume a radical separation between Absolute Consciousness and the relative universe. A stage play is not necessarily autobiographical, but its playwright is not therefore indifferent to the plot. Non-attachment is very different from lack of concern. Nevertheless, the essentials of revelation transcend all human realities.

Revelation is the perception of that which ever was, and ever shall be. The religions of the world, in their systems of belief, concentrate too often on that which in their eyes makes them unique: on the special ways in which their prophets, saints, or masters are different from all others; on the one special grace that animates them alone; on their own way of salvation as the surest for winning divine favor. They describe as "revelation" those truths which, they believe, set them apart from— and of course above—all other religions. Even the explanation of a revelation, however, is not the same thing as the experience of it. Though the explanations be many and diverse, the revelation itself can be only one.

One hallmark of revelation is its innate power. There is nothing vague or mystifying about its experience.

The entire universe was projected from Divine Consciousness. Scriptures born of revelation project an almost palpable aura of divine power. Ordinary books are sometimes written and offered to the world as scripture that are merely mind-born, not superconsciousness-born. Some of them even become widely accepted as scripture. If they lack that aura of divine power, though, they must be classed as human inventions, merely. They are not expressions of true revelation.

In divine power there is another quality also: a vibration of expansive joy. Scriptures based on true revelation are never melancholy, pessimistic, or depressing. True scripture conveys a spirit of infinite hope. For such, through the ages, has been the experience of everyone who has been blessed with the experience of revelation.

The insights on which the Hindu teachings are based were revelation in the highest sense of the word. That revelation is not unique to any religion. No experience of the Absolute may be claimed as the possession of one person or one religion.

An aspect of the greatness of the Indian scriptures, indeed, lies in their own claim to universality. In this, Vedic revelation is, in the words of the American philosopher Ralph Waldo Emerson, "sublime as heat and night and a breathless ocean. It contains every religious sentiment, all the grand ethics which visit in turn each noble poetic mind . . . : eternal necessity, eternal compensation, unfathomable power, unbroken silence."

Chapter Two

What Are Symbols?

Symbols are a means of bringing abstract ideas to a focus. A wedding ring, for example, helps bring to a focus that more abstract reality, marriage. People in East Asian countries remove their shoes before entering a temple; this simple gesture helps them to keep in mind that they should leave their worldly desires and attachments behind them when they pray. A Hindu monk may carry a *danda,* or staff, as a reminder to keep his attention centered in the spine.

Most symbols have meaning only to the extent that we give them meaning. In cultures where other symbols are used to indicate the married state, a wedding ring may be seen as only an ornament. To people unaccustomed to Eastern ways, removal of one's shoes before entering a temple may seem strange. (One imagines the reply: "Can't I just wipe them clean?") Visitors from cultures somewhat aggressively inclined might mistake the monk's *danda* for a defensive weapon. Usually, symbols have meaning only for people who hold the same belief systems.

Because those symbols focalize concepts that are abstract, and often complex, they may assume an importance almost equal to the realities they represent. A standard-bearer in battle will sacrifice his life rather than surrender the flag he carries. To him, to defend that flag is, symbolically, to defend his country. The desecration of symbols is generally considered a gesture of contempt for that which they represent. A symbol, then, is far more than an intellectual concept: It embodies the feelings and emotions that have come to be associated with that concept. To desecrate a flag, for example, is in a very real sense to dishonor the country for which it stands.

A painting of Krishna playing his flute awakens devotion in the hearts of Hindu devotees, because it reminds them of God calling the soul to eternal wakefulness in Him. Would the impact be the same were a person simply to state, "God calls the soul to eternal wakefulness in Him"? Not for the Hindu, certainly. The image of Krishna is inextricably interwoven with numerous inspiring stories of his childhood, each in some way symbolic of God's *lila,* or divine play, in the universe.

Religious symbols and symbolic gestures are an affirmation of affiliation, of belief, of devotion. They may command deep, and sometimes fierce, loyalties. Their appeal to human nature by-passes the necessity of thinking through a concept from the beginning whenever the subject is raised.

The strict rationalist may scoff at symbols as superstition, but in fact logic itself would be impossibly cumbersome even for him, without symbolic thinking: "x" to represent this, "y," that, and so on. A great deal of what human beings do *is* symbolic. Their symbols provide them with mental shortcuts—as much so in daily life as in religious practices. It is impossible to discount their importance, and therefore wiser to use them with full awareness of their true purpose than to brandish them blindly in superstitious ignorance.

It is also wiser not to surround oneself with so many symbols that the sheer number of them causes one to lose sight of their purpose. Simplicity is, after all, the very essence of symbolic thinking.

For bigotry develops when the abstractions brought into focus by symbols are overlooked or forgotten. Paramhansa Yogananda, author of the international best seller, *Autobiography of a Yogi,* once said, "Devotion must be kept in a state of reason, lest it become fanatical." By "state of reason" he didn't mean we should submit every devotional gesture to the scalpel of analysis, but only that we should be aware of the deeper significance behind all that we do.

For everything, ultimately, is symbolic. The universe itself manifests Infinite Consciousness, and in that sense symbolizes it. Nothing in creation is wholly as it appears to be to our senses. Material objects are only expressions of a subtler reality: Matter is but a vibration of energy. Energy is a vibration of ideas. And ideation itself is a vibration of Infinite Consciousness.

In human life, too, everything we do is symbolic in the sense that its motivations are never so straightforward as they appear. The body symbolizes, in a sense, its indwelling consciousness. For our physical postures, or "body language," make evident to others our mental attitudes—whether cheerful or sad, courageous or despairing, energetic or lazy. Not only our postures, but our outer circumstances, reflect our inner attitudes more than most of us realize.

These attitudes, in turn, express (and therefore symbolize) deeper qualities, which again symbolize still more subtle aspects of our nature. For example, why do people seek riches? Is it not because riches represent, to them, importance in the eyes of others? But, again, why do they desire that importance? Because it symbolizes to them the *self*-acceptance that they need. And why do they need self-acceptance? Usually, because they'd like to have a clear conscience. And, finally, why do they want a clear conscience? Because it symbolizes for them their soul's eternal need: acceptance by God and by the universe, through attunement with them.

Everything traces back, ultimately, to the real issues of life: Who and what are we, essentially? Whence have we come? For what end were we made? What is the final meaning of existence?

A painting expresses in symbolic form the artist's consciousness. Creation, similarly, expresses in countless symbolic forms the Creator's consciousness, displaying innumerable symbols of His absolute bliss.

To keep our devotion to symbols "in a state of reason," as Paramhansa Yogananda put it, means not to focus on them so closely that we lose the broader perspective. We should keep in mind that their meaning is larger than the symbols themselves, and we should therefore never lose sight of that larger meaning altogether. This is why certain scriptures advise one to develop "other-mindedness." They want us to preserve an awareness of hidden realities that exist behind all appearances.

Symbols point the way to that understanding. In the last analysis, however, they do only that. Understanding comes at last not through intellectual excursions, but only by the direct *experience* of truth.

Formal religion—the religion we associate with priests and theologians,—to the extent that it examines the signposts but ignores the direction in which those signs point, obscures the truth; it never clarifies it. The real purpose of religion is not to mask reality: It is to show the way to personal, inner spiritual awakening. It is to inspire people to seek the deeper truths for which symbols are simply a focus, but never a substitute.

The problem with organized religion is that it, itself, formalizes abstract realities. All things created are endowed with the dual instincts of self-preservation and self-perpetuation. The same may be said of organized religion. Its representatives, or priests, often deliberately resist attempts to remind people of subtle truths that, they fear, might render their religious structures obsolete. Formal religion owes its very existence to the need for symbols. Religious institutions exert power over people's minds to the extent that they succeed in keeping them bound to symbolism.

At the same time, those institutions *are* necessary. Without them, the very truths they represent are forgotten. It is important only that religious representatives guard against the error of institutional hubris, a "meanness of the heart" which Swami Sri Yukteswar described in *The Holy Science* as "pride of pedigree."

To ward off this error, mankind should not allow any institution to become *over*-organized.

For every religion has an inner as well as an outer aspect. The symbols of religion wouldn't even exist were it not for their inner meaning. Religion itself implies the existence of truths that are deeper than outer structure. And all religions teach, at least to some extent—to the extent, that is to say, that its priesthood doesn't feel threatened by the idea—the importance of *personal* improvement and upliftment. Every religion teaches empathy, self-expansion, kindness, and humility: These themes occur repeatedly, no matter in whose name that religion teaches.

Religion is, universally, that function in human affairs which urges people to seek a fulfillment higher than that granted by selfish gratification. The reason people turn to religion for upliftment is that everyone longs in his heart for a fulfillment that his senses cannot provide. No political system fulfills this inner need, no science, no art, no mere philosophy that doesn't emphasize actual experience over abstract theories.

Thus, for example, there exists in every religion some variant of the Golden Rule: "Do unto others as you would have them do unto you." This fact was presented in the 1950s by a student of the world's religions, Lew Ayres, in a film documentary. Ayres's intention was to prove the fundamental unity of all religions on the ground that they have their roots in this basic truth. The same message was conveyed years later in a book by the author John Ball, titled *The Fourteenth Point*. While I cannot help reflecting that

THE Hindu Way of Awakening

the Golden Rule is only a short step above ego-inspired
common sense ("Scratch my back," as the saying goes,
"and I'll scratch yours"), both Ayres and Ball were on
the track of an important idea.

For all religions do in fact try to motivate people to
refine their understanding of life, to purify their hearts'
feelings, to be compassionate, and to include others'
wellbeing and happiness in their own. Every religion,
moreover, attempts to inspire people toward expanding their consciousness beyond narrow, personal
limits.

The most meaningful symbols in every religion are
those which touch on humanity's deepest needs. A
wedding ring is a meaningful symbol, surely, but it
cannot serve this deepest need for the simple reason
that it symbolizes only the tie between two human
beings. It doesn't remind them of their soul-link to the
rest of humanity and to all Life.

Religion is the only field of activity which has the
specific goal of uplifting human consciousness toward
a higher-than-egoic identity. I do not want to suggest
that meaning can't be found outside the field of religion, for everything we do is invested with *some* meaning, whether or not we consciously understand that
meaning. Downward movement in a painting, for
example, or in a melodic line, can be recognized
instantly by the subconscious as expressing sorrow,
depression, or discouragement. Upward movement, on
the other hand,—depending on how it is expressed—
may be universally perceived as expressing happiness,

courage, or hope. There is a reason for such instinctive recognition.

For subconsciously we relate upward and downward movements to comparable directions of energy in the body. Symbols that reflect this universal awareness communicate meaning more effectively than words ever could, for they appeal to our actual, though deeper-than-conscious, experience of life. For this reason also, certain symbols transcend all cultural differences. Their resonance is universal, not cultural.

There are other universal symbols. One such is the cross. Not uniquely Christian, the cross is an expression of divine aspiration thwarted, or "crossed," by worldly desires—of devotion obstructed by the desire for selfish ego-fulfillment. The cross also suggests *a way out of* this inner conflict. Its message is to view obstructions to our spiritual development as opportunities, not as threats. For worldly desires and attachments can be transformed into compassion for all through spiritual service to them, and through sacrifice of our self-interest on the altar of a greater good. In this way, what appear at first to be obstacles can in fact become blessings, helping us to purify our sympathies until they become divine love.

The conflict between soul-aspiration and worldly desire produces sorrow. Sorrow in its turn, like a whirlpool, draws other thoughts and even other people into its vortex. This inner conflict must be resolved by making a conscious choice between the upward path in life, and the horizontal. The horizontal is the easier, and therefore the one usually selected. But the vertical represents who we really are: our true nature from which no amount of restless noise and laughter can ever separate us. The only way, therefore, to resolve our inner conflict is to choose the vertical path, no matter how difficult we find it.

The death of Jesus Christ on the cross is a refinement of that theme: the *avatar,* or divine incarnation, offering himself up to God in atonement for human sin, and embracing all mankind with the outstretched arms of divine love, that all people be inspired to realize that suffering can be transcended only by rejecting worldly attachments and by reaching up toward God with self-transcending devotion.

Thus we begin to see that symbols may have *in themselves* a certain power to transform. They can inspire us to sublimate deeper-than-conscious tendencies in ourselves, and to offer them up on the altar of universal freedom and love.

Chapter Three

The Power of Symbolism

Symbolism is a bridge between evident and subtle realities. The literal-minded person believes only in the reality of what he sees. To him, matter *is* reality; spiritual vision is an illusion. The literalist (a good designation for him, wouldn't you say?) beholds the world only in terms of its superficial diversity, not of its underlying unity. He is therefore uncomfortable with symbols. His preference is for facts, the more concrete, the better.

In the literalist's makeup there is little poetry. His understanding is neither subtle nor deep. To him, a mountain is a pile of earth and rocks; a lake, merely a body of water. Any thought that he devotes to Nature is statistical: a mountain's height, a lake's depth and circumference, the extent to which the presence of a mountain may prevent rain from reaching the nearby plains.

As a person's awareness becomes more refined, he intuits subtle relationships between diverse phenomena, and between material phenomena and the subtle realm of ideas. With developing wisdom he comes finally to see all creation as meaningful, not chaotic.

For an underlying coherence links everything together. The more refined a person's understanding, the more inclined he becomes to see symbols of spiritual truth everywhere. The dense curtain of material form conceals abstract principles. The tallness of a tree, for example, suggests mental qualities such as divine aspiration, pride, or worldly ambition.

Symbols may be artistic or poetic without necessarily being rooted in truth. They may only please the mind, or clarify some concept for us as cartoons do sometimes in poking fun at political hypocrisy. A symbol may merely serve as a memory peg: a reminder of something to be done, or to be kept in mind. Certain symbols, however, have universal relevance, especially if they derive from superconsciousness. In this case, they may have deep power, resonating with fundamental realities of existence, and thereby amplifying our awareness. Such symbols stir our hearts and uplift our consciousness; they may even awaken us to some degree of soul-recognition.

Motherhood is one such symbol. If universalized, and not depicted solely in terms of a specific mother or child, it can become a symbol of universal compassion. Universalized even more, motherhood can be seen as a symbol of the Divine Mother's infinite love and compassion for Her human children, and for all creatures.

The ocean as a symbol, too, contains spiritual power. If depicted with sweeping majesty and not close up to show only a few waves crashing together, its vastness suggests infinity, especially the infinity of divine consciousness.

I do not mean to imply that symbolism is *inherent* in any form. It is our consciousness that makes it meaningful. But consciousness is, as I've already said, the underlying reality of all matter. Considering the ocean as a symbol, then, divine consciousness is the "ocean" on which appear the innumerable waves of cosmic manifestation.

The more deeply attuned we become to divine consciousness, the more inspiring and uplifting for us are the symbols that represent that consciousness. The more attuned we become to the spiritual concepts behind a symbol, the more immediate its effect on us; it is not gradual, as the intellect labors to understand and absorb them. For symbolism is a bridge not only between evident and subtle realities, but between the familiar and the unfamiliar, the known and the unknown.

Symbols born of deep perception of a spiritual truth may have the power to stir even people who lack spiritual awareness. For a person may be steeped in materialism, and may suppress his spiritual nature indefinitely, but he can never abandon that nature completely. His soul is who he *is,* ineluctably and forever. It is the central truth of his existence, whether he recognizes it consciously or not. Thus, even if the meaning of a spiritual symbol elude our understanding, on some level of consciousness we can hardly fail to respond to it.

A painting of a high mountain, if executed sensitively and with inner awareness, may impress the average viewer as just that: a painting of a high mountain. But if he gazes at it a little longer, he may find that for some reason it makes him "feel good." Motherhood, again, consciously depicted as a symbol of compassion, may impress the "literalist" as merely a painting of a woman with a baby. But if it was executed with deep sensitivity, even the literalist may find himself enlarging on his first thought. Perhaps he'll recall his own wife or mother, and reflect affectionately on that memory. He may even, if he allows his mind the liberty of wandering a bit, surprise himself in the act of reflecting with unaccustomed expansiveness on the meaning of motherhood itself.

There is a potential for symbols to exert a definite power on the mind, more so than most people are consciously aware. For this reason, the ancient *rishi*s, or sages, of India, having decided to give outward expression to their inner realizations, did not limit themselves to simply describing them in their writings. To affect people's consciousness more deeply, they offered also the power of suggestion through symbols and allegories. By suggestive images they tried to build bridges, however tenuous, between the world of the senses and the reality they perceived, permeated with divine bliss.

High spiritual states are not dry intellectual abstractions. Far from it! they vibrate with divine love, joy, and wisdom. The symbols the rishis used, therefore, were often joyful, sometimes quite funny, and always delightful. We should view them in terms of the rishis' own cheerful familiarity with divine Truth. Not for them, the heavy curtain of funereal awe with which worldly people so often drape spiritual concepts!

The literalist may be offended, and certainly will find inexplicable, the classic tale of Krishna's theft, when a young boy, of the gopis' garments while those cowherd girls were bathing in the river. According to legend, Krishna then told them to emerge from the water one by one, arms upraised, to reclaim their property. The cynic must surely ask himself, "Is this any way for a 'divine incarnation' to behave?"

There is a good explanation, however. For God sees all of us with equal clarity, whether clothed or unclothed. It is false modesty on our part to imagine that we can hide from Him anything that we are, and anything that we think or feel in our hearts. To approach Him, we must open to Him our innermost secrets, fully accepting that He knows them already. For only by perfect openness with Him is there any hope of achieving union with Him. As Jesus Christ put it, "Blessed are the pure in heart, for they shall see God." Perfect inner purity is itself a gift of God. We can never achieve it without first "undressing" before Him, or disclosing ourselves frankly as we are to our own innermost conscience.

The poet who gave us this vignette from Krishna's *lila,* or divine play (the story was, I suspect, the poet's own invention) was having fun at the expense of the false shame with which so many people approach God. At the same time, he was offering a deep and important lesson.

It must be understood in advance, then, that the symbols described in this book, though often exuberant, are at the same time rich with meaning. A few of them may even have been *intended* to puzzle us. And a few certainly were intended to amuse.

41

I ask you, therefore, to approach them not only with the furrowed brow of deep thought, but also in a spirit of fun, when appropriate. In this way, you'll derive the greatest benefit from studying them.

Chapter Four

Symbolism in India

Symbolism, for two reasons, plays a greater role in the religion and art of India than in those of other nations. For one thing, India's is the oldest continuous civilization in the world. Its traditions extend back long before recorded history. For another, the Indian mind, having established itself firmly in the belief in a transcendental reality, is completely comfortable with an exuberance in its expression of images and allegories that comes from knowing and accepting that everything is illusory anyway. The profusion that has emerged from this cheerful "come one, come all!" attitude might be compared to an old tree, grown gnarled and twisted with age, its branches of tradition spreading outward in all directions with abandon. Initial symbols produced successive generations, like offspring. Today, even the devout Hindu must sometimes wonder what it is all about.

One of the purposes of the present book is to explain the basis for some of those symbols, and to show that the heart of all that complexity beats with simple, universal, and profound meaning.

India has managed, during its very long history, to adjust to countless turns of time's wheel, from centuries of relative enlightenment to others of widespread spiritual ignorance. Literacy itself, in times of relative enlightenment, was less highly prized than it is today. The symbolism implied by the written and spoken word—words too, after all, are only symbols for the ideas they express—was considered more of an obstruction than an aid to communication. Spiritual teachers enlightened their students by transferring their *experience* of the truth directly. They relied much less on intellectual discussion than teachers do nowadays. Their very style of writing reveals a preference for short, pithy maxims over long-winded discourses.

Even in modern times, a few enlightened masters observe the spiritual practice of *maun,* or perpetual silence. Many others, though not wholly taciturn, are relatively so. They value silence as the secret to divine communion. Even in their teaching they distrust the medium of words, considering it an indirect and unreliable way of expressing truth, since truth cannot really be understood except by direct experience.

Needless to say, the disciples of such gurus must be spiritually advanced also, else they would be unable to tune in to the master's wisdom-emanations.

Paramhansa Yogananda's *Autobiography of a Yogi* contains a significant passage about his *paramguru,* or guru's guru, Lahiri Mahasaya. Swami Sri Yukteswar, Lahiri's disciple, told Yogananda, "Even when Lahiri Mahasaya was silent, or when he conversed on other than religious topics, I discovered that he had transmitted to me ineffable knowledge."

In another passage, Lahiri Mahasaya is quoted directly: "'Please expound the holy stanzas as the meaning occurs to you.' The taciturn guru often gave this instruction to a nearby disciple. 'I will guide your thoughts, that the right interpretation be uttered.' In this way many of Lahiri Mahasaya's perceptions came to be recorded, with voluminous commentaries, by various students."

In ancient times in India, wisdom was normally conveyed by thought-transference. Later, it was committed to memory but not written down, for the record could be preserved more faithfully by the mind than by the written word and subsequent editorial distortion. Only much later, as people's memory became fallible during the general decline of spiritual awareness, was it necessary to begin committing those teachings to books.

The modern mind considers the ability to read and write one of the chief blessings of civilization. This naive conviction is due to the fact that modern man has lost contact with higher consciousness. Granted, literacy is a step upward for those who, doomed to a life of plodding manual labor, live by their instinctual urges like the lower animals. To judge all history by present-day standards, however, is a mark of our own ignorance. There have been ages, in fact, when people generally lived by intuitive wisdom, and not in primitive ignorance as is presently believed.

Much of civilization's history is not the soaring flight toward what we are pleased to consider enlightenment, but an inexorable slide into spiritual ignorance and materialism. Students of ancient history have frequently remarked on the apparently anomalous fact that prehistoric art often shows a steady *decline* in sophistication from earlier, more spiritual levels of sensitivity.

With civilization's decline, the wise teachers of olden times realized that divine wisdom was being threatened with oblivion. Who, living in later times, would understand as egoless such inspiring statements as: "*Aham Brahm asmi* (I am Brahma)," "*Tat tuam asi* (Thou art that)," "*Aham sa* (I am He)"? The unenlightened mind hasn't the capacity to perceive these statements as proceeding from the ultimate refinement of consciousness.

Thus, the lofty teachings of the Vedas and Upanishads had to be clothed in symbolism, and presented in allegories. The purpose of concealing them was in part to protect the truth from profanation, and in part also to ensure their endurance during centuries of spiritual darkness. The hope was to suggest to deep truth seekers, at least, that there are levels of truth beyond any of those suggested by orthodox religion.

"Don't listen to that ignoramus." This counsel, received by the youthful Yogananda from a wise *sadhu* (holy man) in reference to a reputed "scriptural authority," might have been uttered by the rishis of ancient times concerning much that passes for wisdom nowadays.

A fascinating book called *Fingerprints of the Gods* was published in Great Britain in 1993. The author, Graham Cook, did exhaustive research into folk legends the world over, and discovered amazing similarities of tradition among ancient peoples, both so-called civilized and those generally considered uncivilized. It has long been recognized that India's myths of gods and goddesses are closely related to those of ancient Greece, Rome, and the Nordic and Germanic peoples. So similar are they, indeed, that even the days of the week, both in India and in the West, continue to be named after the same deities, who represented the same planets: Sun for Sunday, Moon for Monday, Mars for Tuesday, Mercury for Wednesday (Woden's day in Norse legend), Jupiter for Thursday (Thor's day in Scandinavia; Brihaspati, or Jupiter's, day in India), Venus for Friday, and Saturn for Saturday.

I was being given a guided tour of the Parthenon in Athens several years ago when my guide challenged me: "I'll bet you don't know where the ancient Greek legends came from."

"From India," I replied.

She stared at me in astonishment. "How did you know that? You are quite right, but very few people are aware of the fact."

Graham Cook, after extending his investigation of myths and legends over most of the planet, concluded that in prehistory there must have been some highly advanced civilization from which all those stories derived. He attempted to localize that putative civilization in what is presently the most desolate spot on earth: Antarctica, which has lain buried under a mile-thick layer of ice for thousands of years. But doesn't it seem far more likely, assuming that such a civilization in fact existed, that its extent was as worldwide as ours is today? It is difficult to imagine any highly developed civilization remaining confined to a single continent.

India's traditions extend far back into prehistory. A strong tradition there, even today, is that long before recorded history there existed a high and noble civilization. That some sort of cultural exchange took place seems obvious. The prevalence of the same myths in Europe as in India; the known fact of an Indo-European family of languages; the striking similarity of many traditional myths and images around the world—a quantity too numerous, as Graham Cook makes abundantly clear, and too closely similar to one another, to be dismissed as mere coincidence: These are only a selection of reasons for deducing two strong probabilities:

1) that there *was indeed* an ancient, world-wide civilization, which was subsequently destroyed; and

2) that that civilization was highly advanced even by modern standards, and despite present-day scientific consensus to the contrary.

We shall examine these assumptions, which are admittedly radical, soon. Suffice it here to hint that intriguing remnants of such civilizations (plural, be it noted) are being turned up with increasing frequency all the time, to the equally increasing embarrassment of orthodox archeologists and anthropologists.

My purpose in this book is to present some of the wisdom—much of it hidden and forgotten—behind the ancient symbols. For although the symbols themselves may be misleading if viewed too literally, they cloak insights that are profound. In their profundity, moreover, they are not ponderous or solemn; often they are charming; sometimes they are lighthearted and even, as

I said earlier, delightfully funny. The truths they express, however, are both serious and sacred. In no way are they the mere fantasies of a grotesque and pagan imagination. Nor were the ancient rishis igno rant of objective facts of Nature that have been brought to light only in our present scientific age— some of which, indeed, are still being brought to light by the most advanced physicists of our day.

To state my meaning more clearly, if startlingly: A growing body of research is beginning to suggest the humbling possibility that mankind may actually have been more highly advanced—indeed, far more so, in the past, and perhaps even more than once—than he is now!

More on this subject, then, in the next chapter.

Chapter Five
Dating It All

Where do all those ancient symbols and myths come from? We referred in the last chapter to a time in prehistory when civilization may have been spiritually more highly advanced than ours is today. The very basis for such a claim strikes most people, conditioned as they are by the self-laudatory assumptions of modern education, as absurd. Archeologists reject out of hand the rapidly growing body of evidence that advanced civilizations existed in ancient times, for it contradicts their neatly framed picture of prehistory: primitive hunters settling down eventually to till the land, then building cities, and only slowly and reluctantly renouncing superstition with the dazzling appearance on the scene of Galileo, Newton, and the rest of the gang of scientific ghost busters.

The new myth is that primitive man evolved from the ape a few hundred thousand years ago, and from then onward grunted and clubbed his way through the caves and backwoods of what is called the "Stone Age," to emerge somewhat awkwardly a mere 3,000–4,000 years ago into the relative sophistication of the "Bronze Age." Since then he has strode, increasingly self-confident, into the modern age, where he now stands proudly in the full glory of his bulldozers, tractors, skyscrapers, and spreading pollution.

If anything can tickle the divine sense of humor, it must surely be man's presumption at setting the standards of perfection at his own level of material "accomplishments." This attitude must seem comparable to an ant's airy dismissal of descriptions of an elephant as "absurd exaggerations."

To judge civilization by man's ability to create tools, merely because modern man has achieved some skill in this regard, is too typical of human arrogance to be accepted without the raised eyebrow of skepticism. It must be granted, of course, that not every society has shown our own mechanical skill. The early desert fathers of Christendom, for example, weren't interested in building cities, nor even in developing gadgetry. But wouldn't it be absurd to say that they were therefore less truly civilized than ourselves? The very fact that those hermits, many of them well educated and raised in noble families, despised materialistic civilization suggests that they, at least, considered the simple life they had chosen a better and more intelligent alternative.

The other day an Italian craftsman, justifiably proud of his skill as a tile worker, remarked to me—again, perhaps justifiably—that Michelangelo himself could not have done better work than his. To accomplish to perfection whatever one does is, surely, worthy of praise, and my own praise was sincere. Of course, I couldn't help thinking as he spoke that more than skill is needed to produce a great work of art. Vision, too, is important. Again, more is needed than the skill of crafting and manipulating tools to justify man's boast that he has produced the highest civilization of all time.

Laurens van der Post in his book *The Lost World of the Kalahari* wrote of time that he'd spent among the bushmen of South Africa, whose culture he himself describes—sympathetically, however—as "Stone Age." By anthropological standards, of course, that description is correct. While reading his book, however, I found myself wondering by what right we consider the bushman less civilized than ourselves.

He is not less intelligent. In his own milieu he is far more skilled than the average city dweller could possibly be. He seems to be as sensitive as the most refined of us to noble feelings, to compassion, love, tenderness, loyalty, dignity, and personal honor. Bushmen, according to Laurens van der Post, are excellent artists; the music and paintings they create are beautiful, and reveal amazing sensitivity.

Where, then, shall we begin in our attempt to denigrate them? In many ways, I feel, we have lost a nobility that they may still possess—if indeed enough of this pygmy people still remain, after the predations of so-called civilization, to have preserved their cultural soul.

In ancient India, the criteria of cultural advancement were far more refined than those of present-day Western culture, which might justifiably be termed "toolism." Advancement in those far-off days was judged by *what every human being really wants from life*. The ancients realized that human desires will never be satisfied by material fulfillment alone. The goal of life, they understood, is Self-realization. That is indeed why the human race was created: to realize the essence of all being in Infinite Consciousness.

The most highly evolved human being, according to the ancient rishis, is one who has realized his true essence. And the most highly advanced civilization is that which offers the greatest encouragement toward the attainment of spiritual consciousness.

This criterion is not arbitrary. It is based, as I said, on what every human being *really* wants from life, even if most people seek it misguidedly. For most human beings believe, mistakenly, that money, or human love, or political power will give them fulfillment. But from every quest in those directions they return disappointed. Only the rare person who finds happiness within himself declares unhesitatingly that this is what he was really seeking all the time, even when he knew it not.

Material tools can never fulfill the heart's innermost desire. Nightclubs, a rising stock market, and traffic-clogged highways can't fulfill it. Nothing outside ourselves can ever satisfy us for long; everything disappoints, in the end. Excessive reliance on "toolism" as the means of fulfillment has brought mankind to the brink of self-destruction, whether through atmospheric pollution, global epidemics, or nuclear warfare.

Archeologists object, "If mankind was highly advanced in prehistory, why haven't our excavations unearthed the tools that his advancement should have produced?" Their question simply betrays a materialistic prejudice.

Perhaps, however, some of those tools have already been discovered, and await only modern recognition. It does seem likely that tools didn't command the degree of interest in many ages that they do today, but even so, a number have been found and recognized as such, but rejected as hoaxes because they didn't fit into the neat frame constructed by the "experts."*

An experiment was performed some years ago with a group of cats. From birth they were kept surrounded by only horizontal lines. After some time, they were placed in a room with normal furniture. The cats, unaccustomed to tables and chairs with vertical legs, at first couldn't even see them and kept bumping into them.

I wonder if our archeologists are not conditioned to similar blindness by their absorption in a limited corpus of knowledge they themselves have created.

Maps have been discovered, and reliably attested to by eminent scholars,† that demonstrate convincingly a familiarity on the part of ancient man with both the

---

*Life has taught me to be skeptical of any body of knowledge once it becomes so generally accepted as to have produced "experts" in the field. Most of those experts, so-called, are acclaimed only for having committed to memory the discoveries and opinions of others. The great way-showers of our race are seldom referred to as experts—until their old age, perhaps, when their discoveries have become widely accepted at last.

†Among them Professor Charles H. Hapgood, who taught the history of science at Keene College, New Hampshire, USA, and whose best-known book, *Maps of the Ancient Sea Kings*, so distressed his professional peers that, for lack of more serious objections, they singled out trivia for condemnation and tried to bury him under a mound of what has been described as "thick and unwarranted sarcasm."

existence and the shape of the Antarctic continent. Those maps give the correct outline of that continent, and actually reveal a fact that was unknown until recently: namely, that Antarctica is divided into two large bodies of land.

The amazing thing is that, throughout history as we know it today—indeed, for at least 6,000 years—Antarctica has lain buried under a mile-thick blanket of ice. It was only during Geophysical Year 1958 that soundings revealed its true shape, proving the accuracy of those maps. The tools have yet to be found that made that prehistoric discovery possible. So then, because the tools have not yet been unearthed, will archeologists say that the discovery itself was never made? This reaction would be typical of their record to date for facing historical anomalies.

Unfortunately for their "expertise," the story goes farther still. The correct longitudinal measurements set forth in those maps reveal a knowledge that was redis-covered only toward the end of the Eighteenth Century of our own era, by John Harrison in England.

Archeologists have ways of extricating themselves from the embarrassment of such unwelcome discover-ies. They divert our attention by speaking to us learnedly on more banal subjects, such as the recent excavations on some burial mound in Mongolia. How else, indeed, to preserve their hard-earned status as "experts"?

Knowledge that the earth is round is popularly con-sidered to be a modern discovery; tradition attributes it to Christopher Columbus (though that tradition has been fairly well discredited by now). Yet those ancient maps, and numerous ancient writings that are widely accepted by now, make it clear that this knowledge was fairly common long before 1492, when "Columbus sailed the ocean blue."

It would be a diversion from my present purpose to examine the mass of further evidence for highly developed civilizations in prehistory. A handful of examples must suffice:

Wet cell batteries have been found among ancient artifacts in Baghdad, Iraq. They were recognized as such by Wilhelm König, a German engineer, during a visit to the Baghdad museum.

A hole, perfectly round, was discovered in the skull of an antelope dated circa 100,000 years ago. Such clean penetration could have been caused only by a high-speed projectile, such as a rifle bullet. Any primitive weapon—a spear or an arrow, for instance— would have shattered the bone.

Evidence has been found of the possibility that nuclear explosions occurred in ancient times. Large areas of vitrified sand have been discovered in the Gobi desert and elsewhere, evidence of such intense heat as might not be explicable otherwise.

Extraordinarily advanced architecture, dating back many thousands of years, has been discovered in numerous places throughout the world.

And records have been found in India detailing the ancient existence, and construction, of flying machines.

More and more books keep getting published, reporting discoveries like these. Many of them add testimony from other-than-archeological, but nonetheless scientific, disciplines that flatly contradicts not a few of the fundamental tenets of modern archeology.

The main point to be made here, however, is that to speak of the existence of high civilizations in the past does not oblige us to explain an absence of technological evidence. There is a growing, and indeed already massive, body of such evidence. Archeologists, being human like everyone else, deny this abundance with a sneer. Their best argument seems to be, "It can't be so, therefore it isn't so." There is nothing new in human beings scoffing at evidence that fails to support their own convictions. Napoleon, no bit-part actor on the stage of time himself, described history as "a lie agreed upon."

My present point, then, is to re-state without apology an age-old belief in India that in ancient times mankind reached a stage when civilization was far more highly advanced than it is at present. Indeed, in this light it is amusing to reflect on Mahatma Gandhi's reply to the question, "What do you think of Western civilization?" With a smile Gandhi remarked: "That is a wonderful idea!"

According to ancient tradition in several parts of the world,* the earth passes cyclically through four ages. The highest of these is a time of general spiritual awareness; the lowest, a time of general ignorance and

---

*Greece, Egypt, and the Mayan culture of Central America spring to mind.

materialism. These four ages—*yuga*s they are called in Sanskrit—move in descending and ascending cycles of time, and exercise a dramatic influence on human history.

Whatever else that ancient tradition gives us, it does put into perspective our present-day fixation on the gray sterilities of technology as the last word in human progress.

Back when spiritual wisdom was beginning to lose importance for most people, the great saints and yogis—custodians of India's spiritual culture—addressed themselves to the task of preparing society for approaching centuries of spiritual darkness. One way of addressing the problem was to create what might justifiably be called spiritual "time capsules": symbols in stone, as well as in myth and legend, that would preserve the truth and keep it from being lost altogether. Their purpose was to clothe it in such a way as to remain understandable to those few with sufficient spiritual refinement to desire it, but hidden from others.

The rishis hoped further that in a more distant future, when the general level of understanding was on the rise again, the symbols and allegories with which they'd cloaked those teachings would make it easier for people to re-access the ancient wisdom.

According to current Hindu orthodoxy, the world is presently sliding ever more deeply into an abyss of spiritual darkness—*Kali Yuga,* this age of darkness is called.* The earth is not destined to emerge from this

---

*_Kali_ means dark.

canyon of ignorance for more than four hundred thousand years. A bleak prospect indeed!

Swami Sri Yukteswar, however, guru of Paramhansa Yogananda and not only a great yogi-sage but an astrologer of deep spiritual vision, made the reassuring discovery that this generally accepted tradition is mistaken, and was itself born of the spiritual ignorance of Kali Yuga.

Kali Yuga, Sri Yukteswar proclaimed, is actually of much briefer duration than the 432,000 years Hindu scholars have computed. Its time span is only 2,400 years: 1,200 of them descending, and the other 1,200, ascending. The total cycle of yugas lasts 24,000 years—12,000 of them, again, descending, and 12,000 ascending. The reason for placing the descending cycle first in the sequence is that history as we know it began toward the end of the descending arc, and embraces only the beginning of the re-ascending one. Most of known history took place during Kali Yuga.

The explanation that is generally accepted in India nowadays was arrived at by enlarging on the original figures to produce what, it was concluded, were "years of the Gods." This invention, Swami Sri Yukteswar explained, was an ingenious attempt on the part of scholars in Kali Yuga to account for anomalies that had crept into the official reckonings during the descending centuries of darkness.

Mere antiquity of tradition doesn't guarantee accuracy, even when scripture itself is cited as authority. It is not unheard-of for errors to intrude on supposedly authoritative texts, owing to ignorant tampering.

Discrimination demands that we rely above all on living wisdom, not on an intellectual analysis of dusty tomes. Even texts that have remained free from tampering are often misinterpreted by scholars, few of whom are themselves free from bias. Paramhansa Yogananda in *Autobiography of a Yogi* emphasized that contemporary sages are, as one saint of Bengal, Badhuri Mahasaya, put it, "living volumes, . . . proof against the natural disintegrations of time and the unnatural interpretations of the critics."

A living master is no different from the rishis of old; he is a seer in the ancient wisdom—more exalted than any "expert," whether scholar or technician.

One tradition, supposedly sanctioned by scripture, is that at the end of Kali Yuga the earth will be transformed abruptly into the highest and most spiritual age, Krita, or Satya, Yuga. Nothing in Nature endorses such a sudden shift. The sun passes by degrees from winter to summer solstice, then inches back through the autumnal equinox to winter solstice again. The darkness of night is transformed gradually—never suddenly—into day: Midnight never leaps forward to high noon. The yugas are not manifestations of magic. Like everything else in Nature, their movement is gradual, and cyclical.

Swami Sri Yukteswar explained how this process works. Our sun, he said, has a dual. These two bodies revolve around one another every 24,000 years. From the center of our galaxy, powerful rays of spiritual energy radiate outward to nourish the vast system. During the sun's revolution around its dual it slowly approaches, then recedes from, the galactic center. With its approach, the solar system receives increasing amounts of spiritual energy. Human consciousness is thereby energized also.

An example will help to explain this effect, for it is easy to see the influence of energy on the brain. The real contrast between genius and stupidity lies not in skull capacity, but in *mental energy.* High mental energy is always the mark of genius. Stupid people, on the other hand, always display low mental energy. In this contrast we see the consequences for mankind in general, when our solar system approaches the galactic center, receiving a steadily augmented supply of energy, then recedes from it again and receives energy in diminished amounts. The closer we approach to that source of spiritual power, the more awakened human consciousness becomes.

Another example will explain the broad variations in spiritual awareness that we find in our own age, and that must exist in every age. For we know that a sensitive radio will pick up even weak signals from afar, whereas less sensitive radios may pick up only signals that are nearby. During the depths of Kali Yuga, similarly, certain people possess sufficient refinement to achieve the heights of spiritual realization. Spiritual masters, indeed, transcend the need for dependence on outer influences of any kind. Most people, however, are dependent on such influences to varying degrees, and are more often motivated by them than self-motivated. To such people, the spiritual energy that reaches our solar system during Kali Yuga is insufficient to make them aware of the subtler realities behind material appearances. For mankind generally, matter itself, during Kali Yuga, seems a fixed and absolute reality.

Sri Yukteswar's book, *The Holy Science,* was written in 1894 A.D., when scientists were not as yet aware that all the stars visible to the naked eye are on the outer fringe of one galaxy. Still less did they know of the existence of other galaxies. The sun's position in our Milky Way galaxy was unknown. Its direction of movement was unknown. Many scientists even thought of the sun as posited at the center of the universe.

It was only in 1918 that an astronomer, Edwin Powell Hubble, found that the supposed nebula in the constellation Andromeda is actually another galaxy. Soon more galaxies were being discovered. I myself, when a schoolboy during the 1930s, was stunned to learn from a teacher that there might even be as many as three other galaxies besides our own. (In fact, that number is now computed at something over 400 billion. "Well," as the saying goes, "but who's counting?")

The center of our own galaxy has more recently been located in the constellation Sagittarius. And it is only very recently that astronomers have become aware that a vast amount of energy pours out from that center to the entire galaxy. Our sun's position in the galaxy, and the simple fact as well as the direction of its movement: All this information has appeared only in the Twentieth Century.

Sri Yukteswar's book anticipated some of this knowledge by almost a century. Even the first part of it he anticipated by more than two decades.

His book also stated that the solar system is presently moving in the direction of our galactic center, but is still at a relatively early stage of its return. Astronomers now say that our sun is moving toward the star Vega in the constellation Hercules—an acceptable direction for Sri Yukteswar's claim if one assumes that the sun's movement is, like that of other heavenly bodies, elliptical.

The ascending cycle of Kali Yuga, according to Sri Yukteswar—and the historic facts support his conclusions—ended in the year 1700 A.D. (He rounded out the figure from 1699 A.D. for modern convenience in recalling it). We have already, then, reached the second of the four ascending yugas. This one is called *Dwapara Yuga*, the "second age." The year, then, in which I shall finish the present book will be, if computed in universal terms rather than according to our more time-circumscribed Christian era, 298 *Dwapara, not* 1998 A.D.

Because at the present time we are well into the beginning of an age of relative enlightenment, it is possible for us now to retrieve at least a portion of the wisdom that the rishis concealed thousands of years ago behind a veil of allegory and symbolism. For most educated people nowadays can recognize at least a few of the subtleties in those ancient symbols.

Indeed, much that is thought of as discovery is really only rediscovery. The Earth's roundness, for example, was known in ancient times; this fact is recognized by modern scholars. The fact also that the Earth is not located at the center of the universe was rediscovered only in the Sixteenth Century, by Copernicus. Paul LaViolette, an inter-disciplinary scientist of our own time, has made the startling observation that the ancients may also have known the location of the center of our galaxy. He points out that the arrow in the constellation Sagittarius, and also the tip of the tail in Scorpio, both point to that region of Sagittarius where the center of our galaxy lies. The delineation of these constellations dates far back into prehistory. LaViolette estimates, further, that some 18,000 years ago the arrow and the scorpion's tail both pointed *exactly* to the galactic center.

Numerous other facts, lost sight of during descending Kali Yuga, have been and are being rediscovered at corresponding points of the ascending arc. Ancient Indian treatises, for example, describe the universe as vast—not in the sense that rustics, awed by news that there are continents elsewhere on earth, might understand the term, but vast in the sense of cosmic.

Swami Sri Yukteswar's description of a galactic center was written before astronomers had yet proposed an alternative to the sun as the center of the universe.

The very fact that matter is only a vibration of energy, as Sri Yukteswar stated, was only rediscovered eleven years *after* 1894, when he wrote his book. Today, more than a century later, although astronomers have yet to discover a dual to our sun, many of them have stated that such a dual would explain certain anomalies of movement in the outer planets of our solar system.

During the centuries of Kali Yuga, mankind as a whole was incapable of even imagining that matter is insubstantial. It was only in the early Eighteenth Century, at the beginning of Dwapara Yuga, that Bishop George Berkeley of Ireland proposed the unheard-of concept that everything exists only in thought. To this "notion" even Samuel Johnson, brilliant man though he was, responded by giving his faithful biographer Boswell a kick in the seat of his pants, then demanding, "Was that kick, Boswell, only a thought in your mind?"

The discovery that matter is only a vibration of energy, and is therefore insubstantial, could not have been made until the earth had progressed further into Dwapara Yuga, the Age of Energy. This discovery was announced to the world only in 1905, five years after the termination of a 200-year *sandhya,* or interim period, between Kali and Dwapara Yugas, when we entered Dwapara Yuga proper. In 1894 Swami Sri Yukteswar declared that the world would soon make this discovery.

The ancient texts explain some of the indications of an ascending yuga. One of these is a general increase in human stature. Another is a general increase of longevity. These changes are becoming increasingly evident, world-wide.

Orthodox Hindus frequently cite, as proof of the world's continuing descent into Kali Yuga, the moral laxity of our times. But this laxity is easily explainable as a general sense of release from authoritarian repression. For bondage to form and to rigid structures, typical of Kali Yuga, is being replaced by a new awareness of individual freedom. As people lose their dependence on formal structures, they will cease also to depend so heavily on dogmas and institutions, and will be more inclined to follow their own inner guidance.

The first sign of this new sense of personal freedom has been a tendency to welcome with open arms the easily assimilable advice, "Do whatever feels good": hedonistic counsel, of course, but only a reaction against the older moral code, "If it feels good, it must be a sin!" Gradually, the new energy of Dwapara Yuga is helping people to find *in energy itself* all the guidance they need. More and more they are learning that what really "feels good" is to behave oneself, morally and spiritually—not because someone ordered it, but simply because we were created according to certain universal principles and are wise if we live by them. We cannot eat nails and live: Our bodies simply weren't made to digest them. If we smoke heavily or drink to excess, we abuse our own system and suffer accordingly. No man-made laws are needed to impose the punishment. Human laws are needed to keep people from imposing unduly on the individual freedom of others. Otherwise, Nature herself is our best teacher.

People are becoming more and more aware that to respect natural law as it applies to their bodies and minds is in their own interest. Diet and mental hygiene are being accepted more and more as matters of common concern.

The subtle law applies also to our emotional nature. To act in harmony with it produces happiness. If we act against it, we inflict suffering on ourselves and even disrupt the natural harmony between ourselves and the universe. "To do bad" is, ultimately, "to feel bad." Sensitivity to the flow of energy in our bodies and in our feelings is a surer guide and corrective for right living than whole books of moral maxims.

Thus, the present binge of immorality cannot last, for it is born of an increase, not a decrease, of general awareness—an awareness of energy, especially. What it betokens is greater reliance on personal conscience, rooted not in social and religious strictures but in human nature itself. In time, people will adjust to this new sense of individual freedom and will assume responsibility for it in a way that few ever did during the rigidly structured centuries of Kali Yuga.

Indeed, were today's moral laxity an indication of our continuing descent into Kali Yuga, and were this descent to continue at the same rate for another 400,000 years, one shudders to think what would become of the human race by the end of that time. Would there even be a human race left? Perhaps, then, the earth would be populated only by worms and slugs. Considering the scene about us today, even the dumb animals demonstrate a dignity that is lacking among many of our wilder youths, and a nobility sadly absent from society's behavior generally. I cannot even imagine human beings existing still on this planet 400,000 years from now: They'd have self-destructed.

Fortunately, the present age of energy can only lead to a greater awareness of energy's right and wrong uses, including the way we utilize it in our own bodies.

Chapter Six

Symbolism: Truth, or Imagination?

Paramhansa Yogananda once made a fascinating statement, which I'll paraphrase here: "The sun and moon are symbols of the Father and Mother aspects of God: Wisdom from the sun, Love from the moon. Years ago, for two months, I meditated gazing at the sun daily as it neared the horizon, which is when the rays are not harmful.* From this practice I received great inspirations of wisdom."

Symbols are usually thought of as objective *projections of subjective ideas*. Overlooked is the fact that consciousness itself is not only subjective, but universal. How, indeed, could it not have existed already at least as a potential, for life ever to have manifested it?

According to the Hindu teachings, although God seeks communion with us in our souls above all, He also seeks to guide and inspire us through natural phenomena. The rain, Paramhansa Yogananda said, is a message to us of Divine Compassion; the flowers whisper to us of God's love and joy; the tenderness of Mother Nature reminds us of the consciousness in which She wants us always to live. On the other hand,

*It is important for anyone who wants to practice this exercise to limit it to the first half hour after the sun rises, and the last half hour before it sets. Gaze into it for no longer than a minute to start with, then very gradually increase the time to not more than nine minutes.

Her elemental fierceness is also a warning to us not to live proudly, as if we were above divine law. Symbolism is not only a projection of human imagination: It is inherent in all phenomena.

The materialist believes, mistakenly, that consciousness is merely a product of brain activity: energy moving through a circuit of nerves. He scoffs at religion as idiotic superstition—a by-product of wishful thinking and the fear of eventual annihilation. Materialists themselves, however—amusingly enough—are guilty of the greatest superstition of all. For in comparing the brain to a computer, as they do, they overlook the obvious fact that even computers need people to operate them—and, yes, people also to program them to program other computers. It takes consciousness to produce thought. Thought itself—the sort of calculations, let us say, that computers perform—could never *produce* consciousness.

Carl Jung, the famous psychologist, claimed that certain symbols are universal, in the sense that they belong to what he called the "collective unconscious" of mankind. His term "unconscious" is not wholly felicitous, inasmuch as nothing, really, is wholly without consciousness. In human beings there are powerful urges, such as the instinct for self-preservation, over which people have no conscious control, but which are conscious enough themselves to seize control over the power of both will and reason.

Jung would have done better, I think, to speak of a "subtle network of awareness." For we are all part of one reality. What affects us in a deep way affects all, be it with our suffering or our joy. The enlightenment of one saint uplifts, to however slight a degree, the entire human race. This "network" doesn't exist, however, on lower-than-conscious levels of awareness, but on higher than conscious. In subconsciousness we withdraw into ourselves, away from objective reality; subconsciousness, therefore, separates us from the rest of reality. It is in superconsciousness that our true unity with all life can be experienced.

There are lower levels of consciousness than that which produces conscious thought. And there are also higher. The thoughts produced by human reason are like heavy trucks, shifting gears downward to lumber their way up every grade of rational difficulty. On higher levels of consciousness, however, the mind soars like a bird, high above the mountain peaks of all difficulties. In this greater-than-normal awareness, all that exists participates to some degree. In superconsciousness, even the apparently inanimate rocks play a role. Neither rocks nor most of humanity are aware of the latent superconscious within them, but that level of consciousness never ceases to be aware of them. It knows the slightest movement of every atom.

The ancient teaching of India is that God dreamed the universe into existence. Everything is part of that cosmic dream, even as the waves are part of, and united by, the vast ocean beneath them.

Within the fundamental unity of consciousness, certain symbols possess universal relevance. The ocean itself, as I've mentioned, is one such symbol. So also are the sun and the moon. Another one is the cross.

Still another, the swastika. Other symbols with universal resonance include a tall, straight tree; a round dot or perfect circle; a triangle; a candle or any small flame; a ship sailing calmly on the broad sea; a dark tunnel at the end of which shines a bright light; a high and symmetrically shaped mountain; a freshly opened rosebud; a lotus lifting itself in purity above the muddy water; a rainbow; a flowing river; the crescent moon; a five-pointed star; a six-pointed star or "star of David," one triangle of which reaches upward in aspiration to receive divine grace, descending with the other triangle; a golden aureole; the horizon line of the sea. We may dream of these things superconsciously, regardless of our religious beliefs or social upbringing. Each of them contains eternal and not merely ephemeral meaning.

Usually, the lesser is used to symbolize the greater; the smaller, to denote the larger. At the same time, the grosser symbolizes the subtler regardless of relative size or objective importance. Paramhansa Yogananda described the sun as a symbol not only of the Father aspect of God, but also of the spiritual eye, which is beheld in meditation in the forehead.

Communion with God in Nature is far more than a question of mental projection. Communion in *any* form, indeed, is a two-way process. In calling there should also be listening; in offering, acceptance. God calls to us more openly, however, through certain forms than through others. We find it more natural to commune with Him through the moon or through a beautiful sunset than through a gray sky.

Divinely ordained symbols, moreover, are very different from those which owe their existence to the imagination of man and the consent of society. The communist hammer and sickle, for example, shows symbolic inventiveness, but it doesn't show a recognition of universal resonance. The same is true of other human inventions—the V-for-victory sign the Allies used during World War II; the flags of nations; the reversed swastika of Nazi Germany.[*]

[*]There are many, and conflicting, explanations for the swastika, which symbol has been used in many parts of the world. According to certain explanations, the Nazi symbol had a positive significance. According to others, the significance was negative. Nazi Germany itself, certainly, was devastatingly negative in the outward projection of its energy.

The following explanation is based on an inward, not an outward, interpretation of this symbol.

The clockwise direction of the arms in the Nazi swastika, as opposed to the counter-clockwise direction, made it a symbol of negative power and self-destruction. For the swastika represents a turning wheel. When the direction is negative, it takes the body's energy downward, into material identity.

Two points arise here for which I have not properly prepared the reader and can therefore only touch on them lightly. One is that the direction of rotation is related to a spiral movement of energy in the spine, known in the yoga teachings as *kundalini*. The second is that, in this symbol, the turn is seen as if reflected in the spiritual eye, and not as if viewed downward from above. The spiritual eye is a round circle of light which appears naturally in the forehead during deep meditation.

A positive, counter-clockwise rotation of the spiritual eye is sometimes seen, indicating that the kundalini energy is rising up the spine. A negative, clockwise direction, then, would indicate that the energy was flowing downward. As far as I know, however, this clockwise rotation is not actually experienced, because in meditation it would indicate that the mind was being drawn downward, *out of* meditation into matter-consciousness, and consequently unable to see the spiritual eye. The negative rotation is, therefore, as far as I know, only symbolic.

The use of pendulums to gauge the energy fields of various objects seems to indicate directions opposite to those I've described. This is because, when we look *downward*, the rotation is seen from another perspective. It then becomes *clockwise* when positive, *and counter-clockwise* when negative.

Symbols that are born in superconsciousness have a beneficial effect. If we receive them into the depths of our being, our consciousness is uplifted. Symbols can sometimes be powerful, even when they are not rooted in superconsciousness, for by using them to focus our minds we may enter, or at least touch on, the super-conscious, from which level of awareness wonders can be performed. It is related that Tan Sen, the court musician of Emperor Akbar in India, once plunged the palace precincts in darkness by chanting a night *raga,* or melody, at Akbar's request, while the sun was still high in the sky.

I mentioned that Indian civilization has grown gnarled with age, like an old tree, some of its branches by now twisted and misshapen. As traditions passed down through descending ages, and especially after the earth had entered the dark age of Kali Yuga, additions were made, then accepted as valid, that detracted from the original teachings. That tree, improperly tended, lost some of its shape and beauty.

The disadvantage of symbols is that they may, and often do, acquire a life of their own. New symbols grow out of old ones; each one alters the original a little, until sometimes its very purpose is forgotten. Certain ancient ceremonies have been amplified without due regard for their true meaning.

The story is told of a man who sat in his prayer room to perform what is known as the *shraddha* ceremony for his recently deceased father. During the rites a dog entered the room. The man, anxious to protect the sanctity of the occasion, hastily rose from his seat and took the dog out onto the verandah, where he secured it to a post.

Years later, after his own death, his son in turn performed the ceremony for him. Anxious to get it right, he recalled his father having tied a dog to a verandah post. He possessed no dog himself, but persuaded a neighbor to lend him one. Then, mumbling propitiatory prayers, he ceremoniously tied the animal to what he hoped was the right post.

Generations passed; this sacred "dog ritual" became the central part of that family's shraddha ceremony.

Alterations have been introduced, similarly, into many traditions, including the traditions of religious art. An example is Goddess Kali's tongue. Originally, it extended only slightly beyond the lips, as if in expression of embarrassment. For she had just stepped onto the prostrate form of her husband, Shiva. This gesture of the tongue is a customary way, in India, of showing embarrassment, apology, or self-reproach. In the West, too, people often bite their tongues lightly to express the same sentiments. Implied in Kali's protruding tongue, then, was the thought, "Oh, oh! I've gone too far."

Kali represents Vibratory Creation: Mother Nature in a cosmic sense. Shiva in this image is prostrate to indicate his withdrawal from cosmic illusion. He represents the Vibrationless Spirit beyond creation. Vibratory Creation becomes stilled upon its return to the Vibrationless Absolute.

Kali, nowadays, is depicted with her tongue lolling out as if in blood lust. Her long hair, supposedly symbolic of cosmic energy, is depicted wild and disordered to emphasize her supposedly untamable rage.

Thus, a lofty and inspiring symbol has become distorted, over time, to present a frightening suggestion of universal mayhem. Small wonder the *thugies* (so-called "religious" assassins) of Vindhyachal offered up their strangled victims to Kali, whom they ignorantly considered eager for human blood. It was their own thirst for murder they were satisfying by pretending the slaughter was an act of devotion.

Many words, too, have changed their meaning over the centuries. Sri Aurobindo, a noted scholar-saint of modern times, pointed out that the word *"go"* in Sanskrit, usually understood to mean "cow," means also "light." This double meaning casts the reputed "cow culture" of Vedic times in an entirely new perspective.

There is a story told of a youth in ancient times whose guru entrusted him with a herd of cows. He told the young man to go off by himself and tend them faithfully; then, when the herd had increased in number, to return for spiritual initiation. Obviously, in light of Sri Aurobindo's discovery, what the guru actually bestowed on his disciple was no herd of cows, but a touch of the inner light. Once that light had grown strong, through daily meditation, the disciple could return for higher initiation.

The ancient Vedas, considered by many Westerners to be a compilation of bucolic verses composed by cowherds, were in fact deep scriptures. Indeed, they have always been considered such in India. Although the spiritual meaning of some of the verses eludes modern understanding, highly regarded sages who lived closer to those times, such as the *Adi* (or first) Swami Shankaracharya, expressed reverence for the Vedas. Even Buddha, who denounced the way the Vedic teachings were being abused, never extended his denunciation to the Vedas themselves. All he did was what my own book seeks to do: emphasize the importance of taking personal responsibility for one's own life, and of realizing that truth must be *lived,* and not merely flattered with ceremonies.

Out of respect for the judgment of those great and wise men, the bemused student of modern times would do well to suspend any negative judgment on the Vedas as scripture. For what those sages considered profound must surely contain insights that transcend anything suggested in modern lexicons.

Swami Bharati Krishna Tirth, the Shankaracharya of Gowardhan Math in the Twentieth Century and probably the most widely respected scriptural authority of his time, discovered that the Vedas even contain advanced mathematical knowledge. Himself a gifted mathematician, he found this information buried, so to speak, in passages that appeared to be simple historical references. The meaning of certain key words had changed. The modern student needs access to those meanings. Sri Aurobindo and Swami Bharati Krishna Tirth supplied a few of them. As Dwapara Yuga advances, other people will undoubtedly supply many more.

It is not my purpose to inundate you with explanations. Even these few clues, however, may suffice to steer you around those supreme obstacles to devotion: sneering iconoclasm, on the one hand, and mindless adherence to form, on the other. Indeed, from an understanding of even a few basic symbols you may be able to arrive at insights of your own, which will lead you to the ultimate purpose of all symbolism: spiritual development.

I urge you not to let your intellect become so minutely engaged in the subject that you find yourself lured into a woods of theory and never reach life's supreme goal: divine enlightenment. The truth is simple, always. The true purpose of symbols is to point the way to that simplicity, and not to draw one onto the endlessly meandering bypaths of speculation.

First, then, let us examine the most basic of those truths. For true symbols express, in one way or another, their underlying revelation.

Chapter Seven

Philosophy, Religion, Science, or—What?

To understand the symbolism in Indian art and literature, it is necessary to understand, intellectually at least, the special view of reality that anciently evolved in that country. That view, though not unique, was expressed uniquely. It has been called a philosophy, but properly speaking it was not that. It was a *Way of Awakening.*

Philosophy is a Western term, deriving from two classical Greek words meaning "love (*philos*) of wisdom (*sophia*)." Implied in this term is theory over experience, and *aspiration toward* wisdom rather than wisdom itself. The Hindu Way of Awakening, by contrast, emphasizes experience over theory, and intuition over logic. Its aim is to inspire the longing for blissful union with God.

When Western missionaries first arrived in India and tried to familiarize themselves with its ancient teachings, they were bewildered by such seemingly impious and presumptuous declarations as, "I am Brahman [God]." Where, in these statements, were the traditional sentiments of humility and self-reproach? The rishis didn't lament their lives as sinful! They didn't beg for God's mercy. Beg! quite the opposite, they seemed to expect grace as their divine right. Besides— a lesser point to be sure—where were their religious institutions? their hierarchies of priests? Who, in short, was in charge? In the end, the missionaries decided that those rishis' abstractions belonged, not to theology, but more properly to the realm of philosophy. Only Jesus Christ had the right to say, "I and my Father are one." Moreover, while the statements of those ancient rishis were quite outside any religious frame of reference with which the missionaries were familiar, they resonated with the thinking of a few Western philosophers. Philosophy, then, surely, was the safest category in which to file away their teachings and, hopefully, to forget them.

I took a course in the history of philosophy many years ago. The professor began with a brief reference to the teachings of India, quoting examples from them to describe the dawn of "intelligent speculation" in human history.

But India's teachings were not speculative. They were based on divine revelation. Because the statements were so categorical, a few Indians have proposed that they belong in the realm of science. Indeed, the revelations are so cosmic that they approach more closely the findings of physics and astronomy than the pious pronouncements of preachers.

Scientists, however, unlike the ancient rishis, claim no absolute knowledge of anything. Their knowledge is intellectual, and is based on outer experiment rather than on direct inner experience. Science doesn't even consider the heart's feelings and the intuitive aspects of consciousness, without which human understanding, limited to intellection, is like a man hopping along the street on one leg.

The greatest difference between the ancient rishis and modern scientists is the rishis' apparent lack of dependence on tools and technology. "What, no telescopes?" exclaims the scientist. "No microscopes? How could the insights of those men be more than inspired guesses? Their whole system lacks proper methodology!"

True, the rishis made claims so cosmic that even modern physics seems only to be catching up with them (and realizing, after every scientific breakthrough, that the ancients were there long before them).* Back when Westerners first began reading Indian "philosophy," the statements they found in it far exceeded any insight that science had yet achieved, or even imagined.

Again, on a less cosmic level, India's wise men described our planet Earth (correctly, as we now realize) as inconceivably ancient, and the human race as older than anyone steeped in Darwinism could allow. "Superstition!" scoffed Western theologians and scientists alike. Even as recently as a century ago, the West was still reeling under the impact of the discovery by

---

*The following quotation was a chapter heading in my book, *Crises in Modern Thought:* "Nobody can foresee whether these modern speculations . . . will ever be susceptible to condensation into a social or religious system. Remarkably enough, however, they remind one of certain aspects of the Brahminical Upanishads." —J.H.F. Umbgrove, in *Symphony of the Earth*

geologists that the earth was formed eons ago, and not in 4004 B.C. as theologians had determined.

While the Christian churches lamented the advent of modern science, and regretted intensely a methodology that insisted on investigating every claim rather than taking their own dogmas on faith, at least science didn't intrude into those realms which theologians considered properly their own. Reluctantly, the churches conceded to science the study of natural phenomena, but they were confident that at least the Supernatural would remain their domain forever.

Exposure to Indian "philosophy" threatened their neat division of so-called "expertise." Missionaries could make nothing of teachings in the Indian scriptures, for example, that denied the very reality of matter, and that rejected altogether any suggestion that God is "Wholly Other"—radically different, in other words, from His created beings.

The difficulty they faced in categorizing the Indian teachings continues to the present day. The questions persist: Are those teachings a science? Certainly not in the generally accepted sense. Are they, then, a religion? Again, not in the sense most religionists accept. The only category acceptable, within the framework of Western tradition, remains even today that of philosophy. And Indians, too, seem to have resigned themselves to having their teachings thus categorized; most Indians, too, speak of them as a "philosophy." Many of them, having been educated in Western culture, reject as vehemently as any Westerner the possibility of attaining insights by revelation similar to those which science has gained only by exacting logic and painstaking experimentation.

The Indian teachings, however, are not theoretical, though they are consistent with some of the theoretical speculations of philosophy. A new designation is needed for them. It must be shown that, if not religious in the normally accepted sense, they are *more* religious rather than less so, for they are intensely spiritual.

The missionaries, as much so as archeologists when finding themselves confronted with evidence of great civilizations in ancient times, gave their answer: "It can't be so, therefore it isn't so." They considered themselves the representatives of the one and only true religion in the world. It was they, therefore, who had the duty of setting the tone for what was and was not truly spiritual.

It is human nature to accuse others of any faults one possesses in himself. The presumption of those Christians in India in defining spirituality by the way they themselves lived made it inevitable that they would accuse the rishis of arrogance and presumption for claiming to have realized oneness with God. Their next step, then, was equally inevitable: Hindus, they concluded, are a hopelessly pagan people, amazingly resistant to conversion; they hold bizarre beliefs to which no pious person ought even to listen.

The missionaries wouldn't face the fact that, when Jesus Christ made the same statement, and the Jews accused him of blasphemy for making it, he answered them that the scriptures themselves make this claim for *everyone.**

* "Is it not written in your law, I said, Ye are gods?" (John 10:34)

What the Indian scriptures do, indeed, is fulfill the deeper teachings of every great scripture. For they define, and give substance to, the revelation behind all religions.

The Indian teachings, and the deeper teachings of all religions, offer the only hope there is of bringing the religions of the world into a state of mutual appreciation and harmony. Only thus may religion command once again, in the eyes of all mankind, the respect that is presently accorded only the material sciences.

Such a shift in attitudes is urgently needed, for science has seduced people from high ideals, and in so doing has, though perhaps inadvertently, plunged the human race into a vortex of cynicism, selfishness, and atheism. Religion alone, if reinstated in its former place of importance in people's eyes, could return society to a desperately needed equilibrium.

To every religion there are two sides, as there are to all things created. The first is its exoteric, or outer, aspect; this is the one universally recognized, since it is enshrined in religious structures everywhere. But there is another aspect also, which, like the other side of the moon, remains hidden from our outward gaze. This is the esoteric, or inner, side.

The outer aspect is what attracts congregations, and keeps them faithful and supportive. The inner aspect, because it is so little known, is seldom thought about except by those few who sincerely long to understand life's deeper meaning.

During the twenty-four centuries of descending, and then of re-ascending Kali Yuga, which ended in 1700

A.D., congregational worship was the norm in religious activity. Few people in those times were spiritually refined enough to understand even vaguely the meaning of Jesus Christ's words, "The kingdom of God is within." What, they must have wondered, can possibly be "within" people except blood, bones, and a few organs?

It was believed even then that certain mystics had had supernatural experiences—of angels, for example, or devas, coming down from the heavens. In some cases those experiences were given respectful attention. Even so, the recognition accorded them was screened carefully for the masses, wherever possible. For mystical experience lies outside the power of priests and organizations to control. As a Roman Catholic priest once put it to me, "There are truths we simply can't preach to the people."

The Gnostics of early Christendom believed in seeking personal spiritual experience. For this reason, primarily, they were branded as heretics. The Church succeeded at last in suppressing the entire Gnostic movement.

Sufi mystics were persecuted by their Moslem co-religionists, and found it necessary to conceal their spiritual teachings behind sensual imagery. They made wine their symbol for divine ecstasy. "The Beloved" was their metaphor for God, whom they allowed the uninitiated to imagine as a beautiful woman. Omar Khayyam, the Persian poet whose *Rubaiyat* were translated into English by Edward FitzGerald in the Nineteenth Century, was not the hedonist that

FitzGerald claimed, but a great spiritual master. Paramhansa Yogananda makes this point abundantly clear in his inspiring book, *The Rubaiyat of Omar Khayyam Explained.**

India alone, among the great world religions, preserved the deeper spiritual teachings undisguised and undiluted. It was able to do so precisely *because* religion in India was never formally organized. It had no priestly hierarchy. Anyone could teach what he wanted, and was received in a spirit similar to that expressed by Rabbi Gamaliel in Acts of the Apostles of the Bible. The rabbi, referring to the new sect of Christians, said: "Leave these people alone: for if their teaching or their work be of men, it will come to nothing: But if it be of God, you will not be able to overthrow it, and may even be found to be fighting against God" (Acts 5:38,39). The result, in India, has perhaps been an excessive diversity in the outer aspects of its religion, but it has also been an extraordinary development of the inner.

India has accomplished in the field of spirituality what, in the world of finance, the free market (as opposed to a controlled economy) has succeeded in doing: The individual spiritual seeker has been left free to explore and develop his own spiritual potentials.

Other spiritual traditions, too, have hinted at the deeper truths of inward religion. Other scriptures have declared them. But the priests in every religion seldom

---

*Crystal Clarity, Publishers, Nevada City, California, 1994.

quote those passages, which they rightly see as threatening to their institutional preeminence.

Indeed, the scriptures themselves caution reticence in speaking of deep truths. The masses even today, at the dawn of Dwapara Yuga, are not ready to absorb the higher teachings. Addicts as they are of ego-consciousness, they cannot comprehend that a chasm separates the ego-self from the formless and eternal soul. Even the ancient rishis warned that deep truths should not be spoken of openly to the worldly minded. Jesus Christ expressed this caution colorfully: "Give not that which is holy unto dogs, neither cast ye your pearls before swine, lest they trample them under their feet, and turn again and rend you" (Matthew, Chapter 7).

India concealed deep truths behind a veil of symbolism, and offered only the tip of the iceberg, as it were, for those earnest seekers to see who might want to know more.

Symbolism and outward religion are synonymous. Few people are capable of even imagining transcendental truths. Symbols, for the majority, take the place of that which lies above rational comprehension.

Outward religion may be described as the *Way of Belief*. Although the beliefs, symbols, and rituals of outward religion are many, it is justifiable to describe them all similarly, as the Ways of Belief: the Christian Way of Belief, the Jewish Way of Belief, the Moslem Way of Belief, and so on. The aim of formal religion is to inspire people to embrace higher values: to be truthful, to be honest, to be charitable, and to say their prayers regularly. Those values are stated variously, depending on cultural differences, but basically their message is the same. Because the *symbols* of those values differ, however, and because religion tends to focus especially on its symbols, what people concentrate on is not the similarities, but the differences.

So long as outward teachings remain the primary focus of religion, there is no hope that the various religions will ever come together in a spirit of friendship and mutual appreciation. The less able people are to prove the truths they believe in, the more firmly entrenched they become in their own dogmas and opinions. Only by concentrating on their deep-seated common goals will they ever find a way of coexisting in harmony.

Outwardly speaking, the differences are legion. Religious antagonism has been the cause of bloodier conflicts than the ambitions of kings. The inward, experiential aspect of religion is little recognized by orthodox religionists anywhere, steeped as they are in outward symbolism.

Higher truths belong to those few who, as Jesus Christ repeatedly put it, "have eyes to see, and ears to hear." If, however, any possibility exists for achieving a spirit of appreciation and respect among the religions, it can only come from re-emphasizing the inner Way. For the emphasis of experiential religion is on those timeless truths which form the deep basis of all religions. This emphasis is what I have called *The Way of Awakening*.

Efforts have been made during the past century to persuade the world's religious leaders to come to an agreement on certain articles of faith. These attempts all encounter the same problem: the fact that people are convinced that their own belief systems are infallible, exclusive, and unique. Inter-religious cooperation will never take place so long as the attempt to achieve it demands a sacrifice of commitment to specific symbols. Moreover, in formal, outward religion, universal acceptance is unattainable even in such basic matters as belief in God, in the soul, or in an after-life. Buddhists claim there is no God. Shintoists reject the idea of a soul. Orthodox Jews—many of them—don't believe in an after-life. These are, it must be admitted, fundamental issues.

In their inner aspect, however, all religions have very much in common. For they accept the importance to each one of us of raising our consciousness, expanding our awareness, and deepening our sensitivity to the needs of others. They agree that an expansion of sympathy is important to our spiritual development. And if any of them disagree on anything, it is only because their symbols propose different methods for attaining these goals—Christians insisting, for example, that we take the name of Jesus, Moslems, that we name Mohammed, and fundamentalist Hindus shouting "Krishna! Krishna!" or "Shiva! Shiva!" These are all symbols, only, of formless virtues and abstract truths. The Star of David, the Cross, the Crescent, and the lotus too, may never unite people's sentiments everywhere, but religion basically serves mankind universally as a *Way of Unfoldment and Awakening.*

The outer aspects of religion, which I've called the Way of Belief, represent people's need for a higher purpose in their lives. The inner aspects, on the other hand, represent their need for *personal attunement* with that higher purpose. Every religion offers, apart from its claims to uniqueness, this Way of universal unfoldment and inner Awakening.

It is, as I've already emphasized, a mistake to speak of Hinduism as a *philosophy*. It is correct, however, to include those ancient teachings in this broad category as the Hindu Way of Awakening. The compatibility of this with other Ways of Awakening consists in the fact that its aim is not merely abstract: It focuses on inspiring the individual to live more charitably, and in a spirit of expanding sensitivity toward others, while gradually transcending egoism altogether in the realization that God alone IS. As the Jews put it millennia ago: "Hear O Israel, the Lord our God, the Lord is *One.*"

What, then, *is* the Indian, or Hindu, Way of Awakening? It is its revelation. The revelation is not unique to Hindus. It is as universal as the principles of mathematics. And its truths have been realized by every great master, of every true religion.

No religion outside of India, however, has stated that revelation so clearly, so openly, and so encouragingly for all seekers.

And what is that revelation? Its essence will be discussed in the next two chapters of this book.

Chapter Eight

The Hindu Revelation—Part One

Sanatan Dharma—the Eternal Religion

Western theologians, thinkers, and of course philosophers, comfortable in their assessment of the Indian teachings as a "philosophy," often praise its lofty "concepts," its cosmic "generalizations," and its approach *"even in theory"* to the sweeping insights which science, with advanced technology, has succeeded in proving *in reality.*

A Catholic cardinal in Rome once remarked to me, "Indian philosophy went as far as human thought can go toward probing Life's great mysteries. What it lacked, of course, was *revelation.*" Indian perceptions of reality, in other words, could not be classed as *divine revelation* such as that propounded in the Holy Bible, particularly by Jesus Christ, and even more particularly as interpreted by the Roman Catholic Church. That cardinal was "damning with faint praise" indeed lofty teachings that have given rise to the oldest and most spiritually centered civilization on earth—teachings that could, if they were understood, inspire the world's religions to coexist in mutual respect, harmony, and cooperation for world betterment.

Even the "gods and goddesses" of the Hindu pantheon, scoffed at by many non-Hindus as proof of "paganism and idolatry," have a profound symbolic significance, the comprehension of which is essential for understanding what "Hinduism" is really all about.

I put "Hinduism" in quotation marks here because Hinduism, as the name of India's oldest religion, is a foreign imposition. The indigenous name for that religion has always been *Sanatan Dharma:* the "Eternal Religion." A sect exists nowadays, however, that claims the name, *Sanatan Dharma,* for its own narrow interpretation of the ancient religion. For this reason, I have deemed it judicious at the present time not to associate Hinduism too closely with that name, though in truth Sanatan Dharma has no such limited implications. Its concern is with absolute Truth, not with systems of belief. The absolute Truth is universal, and forever impersonal. No one has a proprietary claim to it.

Sanatan Dharma, rightly understood, is rooted in the foundations of the universe. As a teaching, it excludes no practice that is designed to ennoble and uplift the mind, to awaken selfless love in the heart, to inspire longing for the truth, to loosen the bonds of egotism and selfishness, and to deepen our awareness of what *is* as opposed to what merely appears to be.

Put more simply still, the goal of *Sanatan Dharma* is twofold: the *upliftment* of human consciousness, on the one hand, and the *expansion* of our self-identity through love, on the other, that we embrace all life and all reality as our own. Any practice that inspires people in this *direction*, even if it doesn't define the goal so specifically, belongs rightfully within the domain of *Sanatan Dharma.*

Thus, one may insist that salvation can come only by accepting Jesus Christ. *Sanatan Dharma* offers no objection. If in this faith our consciousness is raised, and our sympathies are expanded, we fulfill the essential conditions of *Sanatan Dharma,* of which direct experience, and not mental or emotional belief, is the criterion.

If, on the other hand, we insist that Jesus Christ is "the only way" but in our narrow devotion we fail to raise our consciousness, or to enlarge our sympathies, then our religion, *as practiced,* is incompatible with Sanatan Dharma, the Eternal Religion. According to *Sanatan Dharma,* we ought not even, in this case, to be considered true Christians, for we ignore the principles that were taught by Jesus, which make Christianity truly a path to God and to soul-salvation. As Jesus Christ himself put it, "Why call ye me Lord, Lord and *do not* the things which I say?" (Luke 6:46)

This judgment applies equally to every religion. Man's beliefs are provisional, merely. Like the hypotheses of science, they must be proved by direct experience, which in scientific terminology is known as "experiment." If people in their belief systems proclaim that only their own beliefs are true, and don't test those beliefs by experience, they are guilty of presumption.

Sanatan Dharma speaks not of static systems of belief, but rather of *directions* of development. A

Christian may cry, "Jesus is the way." A Muslim may reply, "No! Mohammed is God's prophet." A Buddhist may pontificate that the Way lies only through acceptance of the Buddha. The important thing, really, is that a person live according to the highest and most expansive vision of truth that he himself is capable of understanding, and that he aspire toward that truth, expanding his heart's sympathies to embrace all humanity and all life.

If, on the other hand,—I offer this thought as a theoretical possibility, merely—it should develop that any one great teacher really *is* more exalted than any other, this truth will surely be revealed, in time, to the sincere aspirant. There is no need to fight over it. A serious search for truth must bring the realization at last of whatever best way there is.

Granted, the teachings of India's rishis offer no hint of partiality on God's part, or on the part of Truth. Granted again, the introduction of such partiality into the divine scheme of things would contradict the very concept of universality. Yet those ancient sages would never have become excited over any such contradiction of their teachings. The realization of the *Truth,* whatsoever it might be, was their single ideal.

In ancient India, it was traditional not to append a teacher's name to his teachings. Today, when the teachings are so multifarious, it helps to know who has authored an idea. But those far-off days lacked the religious competitiveness that is so prevalent in the present age of diminished spiritual awareness. Who, in reality, has any right to claim "authorship" of a single truth?

There was a second reason for the tradition of authorship anonymity. For truth, though eternal, may need to be emphasized differently at different times and places, and according to different levels of understanding. Words, moreover, can change their meaning with the passage of time. A truth stated at one time or place may require a different statement at another. It isn't that the truth itself changes. To verbalize it, however, is already to qualify it, and thereby to make it less universal. And to qualify it to the extent of *personalizing* it is to take it a step farther away from the central fact of its eternal verity.

The ultimate authority for truth must be, wherever possible, a true sage of one's own time, and not one who lived remote centuries ago. The important thing, always, is that the sage today be as developed in Self-realization as his predecessor. Every age has produced at least a few such great men and women.

An important test of authenticity is *consistency* with the authorities of the ages. If a recent, or still-living, teacher contradicts any fundamental truth that has been taught consistently by great masters through the ages, his teaching must be considered false. It is to underscore this consistency, and not to help them to reach their own conclusions, that great masters generally quote the scriptures. Divine truths differ in this respect from the declarations of modern scientists, whose understanding of reality changes repeatedly as new facts come to light. Realized truth, as opposed to empirical knowledge, is changeless and eternal. This was why the ancient teachings were called *Sanatan Dharma*.

What the rishis taught, be it understood further, was their own *expressions* of *Sanatan Dharma*. We ought not to confuse any expression of truth, however much founded on direct revelation, with the direct *experience* of that truth. This caveat is important, for it is unfortunately common for students, whose approach to the scriptures, often, is only intellectual, to quarrel over the wording of a teaching rather than trying to *intuit* its actual meaning, behind those words. Often, in other words, what appear to be contradictions are actually confirmation couched in different terminology.

In India, the rishis of ancient times are universally recognized as the first proponents of *Sanatan Dharma*. Let us consider a few of their basic insights.

The Cosmic Dream

According to their teachings—based not on deduction but on direct experience, and therefore as much (though, it must be added also, not more so) rooted in "revelation" as any other great scripture—the universe is a dream projected by the consciousness of the Infinite Spirit. Everything in creation, including our own all-too-real-seeming egos, is an illusion. Consciousness predates the creation of the universe. It is *manifested* by the human brain, but could never be *produced* by it.

Matter, to our human senses, seems very substantial. The rocks are hard; the rivers flow and are wet; even jellyfish, so almost-insubstantial to our eyes, have a clear definition of their own. Science, however, paints a very different picture of reality from that which is revealed to us by the senses. In the early 20th century, as I remarked earlier, physicists proved that matter is only a vibration of energy. Before very long, a few were going even farther: They declared that energy itself looks suspiciously as though it were a manifestation of consciousness.

According to the ancient Indian scriptures, Spirit is the Ultimate Reality. Non-Hindus accuse Hinduism of being pantheistic, and so it is, but not in the sense those critics imagine. Hindu pantheism is not, as they claim, a teaching that everything is God.

A wave is not the ocean. No created being can be God. As the Bible puts it: "No man hath seen God at any time" (John 1:8). And as the Bhagavad Gita puts it: "Thou canst not see Me with mortal eyes. Therefore I now give thee sight divine" (Chapter 11). The wave, as Paramhansa Yogananda explained, is not the ocean, but the ocean is all of its waves. Nothing is God, but God, at the same time, is everything in the sense that it was He alone who manifested it. It is not *man*—this human body, these mortal eyes—who sees God. God can be seen only with spiritual vision—with the eye of the soul. The mosquito is only a minute *expression* of the Dreamer's consciousness. Its manifestation of divine wisdom is limited to such merely instinctual knowledge as the way to dilute animal blood before sucking on it.

Even the rocks, according to the ancient teachings, manifest a certain glimmering of awareness. This claim has been made by famous scientists such as India's Jagadis Chandra Bose and Germany's Karl Bonhoeffer, both of whom succeeded in stimulating a response in apparently "inanimate" matter. Their conclusion is that no clear dividing line exists between "animate" and "inanimate" matter.*

"God sleeps in the rocks," proclaim the Indian scriptures, "dreams in the plants, stirs toward wakefulness in the animals, and in mankind is awake to his own ego-individuality." In the enlightened sage, finally, he awakens to the full reality of who he truly is, in His infinite Self. God cannot be defined in terms of any specific manifestation, nor indeed in terms of their sum total. He is beyond all possibility of definition. The Bhagavad Gita, the best-known scripture of India, states this point clearly: "Though I manifest Myself in all things, I am identified with none of them."

The Dream as Vibration

The Divine immanence in all things, manifested *through* all things but never revealed through any of them, was one of the great pronouncements of the rishis of ancient times. God, the Eternal Spirit, set a portion of His consciousness in movement, which is to

*See my discussion of this subject in *Crises in Modern Thought,* Crystal Clarity, Publishers, Nevada City, California. Revised edition, 1988.

say, in vibration. Through that vibration, He produced what our senses tell us is reality, but what is in truth an appearance, merely. This appearance is His cosmic dream.

A portion of cosmic vibration moved, and produced thoughts and ideas. In its next stage of manifestation, a portion of this ideational or causal universe, as it is called, vibrated more grossly, or broadly, producing light and energy. Finally, a portion of that light, which is known as the astral universe, vibrated still more grossly, creating the illusion of heaviness; thus was manifested the material universe. Matter is nothing but energy; energy is only thought; and thought is only a vibration on the surface, so to speak, of the calm Ocean, the Supreme Spirit.

The entire universe, from its subtlest to its grossest manifestations, exists as vibration. The Indian scriptures name this cosmic vibration "AUM." Were AUM, the cosmic vibration, to be stilled, appearances would cease to exist, and even the consciousness of them would sink back into the still ocean of Spirit from which they emerged.

The Holy Bible, by no means a stranger to these truths, begins with the words: "In the beginning God created the heaven and the earth. And the earth was without form, and void; and darkness was upon the face of the deep. And the Spirit of God moved upon the face of the waters. And God said, Let there be light: and there was light. And God saw the light, that it was good, and God divided the light from the darkness."

Dwaita, or Duality

Vibration is an alternating movement in opposite directions from a state of rest at the center. Thus, everything in manifestation, being vibrant, is founded on the cosmic principle of *Dwaita,* or duality.

Vibrations, as is generally known, produce sound. The Cosmic Sound is the "faithful and true witness"* to the divine origin of the universe. It is not what the outer ear cognizes as sound. Rather, it is sound in its subtler, divine aspect. AUM is experienced *within* the body, not outside of it through the ears. Its sound is first heard within the right ear. Later, it is heard and felt throughout the body. With deeper spiritual development, it is experienced in the entire universe. This great sound, concentrated on in deep meditation, draws the mind away from sensory involvement and into a state of inner, divine communion.

Cosmic Vibration is a manifestation of divine consciousness. It manifests not only as sound, but as every other aspect of Divine Vibration. It is easy, intellectually, to comprehend its manifestation as light, since it is well known that light also accompanies vibration. But the Cosmic Vibration manifests also as divine love, as ecstatic bliss, as absolute power, as heavenly peace, as a vast and dynamic calmness, and as perfect wisdom. All that the mind can know of inspiration derives from that vibration.

---

*This quote is from the Holy Bible: "These things saith the Amen, the faithful and true witness, the beginning of the creation of God" (Revelation 3:14). The Amen, here, is the Sound of AUM.

The most compelling aspect of the Cosmic Vibration, because the most steady in its manifestation, is sound. This is the aspect, therefore, that is especially emphasized for those who meditate deeply. AUM is indescribable, since it plays upon the very "strings" of our inner being. It can be vaguely compared, however, to a distant roar—the "sound of many waters," as the Holy Bible describes it.

There are several important passages in the Bible that show agreement with this teaching, and demonstrate its universality. I quote a few of these passages here:

"Afterward he brought me to the gate, even the gate that looketh toward the east; And, behold, the glory of the God of Israel came from the way of the east: and his voice was like a noise of many waters, and the earth shined with his glory." (Ezekiel 43:1,2) The Hebrew word for "east" is *kedem*, meaning forehead, or "that which lies before." The "gate" that looks toward the east is the spiritual eye in the forehead, midway between the eyebrows. The devotee is also taught to look eastward in meditation.

"His voice was as the sound of many waters." (Revelation 1:15)

"Suddenly there came a sound from heaven as of a rushing mighty wind." (Acts 2:2)

"God thundereth marvellously with his voice: great things doeth he, which we cannot comprehend." (Job 37:5)

To chant "AUM" at the beginning and at the ending of a prayer means to offer that prayer up for acceptance by the Universal Consciousness. It is to affirm, "This prayer is rooted in Truth." "Amen" means AUM, and is uttered at the end of semitic-based prayers for the same reason.

A good illustration of the relation of Spirit to Cosmic Vibration is the ocean and its waves. The up-and-down motion of the waves is always equal. Thus, the over-all level of the ocean remains unchanged no matter how high the waves. Every upward movement is offset by a corresponding trough.

The movement of an ocean's waves is infinitely complex. On the surface of every large wave there are innumerable wavelets; on every wavelet, smaller ripples; on every ripple, tiny tremors barely visible to the human eye. The movements of cosmic vibration, similarly, exist in even the minutest tremor of an electron.

No illustration can express fully the truth it illustrates. Ocean waves are only material manifestations, but Cosmic Vibration includes everything in existence. It embraces an infinity of thoughts, feelings, and states of consciousness. The fundamental duality of all things is as evident in human consciousness as in matter. The illustration of the ocean wave explains to some extent also the ups and downs of human reaction and emotion.

The larger an ocean wave, the more it obscures—for a person riding it—the ocean's underlying calmness. The larger the wave, moreover, the deeper its offsetting trough. The more people distance themselves from their soul-center within by seeking fulfillment in outer excitement and sense-stimulation, the more their emotional highs are followed, necessarily, by emotional lows of sorrow and depression. The greater a victory, the greater also, sooner or later, the defeat. The greater the fame, the greater the opposition from others. The greater the success, the greater—perhaps in some other area of life—the degree of failure.

Life and the law of cause and effect known as karma rules all activity, and has no choice but to give us, as the sum total of all our endeavors, that bleak figure: zero. Just as the over-all ocean level never changes, so our central reality remains unaltered and untouched by anything we do and by anything that happens to us in this dream-world of outward manifestation.

The Three Qualities, or Gunas

Duality is self regulated by its own tendency to return to its own central reality, just as surface tension acts upon waves to draw them back to the over-all water level. Thus, implicit in duality is a third quality. Vibrational movement is dual, but the *qualities* of that duality are triune.

This third quality, while not properly speaking a movement, is no mere *lack* of movement, either. Its action, in other words, is positive, not passive. The stilling of the waves is due not only to a gradual dissipation of energy, but to a naturally calming influence, which, in the case of water, we call surface tension. Duality could not even exist were there not this central influence holding it together.

In cosmic duality there are three *qualities* of movement, the third of which acts as a brake, so to speak, on that duality. The Sanskrit word for these qualities is *guna*. The names of the three *guna*s are *rajas* (energizing, or activating), *tamas* (depressing), and *sattwa* (calming).

Sattwa guna is that quality which ultimately stills vibratory creation, causing it to merge back into the Supreme Spirit. In the unmoving Spirit, the gunas cease to exist. A liberated master, having merged his consciousness in the infinite stillness of Spirit, is spoken of as *triguna rahitam:* one who has transcended Nature's triune qualities.

In the realm of outward manifestation—the realm of relativity—the calming influence of sattwa guna is found at every level. In the ocean, surface tension is present over the entire ocean surface, including every wave, wavelet, ripple, and tremor. In the smallest tremor there is surface tension. When a ripple is calmed by surface tension, however, only its own little movement is stilled; the water around it may be as restless as ever.

Sattwa guna is present even where the dualities are in violent opposition to one another. The oppositions are least in evidence however, in sattwa guna, and in tamo guna, most in evidence. The rapid rise and fall of smaller waves, indicating the predominance of rajo guna, becomes slower and more ponderous when they rise to greater heights. With the predominance of tamo guna, extremes are the norm: violent anger, passion, and greed, followed by their inevitable consequences: disgust, depression, and satiety.

All the three gunas interact, however, at every level of cosmic manifestation. For even where duality is the most violent, and delusion consequently the strongest, there is always present to some degree, however slight, sattwa guna's calming influence, and the restless influence of rajo guna. Even the most violent criminal, for example, may also be a loyal son and devoted father.

Again, where the extremes of duality subside to a minimum, there will still be, comparatively speaking, some of the restless spirit of *rajas* and, to an even smaller degree, some of the heaviness of tamo guna. The greatest saint, in whom sattwa guna is uppermost, must still move about (a manifestation of rajo guna), and sleep or relax (a manifestation of tamo guna). He may express occasional impatience (rajo guna), or perhaps sadness (tamo guna) at the folly of others. Obviously, rajo and tamo gunas are present to only a minute degree, relatively speaking, in the case of the saint, whose "wave" of manifestation is closely attuned to the vibrationless Spirit, the Cosmic Ocean. Creation could not exist, however, without the continuous operation of all the three gunas.*

On a human level, it is helpful to visualize these qualities in terms of movements of energy within the body.

Rajo Guna is the energizing current in Nature, and therefore also in man. Rajo Guna in the body, then,

*Inspiring discussions of this subject appear in Paramhansa Yogananda's book, *God Talks With Arjuna,* an enlightened commentary on the Bhagavad Gita. Self-Realization Fellowship, Los Angeles, California, 1995.

manifests as an *upward* movement. Indeed, we associate any surge of energy—a feeling of elation, for example—with an upward flow. With developing spiritual sensitivity it becomes clear also that this flow takes place primarily in the spine. Whether or not our awareness is centered there, an upward flow of energy and consciousness in the body produces a tendency to look upward, to stand or sit up straight, and to *feel* generally "up" about life.

Tamo guna is associated with a lessening, or withdrawal, of energy. The natural direction of *tamas* is downward, similar to the way a trough forms to compensate for every wave. In the human body, this downward flow of energy often produces a sense of depression, the emotional opposite of euphoria. A literal feeling of depression is reflected in what is known today as "body language": a forward stoop, slumped shoulders, the downward-turned mouth, a lowered gaze.

If, however, the movement is not only downward, but inward, the negation of energy manifested by tamo guna may be transformed, instead, into a negation of outward involvement altogether and a reaffirmation of inner, sattwic peace. Thus, it does not follow that rajo guna is *necessarily* followed by a tamasic reaction. With discrimination, rajas can be canceled by a withdrawal into sattwic calmness and even breathlessness, which accompanies deep states of meditation.

Another "ripple" of vibratory manifestation in the body is the breath. With every inhalation there is a subconscious affirmation of rising energy, and a corresponding upward movement of energy in the body. With every exhalation, there is a subconscious affirmation of that upward energy being cancelled, and a corresponding downward flow of energy in the body.

The breathing process may in fact serve as a means of gaining control over the emotional reactive process, and in time of winning release from the unceasing restlessness of *maya,* or delusion. "Breathlessness," Paramhansa Yogananda used to say, "is deathlessness."

The play of *maya* can perpetuate itself indefinitely. As long as the divine impetus toward creation persists, so long will vibratory movement continue. The Indian scriptures speak of cosmic manifestation as a "Day of Brahma." This vast cycle of time endures for many billions of years. A corresponding "Night of Brahma," when creation is withdrawn into the Spirit, is said to endure for an equal period of time. (One wonders how time can even be measured in that state of timelessness, when movement itself ceases to exist. Ah, well! The divine mystery cannot but be fathomless, ultimately, to the human mind.)

In Indian art and literature, the duality of Cosmic Vibration, and the triune nature of the qualities, are constant themes. An understanding of them is important for any understanding of the symbolism through which they are represented.

Ultimately, what the symbols in Indian art depict are not merely cosmic abstractions. They refer above all to the human condition, and especially to man's own search for enlightenment. Literal facts—specific events in history, for example, and the disposition and definition of a heavenly hierarchy—are subordinate to the direction of man's inner development.

Chapter Nine

The Hindu Revelation—Part Two

Duality in the Interrelationship of the Sexes

Duality expresses itself through an infinity of contrasts: light and darkness, heat and cold, good and evil, love and hate, pleasure and pain, health and sickness.

One dualism that holds endless fascination for humanity, and that is treated extensively in Indian art and literature, is the relationship of the sexes.

Considering our discussion in the last chapter, it is natural to ask, do rajo and tamo guna apply also to the sexes? And if so, where does the third guna, sattwa, come in?

All of them do fit into the picture, of course, but it would be misleading to limit these qualities to either sex. The cosmic drama is too complex to allow for simplistic explanations. The qualities alternate in every human being, and in every human relationship. In many cases they shift back and forth as one partner helps to raise—or, possibly, to degrade—the other.

As for sattwa, it operates on the sexes in moments, for example, of reconciliation, or in the harmony they experience together when polar differences between them subside.

In India, the female is referred to as the *shakti* of the male, for she provides the impetus for what he does and inspires him to enthusiasm. Does this make the male principle, the receiver in this case, tamasic? To say so would be, again, simplistic.

There are two relationships in the rapport between the sexes. One is that of parents helping their off-spring. The other is the complementary magnetism between them.

Feminine nature represents feeling; masculine nature, reason. In women, feeling is generally upper-most, and reason, hidden. In men, the opposite is true: reason is generally uppermost, and feeling, hidden. We can bring these qualities into balance within ourselves, as well. This is indeed the ideal condition, and comes about naturally as a person develops spiritually.

Calm feeling is intuition. The intuitive faculty is centered in the heart—or, more accurately, in the dorsal region of the spine just behind the heart. In human beings the quality of feeling is more refined than in the lower animals. Women's breasts therefore develop not on the abdomen, but on their chests close to the heart. The very fact that women have breasts is a manifestation of their hearts' feelings; in turn, they also influence their feelings.

Reason's center is situated in the frontal lobe of the brain, just behind the forehead. Therefore the male skull is slightly ridged above the eyebrows, and is also rather square in shape. A woman's forehead curves back gently at the hairline. The point midway between the eyebrows is described as the seat of the intellect, of will power, and—in superconsciousness—of ecstasy and spiritual vision. By the shape of the skull anthropologists can tell whether a skeleton is male or female.

When the feeling flows upward from the heart toward the brain, and through the brain to the "spiritual eye" in the forehead, perfect mental and emotional equilibrium is achieved. Feeling, if not "kept in a state of reason"—which is when its flow is upward—can become caught up in emotional likes and dislikes, and focused more on its subjective reactions than on objective reality.

Reason, on the other hand, unsupported by feeling, is barren, and loses a real sense of purpose. When reason is divorced from feeling, the mind spins webs of endless theorizing, but lacks the incentive to act upon them.

Feeling and reason are complementary halves of one whole. When they are brought into harmonious balance, the creative flow rises effortlessly from a wellspring of intuitive perception.

Feeling is the *shakti* of reason. It gives the masculine half what is needed, to energize it. On the other hand, if feeling is not directed toward reasonable ends it can lose its grip on objective reality, and even become wild and untamable.

In the rapport between the sexes, man is often motivated to action by drawing inspiration from woman. Women inspire men with the *desire* to create. It is women's nature also to *want* to see that things get done. Without the incentive of feeling, whether generated outwardly by a woman or inwardly in himself, a man is inclined, as I said, merely to mull ideas over in his head without acting on them.

A woman, lacking a man's calming influence, sometimes becomes scattered emotionally. For the heart is the fulcrum, the midpoint, of the spine. The energy from that center can flow as easily downward as upward. If it flows upward, feeling is lifted toward calm intuition. If it flows downward, feeling is plunged into a pit of emotions that are more or less destructive depending on the intensity of the flow. The intuitive faculty is innate in everybody. Emotions disrupt it, however, and funnel the heart's essentially expansive nature into pettiness and a narrowing perception of life.

In the lower animals, and also in people whose feeling quality is dormant, the spinal energy flows naturally downward. Evidence of this downward flow in animals can be seen in the simple fact that they have tails. The tail is an expression of instinctual feeling. Notice how a dog wags its tail when it is happy, and lets it droop when it is morose. Notice also the teats of animals, physical indicators of the degree of refinement of feeling. In animals, they are located on the abdomen, not on the chest as with human beings.

The base of the spine is the body's negative pole. If a person's feelings are centered there, he is spiritually asleep. To rouse himself from that slumber, his energy must be directed upward. Until at least a few rays of this energy rise to the heart level, the feelings remain centered in material, not in spiritual, awareness. From the heart level the energy, known as *kundalini,* must be raised still further for spiritual enlightenment, until it is centered in the forehead.

The negative pole of the spine is associated with the feminine quality in human nature—not, be it noted, with women, but with a centripetal focus of feeling. When the feeling quality in men is centered there, the male organ assumes the function of a false spine, the top of which, like a false head, draws that energy outward, toward physical procreation and material involvement.

The natural direction of unawakened masculine energy in human nature—not, again, men's energy, specifically is outward. Its creative urge expresses itself most commonly in physical procreation. But the more this energy becomes focused at the spiritual eye, the more it causes the mind to be attracted to subtler forms of creativity, either mental or spiritual, and toward an ever-more universal outlook on life.

Feminine magnetism, when not drawn outside itself by masculine magnetism, tends somewhat toward contractiveness, for its natural direction is inward. When balanced with the masculine, it finds outward expression through nourishing life, and through nourishing creativity in others. Many women are less inclined to engage personally in artistic creativity, but when they do so their works tend to emphasize adaptability and harmony, rather than conquest and victory: typically masculine attitudes. Both expansion and contraction, outward creativity and inward absorption, are necessary for achieving balance in human nature. The sexes, then, are spiritually necessary to each other.

Understanding in any case begins not in the head but in the heart. Feeling, more than reason, is the motivating force in every endeavor. And feeling, in the form of devotion, is the prime mover in spiritual development. That is why more women than men dedicate themselves to the spiritual life. Indeed, in every field of life the tendency to get involved is generally found more in women than in men. Feeling is what awakens the energy.

The power that *directs* energy, on the other hand, is the will. The will power, like the power of reasoning, is centered at the point between the eyebrows. (Note how a person tends to knit his eyebrows whenever he wills something strongly.) "The greater the will, the greater the flow of energy" was a favorite dictum of Paramhansa Yogananda's. When awakened feeling is channeled through a powerful will, it can achieve outstanding success in anything it attempts.

The facts I've outlined are important for understanding many of the basic aspects of Indian art. For traditional art in that country places great emphasis on the masculine and feminine qualities—Shiva and Shakti—and on the ideal attitudes and modes of comportment between men and women.

Duality as Expressed in the Universe

The duality of masculinity and femininity is rooted in infinity. God, the Spirit beyond vibratory manifestation, represents the masculine principle. Cosmic Vibration, in relation to the Spirit, represents the eternal feminine. Cosmic Vibration embraces all the three gunas: the outwardly creative force, which produces the waves of duality, and the sattwic call to enlightenment within. Cosmic Vibration as the Divine Mother draws us inward, toward the Self, with the power of divine love. But Cosmic Vibration as tamo and rajo guna, is *Maha Shakti,* the universal creative force, expressing that creativity outwardly, through duality.

Woman, similarly, plays two roles in her relation to man: inwardly uplifting, and outwardly involving. As mother and spiritual partner, she nourishes, heals, and inspires. As an energizing force, on the other hand, she goads him to get involved in things, and as temptress she draws his energy into a downward spiral of delusion. *Maha Shakti,* the feminine creative force in the universe, vibrates waves of consciousness into outer manifestation as rajo and tamo gunas, then holds them in balance with sattwa guna. In outward manifestation, she is cosmic delusion itself. Projecting her power away from the vibrationless state of Spirit, she creates the vibrations of duality. But in her inwardly oriented aspect, She is sattwa guna, the Divine Mother, calming the waves of vibration and eternally drawing Her children back toward oneness with the Infinite.

It is up to us to decide which aspect of Cosmic Vibration we choose to worship: outwardness, and delusion, or inwardness, and soul-communion with the Divine. The outward aspect is Satan. The inward aspect is the Divine Mother. To "worship" Satan may mean nothing more than to be attached outwardly to the cosmic play. It needn't mean consciously invoking

115

evil. Vibration, however, whipped up to extreme opposites—towering waves, profound troughs—inevitably produces those aspects of consciousness which we define as evil: hatred, cruelty, violent passion, and the like. Good and evil are relative terms, but actively to court that force which moves consciously toward violent opposites is to worship what mankind calls Satan. It is to serve that force, and invite it to use one as an instrument. "Worship" in the sense of *attraction* to outwardness, though certainly not Satan worship in the accepted sense, means still to live under the sway of satanic delusion—a fact that becomes clear only when the soul tries to escape the net. In the lives of saints we frequently see the great lengths to which *maya* goes in trying to prevent their escape.

In the metaphysical sense, no human being may rightly be considered masculine. Everything in creation is feminine relative to the One Male Principle: the Spirit beyond Vibration.* Thus, Krishna, in allegory, represents the Infinite Spirit. Around Him the devotees, as *gopis* or cowherd girls, dance in eternal joy.

People naturally have difficulty with imagining the Divine Mother in a dual role of savior on the one hand, and deluder on the other. But cosmic reality is impersonal. Its personal response is one we ourselves draw, whether by love and selfless devotion, or by selfish desires for self-aggrandizement.

When the Lord manifested His creation, He projected out of Himself a creative force. This force, like any directional flow, had inertial power. Once set into

---

*This point will be explained in Chapter Seventeen.

motion, it continued outward into further manifestation. A *gyanic* attitude—one based, that is to say, on impersonal wisdom—finds no difficulty in viewing the Divine Mother as actively lashing the waves of manifestation into a storm of creative activity. For the *bhakta,* or devotee of God, however, this image holds little appeal. The outward flow of divine creativity is manifested as Nature, or *Prakriti. Prakriti* is responsible for bringing everything into manifestation, from the tenderness of flowers and the gentle dewdrops to the untamed fury of earthquakes and hurricanes. The *bhakta,* however, prefers to think of the Divine Mother in that aspect which smiles upon us with loving acceptance and forgiveness.

In fact, as I said, the Divine Mother manifests to the devotee in whatever aspect he himself desires. There are people who worship Her in Her outward, terrible aspect, as *Maya,* or Satan. (Human beings are capable of every conceivable mental aberration!) This is not the sattwic and compassionate Divine Mother, however. It is Mother Nature in her rajasic and tamasic modes: vibratory creation, busy manifesting waves. Those with developed discrimination worship that aspect of Infinite Consciousness which uplifts the soul, but spiritually blind people may seek "supernatural" powers through attunement with the outward power of *Prakriti.* These people get swept away, sooner or later, in the raging waters of *maya,* and eventually lose whatever transitory powers they attained. Falling into mental confusion, they become victims of their own dark ambitions.

For the outward flow of creation sets itself in opposition to the inwardly drawing power of divine love. It acts in satanic rebellion, as it were, against God. *Maya*'s creative power is endlessly self-perpetuating.

We should not, however, think of the Divine Mother as equally bad and good: terror-inspiring on the one hand, and loving and compassionate on the other. The human mind cannot begin to conceive the vastness of God. All that is, exists in Him. Both good and evil are parts of that consciousness. But in her aspect of universal temptress, the feminine aspect is not our Divine Mother. She is that power which would bind us with the coils of delusion.

Perhaps the following illustration will help to clarify the matter. A playwright brings out of himself all the characters in his play. The hero and the villain, equally, are his own creations. While writing the villain's part, he enters earnestly into that state of mind in order to make it convincing. But his *purpose* in creating the villain is to make the hero more attractive. The existence of evil in God's drama, similarly, serves the higher purpose of inspiring us to love the good, and the ultimate purpose of drawing us beyond duality into oneness with Him.

We attract to ourselves whatever aspect of the Divine we worship. The choice is forever ours. If we enter the clear river flowing majestically to the sea of cosmic consciousness, we find ourselves carried along with increasing ease. At no point do we need to do all the work of swimming ourselves. Ultimately, the current carries us to oneness with Infinite Bliss.

We can also, however, if we so choose, enter the other river, which may be described as a channel for the sewage of delusion. If we feel attracted to its stench—and even the lowest vice has its own sordid appeal—by entering that river we find ourselves pulled along not into any cosmic ocean, but into a fetid swamp of brooding delusions. Only remorse, and a deep desire to change ourselves, can extricate us from this putrescence. Hell is described in some religions as eternal, but the rishis said that suffering only seems eternal while it lasts. A finite cause could not possibly have an infinite effect. "Every grief, every wrong," as I wrote once in a poem, "has its ending in song."

For the soul, there is no final destruction. We came from God; our souls are as eternal as He is. *Maya*, though all-but-overwhelming to our senses, is only an illusion. The miasma that rises from the swamp of delusion prevents us from perceiving our own brilliant, ultimate destiny. But when the ego cries out for relief from its nightmares, at first so pleasant and exciting but now tawdry and hardly bearable, our will to return to the wakeful state attracts a willing response from the Divine. For the river of Grace flows forever in the hidden depths of our being. There is no need to cry out loudly to God for help. He is forever near us—nearer than our most secret thoughts and feelings.

The cosmic push to create becomes, in its more violent vibratory extremes, what the scriptures call, Satan. Satan is metaphorically depicted as a fallen angel, arrogantly rebelling against the Lord. He is that aspect of universal consciousness which projects vibration farther and farther away from its initial calm attunement with divine bliss. Satan therefore represents evil, for, in contrast to the good, he tries consciously to make duality attractive to mankind.

There is duality also in these two opposite forces of creation: the outward thrust into diversity, and the inward withdrawal toward a state of oneness. The inwardly drawing force attracts us through God-reminding qualities, tender feelings, Nature's beauties, and soul-elevating art and music. These qualities soften our hearts and uplift our consciousness. But the evil we see around us—the ugliness and the menace: These represent the disharmonious influence of cosmic delusion. They express an actual, conscious force, which endeavors to keep all beings tossing on the waves of *maya,* fearful of drowning in their suffering. Fortunately, the soul's eternal essence can never be drowned. It cannot suffer. It cannot be harmed by what is, after all, only a dream.

Satan exists. He is no mere figment of the human imagination. But he represents the outer fringes, so to speak, of the cosmic dream, and also the outer fringe of any aspect of *maya* that involves us. Cosmic creation may be thought of as a series of concentric circles, the most spiritual of them being those closest to the center, and the grossest being those farthest away. The outer circles represent the tamasic, or satanic, influence in the universe. Every circle, however, is like a broad band, of which the inner edge represents its spiritual aspect, and the outer, facing away from the center, the satanic aspect. Good and evil are not static conditions: They are directions of movement. For a spiritual person to declare, "I want to become a millionaire!" would very probably indicate a step away from the inner gains he had made. But for a lazy fellow to make the same announcement might well indicate a move toward greater good; at least it would mean stirring his tamasic sloth with a teaspoon of energy.

Even in the subtlest inner circle, the one closest to the divine center, the tenderest sentiment contains some hint of a tendency to hold back from the center itself. And even in the outermost circles of delusory involvement there is some hint of divine memory—perhaps an occasional feeling of nostalgia for a purer, more inwardly centered life.

Nothing in this vibratory universe is wholly static. The sincere aspirant must try always to keep his consciousness flowing toward *greater* awareness in God. Because the ego is the main cause of man's limitations and delusions, he should unceasingly offer it up onto the altar of Infinity. God's is, fortunately, the stronger magnetism; it is well always to remember that. There is no cause for fear. The mere *willingness* to enter the divine stream is often all one needs. The Bhagavad Gita puts it beautifully: "If you can do no more, then offer Me your failure." The mere desire to return to God invites the divine compassion. Every soul, eventually, will be drawn back to its eternal source in God.

The outer aspect of Prakriti is experienced through the physical senses. We hear its sound in the wind and in the songs of birds. We see it trembling in the leaves of trees. Occasionally, in outward Prakriti's manifestations, we sense lofty truths drawing our hearts toward communion with the Divine Mother inwardly, in our souls.

Only in the silence of inner communion, however, does She commune with us directly, in the two-way communication that the word "communion" implies. Her manifestation appears to us through the great sound of AUM, audible in meditation. AUM is the "Word of God" described in the Bible in a famous passage: "In the beginning was the Word, and the Word was with God, and the Word *was* God."

The Cosmic Trinity

When God manifested Himself as creation, and thereby dreamt, or vibrated, a portion of His consciousness, He did it by "singing," so to speak, His Cosmic "Song": the Cosmic Sound. In that sound all things exist. They are not themselves that sound, and yet that sound-vibration makes their existence possible. Everything exists as vibration. The Sound itself, on the other hand, is an aspect of God. God is, first, the Vibrationless Void, the Supreme Spirit. He is also the Cosmic Sound through which He brought the universe into being.

In this cosmic manifestation His nature became, not dual, but triune. For in addition to what I have called the Vibrationless Void, untouched by the dream of cosmic creation, and Cosmic Vibration, divinely conscious also (for it was only out of consciousness that creation could be brought into manifestation) there is the vibrationless reflection of the Supreme Spirit as the subtle essence of every atom, of every point of light in the universe.

Without this third aspect of Infinite Consciousness, creation itself would disintegrate in chaos. That poem that I quoted earlier* has another pertinent line: "Without silence, what is song?" It is the perfect stillness at the heart of all movement that holds movement together. This third aspect of Divine Consciousness is known in the Hindu scriptures as *Kutastha Chaitanya*. In the West it has been called, the "Christ Consciousness." Christian theology describes it as "the only begotten Son of God"—and rightly so, for the *Kutastha Chaitanya* is the reflection of God the Father's still presence in all creation.

The Christ Consciousness was realized by Jesus, as it has been by all great spiritual masters. It could never have defined him exclusively, however. Christ defines the enlightened master, but no master, even, can be, himself, a definition of the Christ, just as no wave can define the ocean.

The Hindu Trinity is the same as the Christian Trinity of Father, Son, and Holy Ghost. In Sanskrit this Trinity is called AUM-TAT-SAT: Father, Son, and Holy Ghost in reverse order. Students of comparative religion generally confuse the Hindu Trinity with another trinity, that of AUM: Brahma, Vishnu, and Shiva. This subject we'll take up in Part Two of this book.

---

* "Song of the Nightingale." I composed it for a story I wrote when I was eighteen called, "The Singer and the Nightingale." Crystal Clarity, Publishers, Nevada City, California.

AUM is Cosmic Vibration, the great Sound out of which all things were manifested. TAT is the unmoving reflection of Spirit in creation, the Christ Consciousness residing within everything as the most refined essence of its being. And SAT is the Vibrationless Spirit beyond creation.

The Holy Ghost, in mystical symbology, is also Mary, who was historically the mother of Jesus but who in cosmic terms represents the Divine Mother, the feminine aspect of God.

Every aspect of reality, even the subtlest, is reflected in every other, even the grossest. Divine Love expresses itself in matter, for example, as the force of gravity. Divine Energy expresses itself, similarly, as the blind force of electricity. The Cosmic Trinity is reflected in humanity also, as the human family. Just as the power of Spirit infuses cosmic vibration to produce the universe, so the human father inseminates the mother to produce the child. Again, in the home it is the mother, traditionally, who sees to it that things get done. The father's work takes him outside the home. Their love for one another is cemented by the birth of offspring. Parents who recognize and accept this division of responsibility have the greatest chances of creating a harmonious home.

The human body also reflects the Cosmic Trinity, although, as we shall see later, this trinity of energies is more closely allied to the aspects of AUM.

There are two currents in the superficial spine; they are known as *iḍa* and *pingala*. These currents are connected to our reactive emotions: our likes and dislikes.

They are also connected to the breath. The energy's ascent and descent in the spine is, in a subtle sense, what causes the breath to move in and out. With the movement of the breath, our consciousness is drawn outward to the body. And with the upward and downward movement of energy in the spine, we react affirmatively or negatingly to outer experiences, thereby becoming involved in them emotionally.

When the reactive process becomes stilled, the breath is stilled also, and the energy withdraws into the deep spine, the *sushumna*. It is particularly in these three currents that we find, as I'll explain later, the three gunas expressed in the human body.

A magnetic polarity exists between the base of the spine and the top of the head. The pole at the top is cognized first as the spiritual eye between the eyebrows.

The lower pole in the spine is the negative, or feminine. The upper pole is positive, or masculine. These terms, negative and positive, however, signify only a contractive and an expansive magnetism, and have nothing to do with the sexes, as such.

When, during deep meditation, the energy (called *kundalini*) rises in the deep spine, it passes eventually through the spiritual eye, and becomes united with the upper, positive pole at the top of the head. This "north" pole is known as the *sahasrara*, "thousand-rayed," also called the "thousand-petaled lotus."

From the *sahasrara* numerous rays of energy emanate, suggestive of the energy emanating from our galactic center to the entire Milky Way system. For the body itself is a miniature universe. The rays from the *sahasrara* keep the physical body nourished with energy. Perceived in meditation, *sahasrara* thrills the soul with divine ecstasy.

In this chapter and in the foregoing one I have attempted a brief over-view of the fundamental insights that were expressed symbolically in some of the figures and designs of Indian art. The insights are many, of which I have explained only a few. Certain others will be covered in further discussion of specific symbols.

Hindu Temples as Symbols of the Human Body

One final point remains to be made here. It has to do with the profusion of images in Hindu temples. This sight is often the only impression foreigners receive of Hinduism. The very profusion discourages many of them from pursuing further the subject of Hinduism. Let us, then, briefly consider what it all means.

The human body is the actual temple, within which, in meditation, we can realize God. The Hindu temple, therefore, symbolizes the human body. Most Hindu temples are quite simple, inside, and sparse in their display of symbols. This simplicity represents the stillness of divine communion.

On the outside, however, suggestive of the body's surface, a profusion of symbols represents the sensory world. Here we often see *Maya* displayed in all her exuberance, attempting to ensnare mankind in delusion. The art on the outside of a Hindu temple can be robust—to put it mildly! The artists—most of whom, probably, were themselves steeped in worldliness—seized on the excuse of serving a religious cause to express themselves with abandon.

What one beholds on approaching these Hindu temples can be misleading. Fortunately, this is not true of all Hindu temples, many of which are covered with inspiring scenes from epic spiritual allegories, especially the *Ramayana* and the *Mahabharata*.

The Hindu Way of Awakening is not in itself at all sensual. It encourages transcendence of worldly attachment in divine ecstasy. Nor is the outward profusion, distorted during dark centuries of Kali Yuga, a true indication of the inner teachings of Hinduism.

Regrettably, as I said in the Introduction, Hinduism is often omitted from rosters of the world's religions. Buddhism is advanced in its place as a more sophisticated version of that religion. The lusty scenes on certain Hindu temples, and the almost equally exuberant symbols and allegories expressed in much of Indian art and legend, have induced the uninitiated to dismiss Hinduism itself as a primitive religion, inextricably tangled in superstition.

The purpose of this book is to show underlying truths that are essential to all religions, and indeed central to them. I have selected Hinduism as my main example of this universality precisely *because* its complexity seems so noisily to deny the very theme of essential unity. Behind its exotic, and sometimes even grotesque, masks the Hindu Way of Awakening is as pure and exalted as any religion the human race has ever been blessed to receive from the heart of God.

Chapter Ten

Symbolism—or Idolatry?

Few Hindus are conscious of the depth of prejudice many Westerners hold toward the term, "idol worship." The guide in a Hindu temple may announce blithely to his group of tourists, "Now, over there you see people worshiping the idol of Shiva"; he has no idea that he has opened up a Pandora's box of negative connotations. That glazed look in some of their eyes wouldn't be there if he'd used other words: "image," perhaps, instead of *idol*, and "praying before" instead of *worshiping*.

For Westerners, even if they never go to church, know that the Bible condemns idolatry. "Thou shalt have no other gods before me," is the Lord's commandment to Moses; and, "Thou shalt not make unto thee any graven image, or any likeness of any thing. . . . Thou shalt not bow down to them, nor serve them." The perpetrators of such acts are described as people "who hate me."

The Hindu, for his part, is nonplussed by the Western antipathy to spiritual imagery. Don't Christians, too, have their cross? their images of Jesus and Mary? their paintings of scenes from the Bible and of episodes from the lives of saints? And don't Jews have their Star of David? their holy tabernacle? Where is the harm, the Hindu wonders, in images that remind one of God and that inspire devotion to Him?

Merely to create a likeness of something doesn't, in itself, imply "hatred" of God. To hate God is to turn away from Him—not to wish Him harm, but to be willing to do harm to one's own attunement with the Source of all true happiness, harmony, and love. Images, in themselves, are neutral. Their influence is positive or negative depending mainly on our reaction to them. But certain images remind us more naturally of God and of noble qualities in ourselves. They inspire in us thoughts of love, beauty, and wisdom. If we find an image spiritually uplifting, it would be absurd to claim that it is an "instrument of Satan." Austerely to reject all images as evil results merely in lukewarm devotion. Why be guided by pallid examples—"puritans," for example, to whom, as D. H. Lawrence put it, "all things are impure"—when innumerable saints down the centuries have employed images in their devotions?

The key to understanding the Biblical commandment lies in the words, "them who hate me." A little further on in the same section the Israelites created a golden calf as an idol, and plied themselves to its worship. Their act was a sin for the reason that it implied turning away from God and worshiping something else *instead of* Him. To their minds, the calf represented temptation.

It makes no sense to imagine the Jews worshiping anything so trivial as the replica of a domestic animal! And even assuming that such a mania really engulfed a whole people, God can hardly have denounced their insanity so scathingly. Denunciation is usually reserved for people whose behavior is at least rational.

The calf was made of gold. The implication is clear. The Israelites, after wandering long years in the desert,* were tired of living in poverty. They wanted material luxuries. They wanted wealth.

The story tells us, further, that they were dancing naked before the idol. This added detail suggests they were indulging freely once again in sexual pleasures.

Money and sex: two of the most common temptations to which human flesh is heir. No mention is made of the third: drunkenness. It is easy to infer it, however, from their evidently orgiastic revelry.

The Israelites' "hatred" of God lay in their return to worldly consciousness and the sleep of delusion. Money, sex, and intoxication†: These three delusions are mentioned in countless scriptures as those which most commonly induce mankind to forget God. The Israelites succumbed to these weaknesses and abandoned their spiritual calling. Albeit God's "chosen

---

*Even those forty years can only have had an allegorical significance. Otherwise, a simple glance at any map of the Sinai desert must cause wonder at how a whole nation could have roamed about in that relatively small area for so many years. Surely they'd have strayed over its boundaries repeatedly into settled territories.

†"Wine, woman, and gold" is the traditional wording. Women, understandably, are not happy to be placed in this light. For man also is a temptation, for woman. The traditional wording comes from the fact that spiritual students in those days were usually men. The predominance of the male role in society is a feature of Kali Yuga, when people considered physical force the only, or at least the most effective, means of controlling matter.

people," supposedly, they decided to choose Him no longer, and thereby forfeited their rights in that pact.

It is quite possible that the idol they worshiped was not a calf at all, but a golden image of wealth in their own minds. If, however, there actually was such an image, they must have looked upon it as a symbol of future abundance, since the calf, in time, becomes a giver of milk. Clearly, in any case, it was their hearts' *intention* that God condemned. For the Lord watches our hearts, not our outer deeds.

Scriptural accounts are frequently allegorical, even when they are based on historical facts. If we take them too literally, we miss their message and are left with impressions that are not only unclear but misleading. When scripture seems to contradict common human experience, which it does especially when teaching through allegories, it is important that we not abandon common sense. It helps also to seek guidance in these matters, whether from others who are wise, or from within ourselves, in prayer and meditation.

Religious institutions are not always reliable in their guidance. In many matters they have an agenda based on self-interest rather than on truth. The representatives of such institutions, moreover, may not always be wise, themselves.

Wisdom must be sought from such persons as have gained spiritual insight, born of soul-attunement with the Truth. The true custodians of religion are Self-realized saints. *Living wisdom* is the key even to ancient revelation.

Divine truths never change. In this respect they differ from facts as propounded by science. Truth must be realized by direct experience. No words can ever express it adequately. Truth is *Sanatan Dharma,* the eternal truth of the soul, which the Ways of Belief express variously according to humanity's differing needs. *Sanatan Dharma* transcends the Ways of Awakening, whether Hindu, Christian, Jewish, or any other. The seeds of *Sanatan Dharma* sprout and grow in inner silence.

What must have occurred in that episode of the golden calf was that when Moses went into seclusion on the mountain, people lost, for a time, their living source of wisdom. Lacking the inspiration of his company, they became attracted anew to the pleasures of the senses. The Bible doesn't tell us they had worshiped idols previously. Their reversion to old ways implied the reawakening of old material desires.

It is not in their love for material images that men sin so much as in the nature of that love. To believe that all images are displeasing to God is unreasonable. Imagination is one of mankind's most potentially helpful talents. It cannot be suppressed. If we push our fantasies down into the subconscious they will only rise again, often when we least expect them to. Often, they explode with irrational and uncontrollable force. Imagination can, however, be put to good use if, instead of suppressing it, we guide it constructively. To surround ourselves with inspiring images rather than with those which stimulate worldly desires is one way of transmuting harmful tendencies into beneficial ones.

There is no danger that we'll turn away from God or come to "hate" Him, so long as we keep love for Him alive in our hearts. To exclude imagery from our spiritual practices altogether, however, deprives the fires of devotion of fuel. Sometimes, such rigid exclusion hardens into fanaticism.

Guru Nanak, the first of the Sikh gurus, taught the underlying oneness of all religions. When Muslims, however, insisted on excluding imagery from worship altogether, he pointed out to them, "You bow to Mecca when you pray.* Isn't the Black Stone there an image also?" He wasn't condemning their reverence; he was only pointing out that human nature needs material references of *some* kind, just as a plant needs soil, to grow.

It is an unusual person who can find inspiration in abstractions. Though the highest truths transcend all forms, we live in a world of forms. A tree's branches make it possible to climb to the top. Even so, images enable the mind to climb the "tree" of spiritual experience. From the known we can rise more easily to the unknown than if we ignored the known altogether. From our present level of understanding, more easily than from no understanding at all, it is more possible to rise to ever-higher levels of understanding.

Nonetheless, formlessness *is* the higher reality. Saint Teresa of Avila in Spain once had a vision of what she called the "formless Christ." Her spiritual confessor

---

*Mecca was the birthplace of Mohammed. The city includes the site of the Black Stone, said to have been received by Abraham from the angel Gabriel.

expressed doubt. How could Jesus appear without form? He found corroboration, however, in the writings of Saint Thomas Aquinas, foremost among Christian theologians. The formless Christ, St. Thomas had written, is indeed the higher spiritual experience.

We do not deny that formless state in visualizing images that inspire us. To limit religion to abstractions suppresses its vitality and may reduce it, in time, to a mere catalogue of conventions.

The Hindu doesn't equate the word "worship" with reverential awe. I was struck, one day, to hear an Indian astrologer advise a client, "Worship your gemstone before wearing it in that ring." What he meant, I realized, was simply, "Project energy into the stone; try to harmonize its energy with your own." He was not telling his client to prostrate before it!

There are, as must be evident by now, many levels of meaning to be studied in India's very ancient teachings. I've just mentioned two more points of common confusion: astrology, and gemstones endowed with spiritual power. Perhaps I should explain them briefly.

According to Hindu belief, certain gemstones have a vibratory resonance with certain planets: emeralds, with the planet Mercury; diamonds, with Venus; blue sapphires, with Saturn. To project energy into an emerald, then, is a way of harmonizing oneself with it and also with the vibratory influences of the planet Mercury.

As regards astrology, modern science is discovering the existence of countless electro-magnetic forces and of their inter-relationships with one another. Given this new awareness, it seems no longer reasonable to dismiss the possibility of electro-magnetic planetary influences on our lives. Advocates of astrology quote Isaac Newton, who claimed that this ancient science had been tested *and verified* times without number. My own goal in these pages is to peel away layers of misunderstanding. Idols and idol worship are two such layers. Gemstones and astrology are two more.

Worship, then—to return to our theme—does not necessarily imply, for the Hindu, an attitude of adoration or of superstitious or reverential awe. It may connote these attitudes also, but what it generally means is simply directing one's energy toward some particular focus of concentration. To approach God through images is to use forms as means of awakening love for Him in our hearts. Images are a means of bringing our devotion to a focus. They are reminders of higher, but abstract, spiritual truths. We treasure religious images in much the same way that we treasure photographs of our close relatives. No sensible person would mistake photographs of them for his actual loved ones.

There is a certain happy exuberance in the Hindu's sense of kinship with all Nature. His attitude may be difficult for people to appreciate who consider matter as lacking any vestige of consciousness, and consciousness itself to be merely the product of energy-activity in the brain. The Hindu teachings declare just the opposite. Consciousness, according to them, even in its dimmest manifestations, is *actively manifested* throughout the universe. All things, viewed in this light, are seen to belong to a universal awareness in which we, too, participate. Everything, then, is interconnected—like the members of an extended, and indeed cosmic, family. Modern physics, approaching the matter from another direction, is coming to much the same conclusion. The Hindu, then, may be seen as no mere sentimentalist in his practice of embracing everything cheerfully as his own.

A beautiful Bengali song, *"Gokula Chandra,"* is addressed to Krishna as an incarnation of the Supreme Lord. The singer accuses Him of "cruelty" for leaving Gokula, where he had spent his boyhood years. This accusation is not meant disrespectfully, for it is uttered with love (Would anyone dream of expressing himself with such familiarity to a government official?) A mutuality of love is what keeps this accusation from being presumptuous. The singer is confident in her love.*

Where, in true prayer, is the need for fear or diplomacy? God knows our hearts; He knows better than we do whether we truly love Him.

I will never forget my surprise during my first meeting with a wonderful woman saint of Bengal, Anandamoyee Ma. She had given me a shawl which, as she wanted me to know, she'd been wearing for five years. Deeply moved by this demonstration of her love, I thanked her from my heart. To my astonishment, she replied, "Would you thank your own mother?"

"Why, yes," I replied. "Of course I would!" There ensued a little good-natured badinage over these

---

*People forget, incidentally, that the English "thou" is the familiar pronoun, and was originally used in prayer to imply closeness to God.

differences of social custom. I told her I simply couldn't accept such a gift without saying anything to her: I had to show my gratitude *somehow*. Everyone present laughed kindly at my predicament. It was years, however, before I was able fully to appreciate that, in the cultural context of India, to thank one's own mother would be almost tantamount to accusing her of loving inadequately, since she wanted thanks for demonstrating it.

To the Westerner this seems a strange usage. But I remember a Bengali gentleman once remarking in jest, "If we Indians learned nothing else from the English, at least we got from them this quaint expression, 'Thank you.'"

The typical Indian home is far from starved for love. Indeed, the heart connections I've observed there impress me as perhaps deeper than in most Western homes. For the Indian inclines by temperament to live more centered in his heart.

It is natural for the Indian worshiper to address God with a fondness that amounts sometimes to familiarity. And why not? God is our very own. The Bengali song to which I referred earlier concludes with these words: "I will follow him [Krishna] to Mathura, where he now dwells. And if I find him, though I know his consciousness is as infinite as the ocean, I will bind him with my sari and drag him home with me!" What Western hymnist would dare to express himself to God in terms of such intimacy? And yet, again: Why not? If we really love God, is it not natural to hold Him close?

The Hindu imagines God smiling from the hearts of trees, from the flowers, from the rocks, from the hearts of clouds. The Hindu wife is taught to love her husband as a manifestation of the Lord Himself. The Hindu husband is taught to love his wife as a manifestation of the Divine Mother. Instead of excluding God from daily life, the devout Hindu includes Him in everything he does. And instead of distancing Him—as people do, in effect, when they freeze Him in ice cubes of intellectual definition—the Hindu thinks of God as his Divine Friend, his Cosmic Beloved, his Divine Mother, his Heavenly Father.

Some intellectually inclined Christians, seeking a scientifically acceptable definition of God, refer to Him (or, perhaps one should say, to It) in such abstract terms as "The Cosmic Ground of Being"—a suggestion, if I'm not mistaken, of Paul Tillich's. In fact this concept is too abstract to evokes any image in the mind. Its effect is, instead, to discourage devotional aspiration. Once people's devotion to God as their very own is taken from them in the name of scientific exactness, they often divert "faith" itself to social issues.

To define God in vague terms holds little appeal for the Hindu, despite the abundance of abstractions in the Hindu teachings. What is the point of worship, he asks, if it awakens no enthusiasm in the heart? And how much enthusiasm can a person muster over a "cosmic ground of being"? To the Hindu, worship means love. It means childlike trust. Even *Gyana yoga* (the path of wisdom and discrimination), which focuses almost wholly on abstractions, offers soul-freeing concepts such as expansive consciousness. Its saying, "Thou art that" (*Tat tuam asi*), is very different from stating, "That which He is, thou art not." It is a dull Hindu indeed who satisfies himself merely with definitions, and who scoffs at spiritual enthusiasm as, perhaps, childish and unnecessary.

Jesus Christ, a Jew among Jews, broke with austere tradition in calling Yahweh (the Lord), "Father." This paternal concept enabled his followers to develop heartfelt devotion instead of pondering intellectually the aridities of divine law. The average person, Jesus knew, is not capable of conceptualizing an Infinite Spirit. In effect what he told people was, "God wants your love, not your intellectual subtlety." Carefully chiseled prayers are like pleas uttered before an emperor's throne, anxiously and with fear of being rejected. God doesn't want our diplomacy. He is our nearest and dearest. He is our very own.

Indian devotional songs often express such sentiments as, "I will make Thee a prisoner of my heart's love!" Lest the devotion descend to a level of ego-familiarity, there are allegories also that teach us to seek a divine, not a human, relationship with the Lord. For the familiarity we feel must be of the soul.

The allegory is told of Radha, principal among the woman devotees of Lord Krishna. She and Krishna were walking together one day in the forest. Radha, suddenly filled with womanly affection for her Lord, exclaimed, sighing, "Oh, Beloved, I am so tired!" Krishna, aware of her innermost thoughts, inquired innocently, "Would you like me to carry you?" She was so pleased! "Climb up onto my back," he offered her. Radha did so.

Suddenly, she found herself sprawling flat on the ground: Krishna had vanished into thin air!

"Oh, Lord," she wept, "please forgive me! I realize my mistake now; I won't commit it again." Krishna at once reappeared smiling. There was no need for them to discuss the episode. Calmly they continued their walk in the forest together.

The Hindu, as I said, visualizes the Lord not only as omnipresent but as consciously *expressed* everywhere. In no single expression, nor even in the sum of all of them, is the Infinite Consciousness fully manifested. "The wave," Paramhansa Yogananda used to say by way of explanation, "is not the ocean." Nor can the combination of all the waves ever describe the ocean as it truly is. Even the spiritual masters, enlightened though they are, cannot express fully through their physical bodies the realization they enjoy inwardly. Infinity can never be more than hinted at through a finite vehicle.

Unenlightened human beings express the Infinite Consciousness more fully than do the lower animals, which are less aware. Above the human level exist angels, or advanced astral beings. These *devas*, as they are called in Sanskrit, are less highly evolved than spiritual masters, even if a master is still living on this earth. For the devas, too, are evolving spiritually, whereas a master has transcended evolution itself. In Paramhansa Yogananda's words, "There is no end to evolution. You go on until you achieve endlessness."

Human beings, having achieved some measure of self-awareness, have a duty to help uplift creatures on lower levels of evolution. Kindness to animals helps them in their spiritual unfoldment. It helps us, too, for it increases our attunement to the Source of All Love. The devas, in their turn, hasten their evolution by stooping down to help human beings. To pray to a deva or angel for help need no more imply lack of faith in God than would a request for help from a brother or sister instead of taking all of one's problems to one's parents.

Indeed, the Supreme Spirit seldom, if ever, intervenes directly in the affairs of man. It may be compared in this sense to a power station, the voltage of which must be stepped down by transformers so as not to incinerate the wiring in people's homes. The universe abounds with entities innumerable that actively direct the growth of plants and of motile creatures, the manifestation of new species, and the working out of individual and group karmas.

No created being is comparable to God. The Hindu doesn't even consider the majority of astral entities as deities. We might term them "nature spirits" or even "astral functionaries." On the other hand, these spirits thrive on love, and give us more energy if we offer them our love and appreciation. If they feel unloved and ignored, they withdraw in much the same way people do when their expressions of good will are misunderstood.

The analytical bias of the present age is having a devastating effect on our relationship with subtle forces in the universe. I read the other day that, to derive the same amount of nourishment from a bowl of spinach as people did sixty years ago, one would have to eat *eighty* bowlfuls. The life force is withdrawing from our planet, starved for want of reciprocal affection and appreciation.

There is no need to imagine fairies painting the flowers. All that is required of us is that we love the flowers. This love, alas, is diminishing. Rachel Carson highlighted this fact in her description of the ridicule heaped upon a hapless woman by a town committee for pleading against spraying the roadside plants with herbicide, because, as she'd put it, "They're beautiful."

It is known now that even plants respond to human love. Hindu tradition encourages, as I said, an attitude of happy coexistence with all life. The more love we give out, the more all things respond, reciprocating our feelings with harmony and abundance. Indeed, to express love toward the lower astral "deities" is, in the great scheme of things, one way of sharing God's love, particularly if it offers appreciation to Him, above all, for His inexhaustible bounty.

There are as many attitudes in these matters, of course, as there are human beings. Not everyone is blessed with discrimination. Even the primitive animist, however, shows an appreciation for subtle influences that is sadly lacking in sophisticated modern man. People's sensitivity today is hardened by their exposure to science. If, on the other hand, they are religiously inclined, their sensitivity is stunted by dogmas that declare one must pray only to God. In challenging the starkly purist attitude of this latter position, one may ask: Would an artist take it as a compliment if we refused to look at his paintings, giving as our explanation, "Our interest is solely in the artist"?

I may have been the first Westerner ever allowed into certain temples in India, including the Vishnupad temple at Gaya, where the great saint Chaitanya, centuries ago, was converted from being a professor of logic to an exalted devotee of God.

A temple priest, intrigued to see me there in meditation, asked me afterward, "What do you pray for?"

"Why, for the grace to love God wholeheartedly, as Chaitanya did; for the grace of communion with God; for union with Him."

"Ah, how wonderful!" he exclaimed, as though these goals were extraordinary.

"What are you saying?" I demanded. "Isn't that what everyone prays for?"

"Oh, by no means!" he replied. "Ask anyone. Most people pray for children, or money, or good health."

The *Adi,* or first, Shankaracharya said, "Childhood is busy with toys. Youth is busy with sex and romance. Middle age is busy with money and material security. Old age is busy with sickness and with worries about death. No one is busy with God!"

And Lord Krishna in the Bhagavad Gita declared, "Out of a thousand, only one seeks Me."

Because people everywhere live in ego-consciousness, not in soul-consciousness, what they want most from life is that their egoic desires be fulfilled. If a Christian doesn't pray to devas for this fulfillment, his abstention doesn't mean he wouldn't do so if he thought it might do him some good. Most people simply don't believe that anyone, even God, is really listening, so, resignedly, they try to get along on their own power.

Ignorance, both East and West, Paramhansa Yogananda used to say, is fifty-fifty. Buddha (a Hindu among Hindus, even as Jesus was a Jew among Jews) sought to persuade people not to think of religion as though it were a ritualistic exchange of heavenly merchandise. Vedic ceremonies, he insisted, are not bargaining events where the idea is to get as much as possible with a minimum of personal sacrifice. And, speaking of sacrifice, just see the irony of animal sacrifice! People, knowing that some sort of sacrifice is expected, seek a way around this inconvenience by sacrificing the life of an unfortunate goat! Why burden themselves, after all, with the task of self-transformation?

This, indeed, is a good definition of superstition: the expectation of getting something for nothing.

It is sheer superstition to expect a religious ceremony to flatter the ego of some deva into granting people's desires regardless of their actual deserts. The true goal of the spiritual life is Self-realization. Too many people, instead, use religion to deepen their sleep of delusion. It takes serious effort to find God: the sincere offering of every thought and feeling up to Him.

Few there are in any religion who willingly heed the divine call within. The Hindu's traditions may offer him more *encouragement* in this direction, but the average Hindu, too, is busy nowadays, like the Israelites of yore, worshiping the "golden calf" of materialism. High ideals, however, are still expressed in Hinduism. They are kept alive by sincere seekers. Hinduism, more than any other religion, teaches openly that *everyone* can know God.

I've remarked before that the religion of India resembles an ancient tree: gnarled, twisted, and perhaps in need of trimming. Any attempt to address this pruning task, however, must await the commission of God Himself. For anyone less than a living master to try it, as Keshab Chandra Sen did through the Brahmo Samaj movement in the Nineteenth Century, would be presumptuous. Meanwhile, the tree is still alive, at any rate, and flourishing. Its vitality is still strong, even so many centuries since other ancient civilizations have disappeared.

The images worshiped in Hinduism are foci, as I said, for people's devotion. Even in primitive religions, images are intended to direct people's energy toward subtler realities. In animism, these "subtler realities" may in fact be relatively gross, and may even be demonic. In any case, true idol worship has little to do with material images, as such. Idolatry means the worship of anything *instead of* God. The supreme error of idolatry is that it ignores the need for purity of heart, selfless love, expansive sympathy, and other qualities that uplift our aspirations toward God.

History suggests that the episode of the golden calf occurred during the descending age of Kali Yuga. It was approximately at that time that Buddha lived in

India. The people of that era needed an unusually stern warning, evidently, against material involvement. Great masters are seldom so denunciatory.

Most saints, past and present, have worshiped God in *some* kind of form, and have usually described Him in humanly approachable terms. Shankaracharya, an *advaitin* (a proponent of non-dualism) whose mission it was to remind people of the transcendent truth above all forms, composed a book of devotional verses to the Divine Mother. Ram Proshad, an Eighteenth Century Bengali devotee of God in the aspect of Divine Mother, wrote in a song of his, "Oh, a thousand Vedas declare it: My Divine Mother is formless (*nirakara*)."

The ultimate purpose of imagery is to lift the mind into communion with the Absolute. Always, the quest must be for transcendence. Paramhansa Yogananda used to say, "Even if God comes to you in vision, as for example the Divine Mother, try to see shining in Her eyes the consciousness of Infinity. Don't be attached to form of any kind, but concentrate on achieving union with the Absolute."

In light of Yogananda's statement, and of everything else we've discussed so far, it would be well to add that the deeper a person's devotion to God, no matter what his religion, the less interested he will be in its outer forms and symbols. Why, indeed, study the advertisements for a product when you have the product itself in your hands? As your devotion grows, you will naturally incline to seek God more in the formless Self within.

The Way of Belief belongs to outer religion. It may be called the Hindu Way of Belief, the Christian, the Muslim, or any other Way of Belief. The Way of Awakening, on the other hand, is the inner Way. It is universal. To follow the inner Way of Awakening is to withdraw somewhat from the social aspects of religion—its rituals, dogmas, and traditions—and to become more centered in the inner, spiritual quest. The Way of Awakening gradually leads the mind to perfect stillness, within.

Only by recognizing this Way of Awakening in their own teachings will the world's religions ever reach the point of interacting together in a mutual spirit of respect and appreciation. For each one, in its outer Way of Belief, is in certain ways unique. Who can say whether any one Way of Belief is better than all the others? People who believe in the need for agreement among the great religions must, if they equate religion with outer practices, be willing to dilute tenets that, to each religion, are important. For the differences *do* exist. Only by drastic compromise can people persuade themselves that Christians, Moslems, Hindus, and Shintoists are all saying the same thing.

Traditions, moreover, that people find meaningful who were raised in one religion may hold no appeal for those raised in another. The Christian crucifix—a good example—holds no special meaning for Hindus, and only negative connotations for Jews. If a person feels an affinity with some tradition other than his own, he is unlikely to feel it equally with all of them.

I myself, on entering a Hindu temple—and I consider myself a Hindu according to the true meaning of *Sanatan Dharma*—prostrate with love and devotion before the form I see displayed there, but afterward I close my eyes and meditate on the formless Spirit within, for which those forms are but symbols. I worship above all that One who resides in my own heart. For the true temple is the human body.

It is in this inner awareness, primarily, that I am a Hindu. In this same awareness I am also a Christian. And although I am less familiar with other Ways of Belief, should the occasion arise I would declare myself just as sincerely a Jew, a Buddhist, a Muslim, a Sikh, a Jain, a Zoroastrian, a Hopi Indian or a Sioux—not as a follower of their outer Ways of Belief, but as one who sincerely believes that all those ways are rooted in the universal goal of spiritual awakening.

Non-Hindus may feel no special attraction to Hindu deities, and may even be put off by a few of them. Certain Westerners do, I know, embrace the entire Hindu pantheon, but if theirs has been an outward conversion it amounts to little more than changing their clothes.

On the other hand, people who have been raised as Hindus, and who feel a deep affection for the elephant-headed Ganesha, for the monkey god Hanuman, for Rama and Sita, and Saraswati, do not deserve the label of idolaters. Their devotion is normal, and often beautiful. But even they would do well to recall these words of Swami Vivekananda: "It is a blessing to be born into a religion, but a misfortune to die in one." The Hindu if he is deeply committed never allows outwardly directed devotion to distract him from inner communion with God.

My purpose in writing this book is partly to help demystify the multiplicity of symbols in Hinduism for the sake of those who find them a barrier to spiritual understanding. It would defeat my purpose to explain every symbol, or even too many of them, in exhaustive detail. The reader might derive a little knowledge from such a book, but he wouldn't gain in wisdom thereby. My purpose, then, is to concentrate on a few of the more universal symbols, and to show that deep spiritual truths underlie all that apparent confusion.

If you want a more detailed explanation of Hindu symbols, I suggest you study several excellent works, among them David Frawley's *From the River of Heaven* and others, Heinrich Zimmer's *Myths and Symbols in Indian Art and Civilization,* and "Indu" Inder Jit's *Science of Symbols—A Deeper View of Indian Deities.* My goal here is above all to help the sincere truth-seeker to appreciate the revelation *behind* Hinduism's outer multiplicity.

For Hinduism is the most ancient expression of *Sanatan Dharma,* the eternal and universal religion. The true message of Hinduism, as it is of all other religions, is inward, not outward. It is a message of soul-upliftment, of inner purification, and of deepening awareness and love. Behind all its symbols, what Hinduism teaches is communion with God, and the upliftment of the individual's consciousness into ever-broader, ever-deeper perceptions of Truth.

Part Two

The Symbols

Chapter Eleven

Brahma, Vishnu, and Shiva: The Trinity of AUM

The number *three* has a universal resonance. The German philosopher Georg Hegel (1770–1831) discovered even in the prosaic subject of logic a kind of trinity, which he defined as *thesis, antithesis,* and *synthesis*. Despite the unfortunate consequences of this "dialectic," as he called it, which later became the basis for fascism and communism, the number three *is* basic to logical thinking. In plane geometry a basic figure is, again, the triangle. And in the Indian tradition, the number three appears repeatedly.

There are, for example, three nerves in the astral spine: the *ida, pingala,* and *sushumna nadis,* or channels of energy. These channels are indicated symbolically at the sacred *Triveni* in Allahabad, where two visible rivers, Ganga (the Ganges) and Jamuna, converge with a third, Saraswati, which is invisible though said to flow underground. This confluence is interpreted as representing the base of the spine, where the *ida, pingala,* and *sushumna nadis* meet. *Ida* and *pingala* are currents of energy that flow through the superficial spine, and manifest in the physical body as the sympathetic nervous system. The subtler current, called the *sushumna,* flows through the center.

We discussed previously the three gunas, or qualities, inherent in Nature. In addition to the gunas there are the "three worlds," described in other religions also: earth, heaven, and hell. A fuller understanding of these three worlds yields the three stages of cosmic manifestation: the causal (or ideational), astral, and material universes. And there are also the three bodies that encase the soul, which correspond to the three stages of universal manifestation: the causal, astral, and physical bodies. Spiritual liberation comes only after the soul has transcended every material, astral, and ideational attachment, at which point it is freed at last to unite with the bliss of infinite Spirit.

There are other important numbers also. Cosmic creation begins with the division of the one Spirit into two: the duality of vibratory movement. There are five bodily energies (*prana, apana, vyana, udana,* and *samana,* related to inhalation, exhalation, digestion, elimination, and assimilation). There are the twelve zodiacal houses of the horoscope; the four Vedas or seminal Hindu scriptures; the four stages or *ashram*s of life*; the four aspects of human consciousness (*mon, buddhi, ahankara,* and *chitwa,* translating as mind,

---

*The four ashrams are *brahmacharya, grihastha, vanaprastha,* and *sannyas.*

Brahmacharya, the first of them, is the student stage. During this period, which ideally lasts until the age of twenty-four, the maturing youth is asked to remain single, to practice self-control, and to develop harmony of body, emotions, will, and intellect.

The *grihastha* stage lasts—again, ideally—another twenty-four years. This is the time for marriage, children, and gainful labor.

The *vanaprastha* stage ideally occupies the next twenty-four years until the age of seventy-two. This is a time for gradual withdrawal from worldly concerns, and for sharing one's wisdom with others.

intellect, ego, and feeling); and the four social castes, which I'll discuss in a later chapter.

The things related to human life and to earthly existence in general might be described as "four-square." For in addition to the sets of four listed already there are the four *yuga*s or ages of time, already discussed in this book; the four seasons of the year; the four compass points; and the four periods of the day (dawn, noon, sunset, and midnight), each one signaling a shift in the Earth's energy at one's present location on the planet.

The number *two* signifies the basic duality in everything that exists: the oppositions of male and female, joy and sorrow, love and hate, pleasure and pain, heat and cold, and the balancing scales of outer experience: the ups and downs of life that succeed one another ineluctably as long as consciousness is identified with the world of *maya*.

Numerology in its present stage of development is not really a science, but it has the potential for becoming one. For everything in existence is reducible to numbers and numerical combinations. Even the computer on which this book is being written, and the music we hear on a compact disc, function on the binary system using the numbers one and zero.

The number *three,* generally, indicates the subtler mysteries, of which AUM, the Cosmic Vibration, is

The fourth stage, *sannyas,* lasts until the end of life. Ideally it is devoted to meditation on God and the eternal verities. During this stage the *sannyasi* is encouraged to sever all human ties, both gross and subtle, that bind him to external existence, or *samsara.*

These four ashrams are discussed at greater length in my book, *Education for Life.*

itself the outstanding example. AUM has three frequencies of vibration, according to whether it is bringing creation into manifestation, maintaining it in that manifested state, or dissolving it back again into the Infinite Spirit.

An example, familiar to most people, may help to explain these frequencies. When an automobile starts off quickly down the road, its motor runs somewhat loudly at more revolutions per minute, and its sound is relatively high pitched. As it reaches cruising speed, it shifts gears, producing fewer revolutions per minute; the motor hums more softly at a lower pitch. Finally, as the car comes to a halt, and just before the motor is switched off, its sound is lower still in both pitch and volume.

The sound made by the cosmic "motor" is similar, in a sense. Its vibratory frequency is highest and loudest in its creative mode, lower and softer in its preserving mode, and lowest in its dissolving mode, which brings universal manifestation to an end. The sounds emitted by these three vibrations are otherwise different from those of a motor, but they are pitched accordingly: high, medium, and low, and the same is true of their volume.

The Book of Revelation in the Christian Bible contains the following description of AUM: "These things saith the Amen, the faithful and true witness, the beginning of the creation of God" (Revelation 3:14). Paramhansa Yogananda explained this passage to mean that AUM testifies to the divine source of cosmic creation. To listen to, and meditate on, the sound of

AUM produces deep bliss, and assures the devotee that he is in contact with divine realms. Just as the sound of a motor testifies to the fact that the motor is functioning, so the sound of AUM testifies to the fact that, pervading the entire universe, a divine power and purpose exist.

The word AUM, when written properly, contains three letters, signifying the threefold nature of Cosmic Vibration. In English, this word is often written *OM,* because the vowel "O" is pronounced as a diphthong. I myself stopped writing it this way when I found speakers of other languages mispronouncing it to rhyme with our English word, "from," instead of with "home." *AUM* should be pronounced correctly for its mantric power.*

The "A" in AUM represents the cosmic creative vibration, and should be pronounced short, rather than long as in "arm." When this sound is heard in meditation, it is pitched highest of the three.

"U" (pronounced "oo" as in "moon") is the cosmic vibration of preservation. It maintains all creation in a state of equilibrium. This sound, when heard in meditation, is pitched somewhat lower than the first.

"M" represents the vibration of cosmic dissolution, which draws all creation back into the Absolute at the

---

*A mantra is a word or combination of words that exerts a vibratory influence. Mantras can affect events objectively as well as states of consciousness subjectively. The very sound of the word "peace" in English, for example, has a calming influence. Particularly powerful are words that were brought into being purely for their vibrational resonance. To utter with calm feeling the supreme mantra, AUM, even if it doesn't suggest any particular meaning to the mind, has a transforming effect on every level of one's consciousness.

end of a universal cycle. The time allotted to cosmic manifestation is known as a Day of Brahma, and spans a period of billions of years. This vibration of the AUM sound, when heard in meditation, is pitched lowest of all, like a deep rumbling.

The fact that all three sounds are audible in meditation is proof that their activity is constant, and not only sequential in cosmic time.

The "threefold AUM," a chant common in India, is a reminder of AUM in its three aspects. The notes of the first "AUM" are higher, and should be sung loudly. The second note-sequence is a little lower, and is sung more softly. The third sequence is lowest, and is the softest of the three.

A final point should be made here: When chanting AUM, the "M" should be given equal emphasis to the preceding two vowels.

Hindu mythology has personified the three aspects of Cosmic Vibration as Brahma, Vishnu, and Shiva. So real have these "persons" become in popular fancy that it would be a mistake to describe them as mere myths. For devotion has given them objective reality. Myths are made real by the power of human thought. To the extent that they bring truths to a focus in our minds, they become channels for those truths, and help us to attune ourselves to them.

If a person visualizes God as Vishnu, for example, and if his devotion is deep and sincere, the Infinite Spirit may actually appear to him in that form—"crystalized," as it were, by his devotion. This divine manifestation will vary according to the character and customs of the worshiper. The Virgin Mary has appeared differently, depending on the circumstances. At Guadalupe, in Mexico, for example, she showed herself as having brown skin like that of the peasant to whom she appeared.

Swami Sri Yukteswar put it clearly in *Autobiography of a Yogi,* as quoted by Paramhansa Yogananda: "In order to please His beloved devotee, the Lord takes any desired form. If the devotee worshiped through devotion, he sees God as the Divine Mother. To Jesus, the Father-aspect of the Infinite One was appealing beyond other conceptions. The individuality with which the Creator has endowed each of His creatures makes every conceivable and inconceivable demand on the Lord's versatility!"

The devout Hindu looks upon his gods and goddesses as divine realities, not as mere symbols of cosmic forces. The modern mind, on the contrary, dismisses all anthropomorphic images of God as "superstition" and incompatible with the "enlightened" knowledge of science. According to the ancient teachings of Sanatan Dharma, however, both these concepts are valid and not mutually exclusive. The forms God reveals to His devotees in superconscious ecstasy are as real as, and indeed far more real than, any material form, for the sensory awareness normal to waking consciousness carries with it always a certain dreamlike quality of unreality.

The question of reality versus unreality has been debated for centuries in India. Some have claimed that forms, including especially the visions beheld in ecstasy, are eternally true. Others have insisted that no form is real, that appearances of all kinds are illusions only and therefore non-existent. To many intellectuals—non-dualists by persuasion rather than by actual Self-realization—even visions are illusory.

Paramhansa Yogananda's solution to this age-old debate was quite simple. He pointed out that our dreams, too, are real, *as dreams;* that it is therefore incorrect to say that the universe has no existence at all. It is right to say only that, upon divine awakening, the dream ceases to impose its thralldom.

Subconscious dreams are only subjectively real. Conscious awareness is objectively real, but more or less so, only: for although we are all aware that we live in the same world, people's perceptions are distorted by their emotions and by their degree of mental clarity.

Superconsciousness is the state of absolute awareness; it is subjective and objective, both: subjective, because deeply personal; objective, because it strips away every last veil of illusion and reveals the central truth of everything in existence.

The cosmos is God's dream, not man's. It continues to exist even after cosmic consciousness has been attained. The dream can be recalled at will, moreover, after the soul attains liberation from it. Even our own ego-individuality, absorbed as it is into the Infinite after soul-liberation, remains forever real in cosmic memory, and can be re-manifested at any time should the need arise—as it might, for instance, in response to the loving demands of devotees.

In this connection I recall a saint I met years ago in India who was lying in a coma on his death bed. The hospital staff members were unable to awaken him to any response. A disciple, however, visiting one day, whispered lovingly to him, "How are you, Swamiji?" Softly the saint replied, "Very well!"

Brahma, Vishnu, and Shiva are cosmic realities. But as such they are expressions of Infinite Consciousness, and can be drawn to respond personally by the attractive power of devotion. Any divine form they display in vision is transcended in deeper meditation, at which point it is realized as but an aspect of AUM—forever impersonal, formless, infinite.

Ultimate Truth transcends whatever symbols we use to represent it. In that transcendence lies the essential truth of religion, as well as the hope of bringing a needed harmony to the religions of the world. Brahma, Vishnu, and Shiva may never become valued as objects of devotion by the members of other religions, but AUM, the Cosmic Vibration, can be communed with regardless of belief. It is an Absolute Truth, accessible to all. Indeed, to shun AUM is to shun God.

To shun it is the one sin Jesus Christ described as unforgivable.* Prayer, grace, and the blessings of saints and masters may bring "forgiveness" in the sense of healing man of the consequences of other sins, but not of this one. To blaspheme against the Holy Ghost means to shun the truth of one's own being. This sin,

---

* "All manner of sin and blasphemy shall be forgiven unto men: but blasphemy against the Holy Ghost shall not be forgiven. . . . neither in this world nor in the world to come." (Matthew 12:31,32)

and the deep inner restlessness that results from it, can be expiated only by each of us individually. We must give up living disharmoniously, involved in egoic desires, and seek inner communion with God, our higher and true Self. Above all, so Jesus implied, we should develop communion with the Holy Ghost, which in this passage was the name he gave AUM.

AUM—the Holy Ghost, the Word of God, and the Amen of the Christians; the "Sound of many waters" of the Jews; the Amin of the Muslims; the *Ahunavar* of the Zoroastrians—AUM is the over-arching truth of all existence. It awaits no sanction of sectarian approval, but only our own deep inner communion with it. Even intellectual recognition of this supernal truth carries with it the potential for bringing reconciliation to the world's religions. For AUM *is,* essentially, what religion is all about. AUM transcends the conflicting Ways of Belief, and offers mankind a universal highway of Awakening.

The trinity of AUM is quite different from the Christian Trinity of Father, Son, and Holy Ghost. These are often confused with one another. The Hindu equivalent of the Trinity in Christianity is, as I explained in an earlier chapter, AUM-TAT-SAT. AUM is the Conscious Vibratory Creation, often referred to also as the Divine Mother. TAT is the Christ Consciousness, or non-vibrating reflection of the Supreme Spirit in all creation (the "Only Begotten Son" in Christian theology, because it is all-pervasive). And SAT is the Supreme Spirit, the Father beyond creation. The trinity of AUM is different from that of AUM-TAT-SAT.

AUM's trinity refers to the three basic functions of Cosmic Vibration in the manifested universe.

The three aspects of *AUM* are of course sequential, but they are also coexistent. Their universal function embraces everything, individually. Everything we ourselves do has, like cosmic creation itself, a beginning, a middle, and an ending. These three stages are also coexistent, for every ending is implied, potentially, in its beginning; and beginnings are implied, like a distant echo, in every ending. To paraphrase William Blake, the secret of infinity is concealed in a grain of sand, and the key to eternity, hidden in an hour glass. For infinity is a product of the same energy as that grain of sand: The ultimate secret of both is the same. And although the sand moves in an hour glass, the contents of the hour glass never change except in appearance. Time is spherical; Its beginnings and endings have no intrinsic reality: They don't really exist, except as projections of thought. Like sunrise, day, and sunset, time is a melody endlessly repeated, with endless variations to preserve its fascination. We, too, are like grains of sand: To solve the riddle of our own being is to solve the riddle of the universe.

Again, like that moving automobile, the vibrations of creativity on a human level differ from those required to keep life proceeding on an even keel. Both of these differ, again, from the vibration, or mental attitude, one needs to abandon a project, or to renounce attachment to it and accept change.

People tend to manifest primarily one or another of these vibrations in their lives. A person who tries to keep everything flowing evenly may be described as a "Vishnu" type. He may define himself so rigidly by this mental attitude that he feels uncomfortable in the presence of creative people—the "Brahma" types, who in a sense vibrate at a higher frequency. Both types, again, may feel uneasy in the company of "Shiva" types, with their lower-pitched vibrations and their negating response to every proposal, "It won't work."

The first reaction of the "Vishnu" type to challenges is to ask, "How are these situations generally handled?" The "Brahma" type, on the other hand, meets challenges energetically, declaring, "There must be some new and better way of handling them." And the "Shiva" type, finally, scorns the challenges, perhaps shrugging his shoulders as if to say, "Whatever we do or don't do, it's all the same anyway. The more things change, the more they remain unchanged."

It would of course be simplistic to describe anybody as purely one type or another. Everyone is a mixture of all three—and necessarily so. Indeed, the ideal human being brings the three types of vibration to a harmonious balance within himself. He is innovative, when it is appropriate to be so; conservative, when true values are at stake; and prompt to combat evil, if he sees it to be menacing the good.

There are also positive, negative, and neutralizing qualities in each type of person. Positive "Brahma" types are dynamic in their creativity, especially if what they do seems to them meaningful or worthwhile. Negative "Brahma" types, on the other hand, may direct their energy toward "creating" havoc. They are not interested in "doing good," and may pronounce those very words with a sneer. Again, negative "Brahma" types may exert themselves to nullify other people's creativity. An example is sometimes evident in professional critics, in whom the creative urge is often real, but who have found their creativity blocked by an excessively analytical tendency. They seek revenge for the frustration they feel over their own block by mocking the creative efforts of others. The neutralizing tendency, finally, arises in "Brahma" types during deep meditation, when their creative urge is transformed into an intense offering of the heart's devotion to God alone.*

"Vishnu" types, in their positive aspect, strive to preserve established traditions, which they are predisposed to consider just and true. In their negative aspect, however, "Vishnu" types may dogmatically block change of any kind, even if it seems promising. The neutralizing aspect of this "Vishnu" vibration manifests itself when the consciousness flows inward in meditation. Absorbed in the inner silence, they abandon their concern for outer traditions with the discovery of a divine security in the eternal changelessness underlying all change.

Positive "Shiva" types, finally, derive inspiration from exposing and combatting evil. Negative expressions of this type, however, delight in destruction

---

*St. Thomas Aquinas, foremost among Catholic theologians, never completed his greatest work, *Summa Theologiae*. "Such things have been revealed to me," he commented, after receiving a profound mystical insight one day, "that now all I have written appears in my eyes as of no greater value than a straw."

simply for the sake of destroying.* The neutralizing "Shiva" vibration in human beings turns their minds inward in introspection. As they become more meditative, they develop a spirit of ego-transcendence and intense renunciation, which arises from their growing disinterest in the things of this world.

A friend of mine in Vienna, Austria, many years ago displayed some of the "Shiva" tendency quite amusingly. He wrote, and distributed, a pamphlet in which he urged his readers to "Kill! Kill!" His father, a nobleman, was so angry that he disowned him. A mutual friend, puzzled because this friend of ours had always shown himself possessed of a peaceful nature, asked him what on earth he wanted people to kill. "Why," the youth exclaimed in naive astonishment, "the ego, of course!"

My purpose in writing this book is not to delve into the vast array of Hindu deities and their symbols, but only to explain a few of them to convince the reader that "there's gold in them thar hills." In other words, I want to help people to see that Indian symbols frequently contain a wealth of inspiration and wisdom. From among that vast number, however, I cannot in all justice omit one of the very favorite gods in Hinduism: Ganesha. Although it would be inappropriate, in light of this book's theme, to devote a chapter to Ganesha, perhaps I can safely introduce him here in connection

---

*There is a disturbing prevalence of this negative tendency nowadays. Among the most popular scenes in Hollywood movies, so it has been said, are those which depict the destruction of beautiful furniture and priceless works of art.

with Shiva. For Ganesha is Shiva's son, and represents Shiva's vibration in its benign aspect.

The Hindu worships Ganesha as the destroyer of obstacles. He seeks his help before every undertaking, and his blessings on his own prosperity and well-being. To tell many a Hindu that Ganesha is only a symbol would be to risk a "Shiva"-like reaction of the most negative kind!

Ganesha, though he possesses a human body, has the head of an elephant. He has a "vehicle" also, which is, surprisingly, a rat. There is both comedy and meaning in this ridiculous juxtaposition. For although the elephant is, of course, a symbol of wisdom, its size and strength also enable it to ram its way through the jungle, whereas the rat, because of its small size, can burrow *underneath* the jungle's obstacles and arrive at the same end, and perhaps just as quickly. The rat's forte lies in subtlety rather than in strength. Both might and subtlety are necessary for success in life, depending on the obstacles to be overcome.

Ganesha is shown as pot-bellied and affable. The pot belly indicates affluence; the affability, beneficence, these being the blessings his votaries ask of him.

Meditation on Ganesha helps us, above all, to invoke positive "Shiva" qualities in ourselves, whenever we are beset by life's difficulties.

The three vibrations of AUM, then, function not only at the cosmic level in the creation, preservation, and destruction of the universe. They are present also in the minutest ripple of universal manifestation, which includes every aspect of human existence. As such, their diversity and complexity are both infinite and infinitesimal.

Whatever simplicity the ancient rishis brought to these truths has been complicated by the fact, first, that the rishis themselves were fairly numerous, and were far from unanimous in their selection of symbols. Secondly, complication stems from the fact that not all of the old myths and symbols were invented by persons of wisdom.

In humanizing the triune aspects of AUM, I have tried to make them more immediate, humanly speaking, than do the traditional figures, which depict Brahma with four heads, Vishnu with a discus, and Shiva with matted locks: images, in other words, that, while anthropomorphic, seem to have little direct bearing on our lives. Rather, the three phases of cosmic vibration are living, daily realities in the lives of all creatures, just as AUM itself is all-pervasive in the universe. To develop an awareness of them in ourselves, above all in meditation, is ultimately to cross the bridge that spans human and divine consciousness. AUM, itself, *is* that bridge.

Even during times of outer activity, our consciousness should be directed inwardly at least to some extent, in the recollection of the truth of our own being. Ultimately, in no matter what aspect we seek communion with God, our meditations should bring us to that point where we can listen to, and absorb ourselves in, the mighty AUM itself.

Chapter Twelve

The Symbolism of Brahma

The triune gods, Brahma, Vishnu, and Shiva, are treated somewhat ambivalently in Hindu symbology. AUM, which they represent in its three aspects of creation, preservation, and destruction, is itself part of a larger trinity: AUM, TAT, and SAT, all different aspects of the One Divinity—as indeed they are also in Christianity, as Father, Son, and Holy Ghost. As the Bible puts it, "In the beginning was the Word, and the Word was with God, *and the Word was God.*" AUM, too, *is* God.

And here we come to the ambivalence. It arises because Brahma, Vishnu, and Shiva are sometimes seen as personifying, not the three aspects of AUM, but rather the Supreme Spirit: SAT.

Hinduism has never been formally structured, has never had a formal hierarchy, and has never had an official priestly body with the power to enforce theological niceties. Consequently, there has been no consistency in its symbology. Hinduism *is* consistent in its *underlying truths,* but not in the means through which those truths are expressed. This is why Hinduism, more than any other religion, needs to be approached first through its central revelation rather than through a peripheral study of its symbols and writings. This lack of superficial coherence, however, has been Hinduism's strength, not its weakness.

For it has enabled the cream of wisdom to float openly to the surface, where it has faithfully nourished people's hunger for understanding rather than allowing that cream to be skimmed off surreptitiously by bureaucratic manipulation. India, like the open-aisled supermarket in modern times, has thrived on the assumption that, even if uncontrolled access to the truth may encourage a certain amount of spiritual dishonesty, it will also promote a greater longing for the truth itself. And such, indeed, has proved to be the case. The underlying *truths* of Hinduism have remained ever visible, inviting intelligent inquiry. The people themselves, and not a controlling priesthood of "specialists," have seen to it that high quality is maintained.

Error has been held in check also by the repeated appearance of great masters who, free from restraint by "authorities" less enlightened than they are, have been able to bring the general level of understanding back to the central issues of Sanatan Dharma. Like Rabbi Gamaliel in the Christian Bible's "Acts of the Apostles," India has always maintained that if a teaching is of God, nothing mankind can do will be able to destroy it, and that if it is not of God, it will be naturally forgotten in time. Hinduism, with the help of living saints, has kept its grip on the essential spiritual truths. It has been inconsistent only in the manner of presenting them. And this very inconsistency has often been due, simply, to the varying needs of the times.

Theologically, the explanation that AUM *is* God presents no overwhelming difficulty. Complications arise, however, when AUM is considered—not in its triune nature, but as three separately personified deities. For in Hindu symbolism, the trinity of AUM invites a focus on each of those forms. Sometimes one of them is identified with the Supreme Spirit, but the others not. And the exuberant rivalry that has been fanned among Brahma, Vishnu, and Shiva goes far beyond the reasonable demands of symbology. In fact, most of the tales on this subject are difficult to take seriously. There may be, lurking somewhere underneath all that confusion, a profound truth, but, frankly, one doubts it. They seem the mere inventions of storytellers, eager to please and amuse the crowds. In any case, the important thing here is to keep in mind the salient truths of Sanatan Dharma, and not to get buried under a ticker-tape flurry of gay myths.

A further complication in the treatment of AUM in its three aspects is not a question of ambivalence, but only of the cosmic vastness of those truths. AUM, as explained in the ancient teachings, is a far more sophisticated concept than its counterpart in Christian theology, where the Holy Ghost is never really explained except in terms of the action of divine grace in the soul.

The Indian teachings explain AUM, the Cosmic Vibration, as having an outward function as well as an inwardly inspiring one. We saw this duality of function in the last chapter in connection with mankind, where Brahma-, Vishnu-, and Shiva-like influences are

171

observable on a micro-cosmic level in the lives of all human beings.

AUM, in the cosmic sense, serves the function of bringing Spirit into vibrational manifestation, of preserving that manifestation through eons of cosmic time, and of dissolving it again at the end of a "Day of Brahma." AUM, the sound communed with in meditation, is an aspect of God, but in its outward function it casts the veil of delusion over the Divine Truth.

The outward activity of AUM reveals itself to us through the senses—in the sound of the wind, in the wetness of rain, in the very noise of car horns and of people chatting. AUM in this aspect is the very veil of *maya*.

AUM, however, as the sound heard in meditation, is the Divine Mother, tender, compassionate, seeking ever to draw souls back to God by the magnetic attraction of divine love.

When any one of the three—Brahma, Vishnu, or Shiva—is referred to as the Supreme Lord, AUM becomes, symbolically, the Mother. In the image of Krishna, for example, who is commonly viewed as an expression of Vishnu in the aspect of Supreme Lord, we see him playing his flute to draw all souls back to their eternal home in God. Radha, in this symbol, and the other *gopis* (cowherd girls) around her, symbolize the eternal play between the Lord and His creation. In the relationship between Spirit and the universe, AUM (Vibratory Creation) plays the part of Mother Nature. She creates all manifested forms. She receives power from the Absolute to conceive and give birth to the

Christ Consciousness (the *Kutastha Chaitanya*), which She "cradles" at the motionless center of every atom.

There is, to use the Taoist expression, a *yang* and a *yin* in all manifestation: a masculine and a feminine, an outward thrust and an inward recall. Brahma, Vishnu, and Shiva, in their role of cosmic manifestation, are balanced in this role by their feminine counterparts, or "consorts." In outwardness, they are depicted as masculine, and their "consorts" represent the inward attraction of all-transforming love toward oneness with the Supreme Spirit.

On the other hand, when one of them is depicted as the Supreme Spirit (Brahma in this case is usually called *Brahman*), their feminine counterpart is the infinite AUM, the Divine Mother.

The symbolism here, couched as it often is in a multitude of allegories, takes on an infinite complexity, and an infinite inconsistency. I suggest taking a short-cut through this jungle. Divine truth is, after all, basically simple. Divine love, too, is simple. In the labyrinth of puzzle-solving, however, it is easy to lose oneself and become a prey to the Minotaur of paralyzing doubt.

Where one of the masculine deities, Brahma, Vishnu, or Shiva, is shown as inactive (they are often depicted as supine in this role), it is usually to represent the Supreme Spirit. In this case, his feminine consort, or *shakti,* becomes his energetic outward expression as cosmic manifestation. As his *shakti,* in either of his two roles, her own role corresponds to his. In relation to the Supreme Spirit, on the one hand, she busies herself with the "housework" of creation. In other images, however, she is absorbed in adoration of her Lord. In her first role, she is Mother Nature playfully inviting all creation to join her in the cosmic "game" of *maya*. In her second role, she is the Divine Mother Herself, reminding us of our eternal reality as children of the Infinite Father.

The example of Brahma's consort, Saraswati, may help to explain this ambivalence.

Saraswati, in her outward manifestation, is the goddess of speech, music, and wisdom. Brahma, in this context, is *Brahman,* the Supreme Spirit. But when Brahma is depicted as symbolizing the creative aspect of AUM, his consort Saraswati balances the outwardness of that creativity with an inwardly creative flow.

Saraswati is also described, confusingly, as Brahma's daughter. The apparently incestuous nature of this relationship is one reason why many Indians, unaware of the deep symbolism involved, cannot bring themselves to worship Brahma. It was, of course, Brahma who created everything, so he couldn't actually have got himself a wife at all unless he first manifested her! The meaning behind their marriage, however, is subtle, and will be explained shortly.

First, let us consider Saraswati as goddess of speech and music. The creative flow of AUM, when manifested in human nature, is particularly evident in these two expressions, speech and music. Saraswati represents the *shakti,* or energy, of outward creativity, both macro-cosmic and micro-cosmic, in relation to which

Brahma is Brahman, the Absolute Spirit beyond Creation.

But *shakti* has an inward flow also, which is evident on a micro-cosmic level in its influence on man. In home life, for example, the feminine side of human nature is usually responsible for making the home beautiful and for keeping it in good order, while the husband's role, as breadwinner, prevents him from getting too closely involved in domestic matters. The feminine side of human nature is more inward in its influence; the masculine side, more outward. Every human being contains both these aspects in himself, although women usually manifest the feminine side more openly, and men—again, usually,—the masculine. The *shakti* that finds manifestation in women, for example, usually inspires men to creativity rather than arrogating to the woman herself the task of creativity.

Saraswati, as the divine counterpart of Brahma the Creator, represents the inward flow necessary to balance his outward creative endeavors. True creativity is impossible, in fact, unless it keeps its attention directed also inwardly, toward the true fountain of inspiration. No act is truly creative that does not draw inwardly on the intuitive flow.

Even in the creation of children, the Hindu scriptures recommend that the act of physical union not express too much passion, but that the aroused feelings be directed also inwardly, in uplifted consciousness. In this way, a spiritual soul may be attracted into the family.

175

Saraswati, in representing the inward flow of energy, symbolizes also the *sushumna,* the nerve channel that rises toward the brain through the deep spine.

When human energy in deep meditation is fully centered in the sushumna, consciousness flows upward to merge at last into the Supreme Spirit. Divine awakening is the soul's greatest act of creativity, for it brings rebirth onto the highest level of awareness.

Even a partial upward flow of this energy opens the mind to creative insights that alone can produce great works of art, music, and literature. This partial flow, however, provides no more than a glimpse of the Divine. When the flow is full and complete, it bestows the priceless gift of wisdom. Saraswati is therefore described also as the goddess of wisdom.

The intricacies of Hindu mythology belong mostly to the Hindu Way of Belief. They are of special interest to scholars, theologians, and people who draw inspiration from fairy tales. No one could possibly follow the inner Way of Awakening except trudgingly, so long as he was burdened by such details. The myths are not what Hinduism is really "all about." Indeed, more than any other religion, true Hinduism *is* its revelation. It is not, but very definitely *not,* the abundance of quaint stories that have grown like barnacles upon the supporting hull of its traditions.

The special fascination of those myths and symbols is that some of them are in fact deeply relevant, even to our own human realities.

The symbols of Brahma—our present example—are rich with deep meaning for us as human beings. That

176

meaning is spiritual, not profane, though it may also have a mundane aspect. The symbols relate to what everyone really wants from life: an end to suffering, and fulfillment in perfect, ever-new, unending joy (*satchidananda* is the Sanskrit term for divine bliss).

All three deities have "vehicles." Brahma's is the swan. The Sanskrit word for swan is *hamsa* (or *hansa*). Swans symbolize two important truths. First of all, they are a symbol for discrimination, based on the fact (or perhaps only the belief) that milk in a swan's beak separates into its natural components, curds and whey.* Discrimination, similarly, is the ability to separate reality from false appearances.

The highest spiritual title in India is *paramhansa*, or "supreme swan." A *paramhansa*'s perfect discrimination makes him lord of himself, no matter what his outward role on earth. In his self-mastery he resembles the swan also in its ability to be at home equally on water, on the ground, and in the air.

The word *hamsa* has a further meaning. For this word also means "I am he" ("*Aham sa*"). *Aham*, pronounced *Hong*† in mantric form, becomes a *bij*, or seed, mantra, vibrating with the inhalation. Its vibration, and the movement of the breath itself, also correspond to the ascending current in the superficial spine, in the *ida nadi*, or nerve channel.

Sa, or *Sau* (my guru pronounced it to rhyme with "saw"), vibrates with the exhalation, and also with the descending current through the *pingala* nerve channel.

*If indeed fact, secretions in the swan's beak must cause the separating process. The books are vague on the subject, however, and seem almost to suggest the operation of some sort of magic.

†This is how my guru, Paramhansa Yogananda, taught us to pronounce it.

Thus, the "swan" as Brahma's vehicle denotes the breath itself and the corresponding upward-and-downward movement of energy in the *iḍa* and *pingala*. This movement of energy, furthermore, corresponds to the breath in the astral body. In the physical body, Brahma's creative manifestation begins with a baby's first cry at birth: its protest at being rudely thrust out again onto the shaky stage of earthly existence![*]

Why was it necessary for Brahma actually to *marry* his daughter? The reason is deep, and is not fanciful. What is implied here is union, not eventual separation with a father's blessing. In the "marriage" of the superficial currents at the base of the spine with the central *sushumna*, spiritual awakening becomes possible. To a lesser degree, the inspiration that accompanies all true creativity results also from this union. Without this balancing upward flow, outward creativity would soon lose itself in meaningless forms, becoming merely—to quote a Western fad—"art for art's sake."

In this context, then, Brahma is the outward manifestation of creativity, and Saraswati, the correspondingly inward flow of creativity with the withdrawal of energy up the *sushumna* toward spiritual vision and enlightenment.

Symbols have a certain actual identity with the truths they represent, especially if the faith engendered by them is rooted in superconsciousness. Even our thoughts are substantial. Devotional vibrations, for example, are often tangibly felt in places of worship.

---

[*]The subject of reincarnation, merely hinted at here, will be discussed at some length in Chapter Seventeen.

Devotional chants, too, can acquire vibratory power by the fact of having been sung for centuries, or even once only by a Self-realized master in a state of divine communion.

Saraswati, for those who call to her with devotion, represents a channel for higher inspiration. In this respect, the Ways of Awakening and the Ways of Belief converge, even if the latter are no more than shadows of the former. When the shadow is proffered as the reality, however, and the truth that produced it is ignored, the barbarian hordes of Rivalry and Persecution sweep out upon the scene with slashing swords of intolerance. Hope of inter-religious dialogue then becomes lost, or is at least buried in silence by thoughtful people. The shadow represents the form; the truth, standing illumined by the Divine Light, represents the spirit.

For Brahma's "marriage" to Saraswati to occur, the currents of energy in the superficial spine must be equalized and, in calmness, internalized. This truth is basic to the teachings of yoga, and to the understanding of anyone knowledgeable about meditation. This truth seems at first glance, admittedly, so far removed from common experience as to give most people every excuse for returning to the Way of Belief. For at least those outer forms relate to ordinary human experiences. A deeper look at this teaching, however, reveals its relevancy to daily life as well, and in the most practical sense.

Spiritual teachings, even the deepest of them, have direct relevancy to all levels of human life. In the present instance, the commonest experience of every human being is the way we *react* to the world around us. Indeed, our reactions most truly define us as the kind of persons we are.

There is an intimate link between the reactive process and one's breathing. There is, furthermore, a link between the breath, the reactive process, and the ascending and descending energies of the spine. For the breath and the ascending and descending energy are responsive to the heart's feelings.*

To understand this phenomenon in the light of your own experience, think of your body as a laboratory, and conduct in it this little experiment:

Notice how, whenever you react joyfully to good news, you tend automatically to inhale. Simultaneously, notice an upliftment of consciousness, the result of the rising energy in your spine. Note how you sit or stand up straighter. You may lift your eyebrows, or look upward. Your mouth curves upward in a smile. You lift your chin. In other ways also, your physical posture expresses this inner upliftment of energy.

But what happens on the receipt of bad news? Dejection produces the very opposite symptoms. You exhale, and perhaps even sigh heavily. You look down, and perhaps slump forward. You lower your chin. Your eyebrows become knit in a frown. The corners of your mouth curve downward. In other ways, also, your body reveals this downward flow of energy.

---

*Medical science has found that the breath and the heartbeat are both regulated by the medulla oblongata at the base of the brain. From the medulla oblongata, the currents of *iḍa* and *pingala* separate and descend into the human body.

Since life cannot but manifest the principle of duality, all our emotions are succeeded, sooner or later, by their opposites. Elation is never a permanent peak: Inevitably, it alternates with valleys of dejection. Sorrow is a sigh following every emotional joy. Joy's full-lunged euphoria is like the dawn, after a long night of sorrow.

People, sometimes, tired of bouncing up and down as if on a yo-yo of likes and dislikes, develop an attitude of apathy. But apathy, too, has its opposite state: the hope that something—anything—will stimulate their interest in life once again. That sun-drenched cottage by the sea, with its fragrant roses and hollyhocks, brings on eventual boredom: The ego begins to mutter plaintively to itself, "Enough of roses and lapping waves: Give me a good storm!"

The emphasis in yoga on calming the emotional reactions through control of the breath* is a scientific aid toward accomplishing something that is taught in every religion, namely, that we should rise above likes and dislikes, simplify our life, relinquish our desires, and abandon ourselves in faith and freedom to the divine will, which is to say, to the intuitive flow.

Jesus Christ expressed this teaching in the following words: "Take no thought for your life, what ye shall eat, or what ye shall drink; nor yet for your body, what ye shall put on." He was offering the mental corollary

---

*Offering, the Bhagavad Gita says, the *pran* (the inhalation, or upward flow of energy) into the *apan* (the exhalation, or downward flow), and the *apan* into the *pran*, this concentration on balancing the two spinal energies brings the mind at last to a state of interiorization.

181

to the teaching of yoga. Indeed, without that mental corollary yogic breathing exercises would have little effect. Many yoga students make the mistake of focusing so completely on their techniques that they forget the need for right attitude.

Jesus Christ's statement here, and many similar ones, define the Christian Way of Awakening. Its truths are universal. In every way they complement the teachings of yoga.

The Ways of Belief, however, intrude themselves on those essential teachings with the non-essential compromise of ego-motivation. Worse still, they encourage the ego to adopt cunning ways of getting around those teachings. The dogmatic Christian, lacking wisdom, may display his "faithfulness" to the teachings of Jesus by declaring, "Oh, as for me, I never worry about what I'll eat or what clothes I'll put on. I let my cook and my valet do the worrying for me!" Wealthy Indians, pretending faithfulness to the scriptural commandment to live simply, have been known to eat their meals off of a banana leaf as commanded, yes, but to consider it a mere bagatelle that, between the banana leaf and their meal, they insert a plate of the finest gold. And Buddhists (certain ones, not all of them) honor the Buddha's proscription against killing by purchasing their meat in the market place—or, better still, by sending servants out to buy the meat for them. ("After all, *we* never kill the poor animals ourselves!")

The Ways of Awakening have practical application on every level of life: spiritual, mental, emotional, and physical. In developing equanimity on any level, the calming effect on our feelings generally helps the energy and consciousness to become centered inwardly. This "recollectedness," as Christian mystics have called it—*pratyahara,* or interiorization of mind, as the yoga teachings call it—entails no sudden and dramatic shift in consciousness. A shift, yes, but gradual and, above all, natural. Accompanying it is a steady rising and awakening of energy and awareness, which takes place in the deep spine, or *sushumna,* over which Saraswati presides. Even when this awakening is only partial, it permits high forms of creativity.

The need for balancing outward, masculine creativity with inward, feminine inspiration is especially great in the present age, when creativity has become so generally associated with emotional extremes, stormy likes and dislikes, and so little control over one's reactions that creativity itself seems virtually equated with violent mood swings rather than with emotional balance and mental clarity.

Brahma and Saraswati, together, provide the key to higher creativity at every stage of human development, including the highest, that of spiritual awakening. In so doing, they prepare the way for attitudes that are more properly expressed through the symbols of Vishnu and Shiva, whose influences preside over the development of balance and wisdom in our daily lives.

Chapter Thirteen

Brahma's Secret

The most notable feature in images of Brahma is his four heads, each traditionally oriented toward one of the four cardinal points. Tradition has it that those four directions represent the four Vedas: the *Rigveda, Yajurveda, Samaveda,* and *Atharvaveda.* Implied in this association of India's seed scriptures with the Creator is that, in bringing the universe into existence, Brahma established it on the firm ground of *dharma,* or righteousness.

Apart from the obvious discrepancy between Brahma's establishing dharma on the one hand, and his supposedly incestuous relationship with his daughter Saraswati on the other, there is an even greater contradiction: the image of the creator god not actually creating anything, but rather declaring to the four compass points, in effect, "This is my truth. Accept it, or perish." Cosmic creation should do more than declare ground rules: It should seek ever new and inventive ways of manifesting the three universes within the framework of those rules.

Indeed, the creative spirit would almost feel obliged to test the farthest limits of those rules. But what Brahma seems to be saying, if his heads really do represent the Vedas, is, "Beware of innovation. What has been done can never be improved upon. Listen to, and be guided by, the voice of tradition." Surely the Creator would not oppose novelty. Error, yes, but even truths may be approached by first erring. Without innovation, there cannot be creativity.

What we have, in short, with the traditional explanation for Brahma's heads is an endorsement not so much of scriptural truths as of those whose appointed duty it is to protect those truths: the established priesthood. To identify Brahma's consciousness—which is what his heads must represent—with the Vedas is to suggest the need for dependence on complicated, often incomprehensible rituals, and on the few who know Sanskrit well enough to perform them and explain them correctly.

Left out of the reckoning are countless saints of Self-realization in India and elsewhere whose command of Sanskrit is meager to non-existent. This is religiosity, not spirituality. Brahma, the Creator of countless galaxies, must necessarily be far beyond sectarianism.

Established religion is never attuned to the voice of living wisdom. There is always in orthodox religion a certain intolerance of intuitive insight. Its dismissiveness of inspiration as a threat to rule and order was once exemplified for me by a swami, who insisted that God accepts no chant unless it is intoned correctly. The swami turned a deaf ear when I tried to point out that the scriptures themselves declare that what attracts divine grace is, above all, heartfelt devotion.

Because orthodox religion is so heavily weighted in favor of priestcraft, the thoughtful person cannot but

185

question the source for any exclusive identification of Brahma's four heads with the Vedas. Though a box contain air, can air itself be defined as that which the box contains? Human consciousness is box-like: How can it squeeze Infinity to fit into the narrow dimensions of any man-made definition? How, indeed, can it insist except foolishly that any particular spiritual path is uniquely right, and that other paths are, by definition, deficient?

Probably, the association of Brahma's heads with the Vedas was a product of Kali Yuga, a period of time when religion came to be narrowly identified with the Ways of Belief. Kali Yuga mentality could not think cosmically. Still less could it have imagined that the vastness we now know to exist is all a cosmic dream. Even today, the discoveries of science have converted countless millions to atheism. In the relatively cosy universe of past centuries, it was easy to believe that God's main focus of interest was mankind, especially *important* members of the human race like popes, kings, and maharajas. But in the universe as we know it today, seemingly too vast to be so personal, it is difficult for educated people to believe that God, even if He does exist, is not too absorbed in that vastness to spare a thought to man.

The Kali Yuga mentality confused its definitions of truth with the truth itself. Few during those centuries of spiritual darkness were intellectually subtle enough to understand that a definition can only diminish whatever it defines.* The Kali Yugi (one, that is to say,

---

*Definitions, it may be added, are also an aid to reasoning, up to a certain point. They give the mind a framework within which to think. As I pointed

who lived during Kali Yuga and was a true product of that age) was so convinced of the reality of matter that one wonders if he ever had an abstract thought in his life. Scripture, to him, *was* the Word of God, even though printed to be read by priests. Even today, many orthodox religionists hold that opinion, not only in India but throughout the world. The scriptures themselves don't endorse this view. The Christian Bible is as cosmic as the Vedas in some of its statements, for example: "In the beginning was the Word, and the Word was with God, and the word was God." Obviously, no scripture can have been written before the very universe was made!

We might accept orthodoxy's claim to a monopoly on the explanation of Brahma's heads, were it not for the fact that other symbols associated with him have such a deep spiritual significance. The Hamsa or swan, as we have seen, is an example of the highest traditions of mysticism, and of yoga. The fact, again, that his consort Saraswati is the goddess of music and wisdom has been shown to have profound spiritual significance. And, finally, the fact that ancient tradition assigns the name Saraswati to an invisible river, supposed to conjoin the Ganges and the Jamuna at the Triveni outside Allahabad, suggests truths that far transcend mere theological pedantry.

out in a book of mine called, *Crises in Modern Thought,* the classic definition proposed by Thomas Aquinas, "Man is a rational animal," opens up a wealth of philosophical possibilities. At the same time, however, his definition limits our understanding. If we depend on it too heavily, we cannot but ignore those aspects of human nature which are neither rational nor animalistic.

Let us consider, then, the possibility that an explanation exists for those four heads that is consistent with the modern, scientific view of reality. For civilization itself in ancient India must have been much more highly developed than people have long thought, to have produced, or even to have accepted, so cosmic an image as Sagittarius with his arrow, and Scorpio with its tail, both pointing toward what is now known to be the center of our galaxy.

It seems reasonable, in short, to postulate a Dwapara Yuga alternative to what seems a very Kali Yuga explanation for those four heads of Brahma.

A suggestion of this possibility lies in a statement made by Paramhansa Yogananda in *Autobiography of a Yogi*. He gives a fascinating description of divine vision as "center everywhere, circumference nowhere." This description, surely one of the most graphically clear and profound ever written, has a relevance that is, quite literally, infinite.

For everything in Nature owes its existence to an expansion in all directions from an inner center. Nothing develops inwardly from its periphery. Life itself grows like a pearl. The irritant of the grain of sand in an oyster may be likened to the initial movement of vibration from the stillness of Infinity. Astronomers theorize that the very universe began at a specific point with what they've named the "big bang": a mighty explosion that continues to expand toward an unimaginable infinity.

At the same time, every atom, so physics tells us, is itself a complete system. It has its own center, its own "planets." Every point of space may be likened to the center of a wheel, its influence radiating outward in all directions like spokes. Indeed, a better analogy—though one that is more difficult to comprehend within the confines of linear reasoning—would be an expanding sphere, its spokes radiating outward in all directions three-dimensionally.

Every point in this "center-everywhere" universe is a central point of reference from which the universe can be understood. And from each point the view, and therefore the understanding, must be in a sense unique.

We see here a meeting point between science and religion. Materialists sometimes criticize religious experience as a withdrawal from reality. In fact, only from a center of deep awareness in oneself is it possible to understand anything at all. The more deeply centered that understanding, the greater the possibility of perceiving anything, anywhere, as it really is. Peripheral perception is borrowed, and is basically meaningless.

Human thought is based on sensory experience, and therefore reasons at the circumference: from causes to effects, from one episode to the next, from a beginning to an ending. This, too, is a reason why Brahma is not so commonly worshiped in India as Vishnu and Shiva: It is easy to view Brahma's creative act as something finished and done with. Cosmic beginnings, when events are considered serially in time, seem so far removed from present realities as to seem irrelevant.

Human thought is peripheral. Whenever a human being seeks to understand something, his tendency is to approach it from its outside. Rarely does anyone begin with a search for central issues. Nature herself doesn't endorse this approach. A good example of the difference may be seen in the contrast between synthetic and natural fibers.

The center of a natural fiber is always hollow, to allow passage for the life fluids. Man-made fibers, by contrast, contain no such passage: They don't need it, for there is no life-activity to accommodate.

Human beings tend to think of appearances, first. They judge real worth in terms of those appearances. Illusion, to them, *is* reality; they take for granted that what their senses reveal to them is the way things are. Human eyes cannot see the countless billions of electrons in the head of a pin. Our taste buds cannot accept that a delicious-looking meal, if resolved back into its essential energy, might be reconstituted as a very unpalatable bar of lead. A man sees a beautiful woman and "falls in love" with her, deliberately ignoring what he knows to be a fact: namely, that her beauty is but a veil that covers a quite unattractive system of blood, bones, veins, nerves, and bodily functions, the simple contemplation of which provokes an inner struggle against instinctive disgust.

It would not be inaccurate to say that the human view of reality is diametrically opposite to the divine. Our senses tell us that reality is "circumference everywhere, center nowhere."

When a person decides to carve a piece of sculpture or construct a wooden table, his first thought is, "What shape shall I give it?" Only an artist of exceptional insight begins by contemplating the *essence* of what he knows and feels. True creativity begins only at that center within oneself.

This secret of creativity is implied in the symbol of Brahma's "consort" Saraswati, especially in her correspondence to the *sushumna nadi,* or nerve channel. Divine creativity lies in the eternal interplay between outward creativity and inward awareness. So also, on a micro-cosmic level, does human creativity. Artists who create only with the thought that a certain style is fashionable may enjoy a vogue for a time if they are skillful, simply because people generally share that way of thinking. The creative works of such people, however, lack the inner life of which I am speaking. Their influence, therefore, such as it is, fades gradually and is forgotten, as dreams are forgotten. Only true greatness, because its life begins at its inner center, remains fresh and alive even centuries after the body that housed it dies and becomes dust.

Because true insight develops from one's own center, the secret of true creativity lies in attuning oneself from his center to that of his subject. In this kind of attunement, creativity begins.

All true understanding, in fact, whatever one's field, is achieved in this manner. To understand other people, for example, try to understand them by first feeling them in yourself; by empathy, take on their reality. Paramhansa Yogananda put it this way: "To understand others, hold deep compassion for them in your heart."

Even to understand abstract principles, approach them intuitively, as it were with empathy. Never confine the process to mere analysis. Great mathematicians have said that numbers have "personalities." Indeed, why not? Numbers, too, are part of the cosmic dream, and cannot be lacking in cosmic relevance.

The tradition that Brahma's heads represent the four Vedas is not wrong; it is merely limited. It is static, not dynamic. Worst of all, it is not creative as the Universal Creator ought surely to be depicted. Moreover, those cardinal points, like the Vedas themselves, could not have existed already before the universe was made. This tradition implies wordlessly: "What I have done shall remain unaltered forever." The very image of Brahma gazing outward in all directions suggests, not an act of creativity, but only a commitment to preserving what has already been established.

Brahma—to compound the difficulty—is said to represent rajo guna, the active principle in Nature. But there is nothing active, either, in the motionless pose of those four heads. There is nothing even in the pose, as interpreted by tradition, to suggest the vital quality of the other symbols associated with this god: the swan or *hamsa,* his "consort" Saraswati (whose "steed," incidentally, is also the swan), and the red color traditionally assigned to him. Nothing, certainly, in the mere act of gazing suggests the dynamic act of manifesting the entire universe. Nothing in such passivity suggests even the spirit of creativity on a lesser, human scale.

But now think of those four heads as *directing energy outward* from their common center, as if all of them possessed the same medulla oblongata. If we view their consciousness as creatively expansive in all directions, and not as merely *viewing* what has been created, there comes into focus an excellent symbol for Infinite Creativity. Dynamic thought and energy, then, can be visualized as expanding ever outward—not from one point only, but from an infinity of points, or centers, throughout the universe. Nor could such expansion be circumscribed; it would truly be "circumference nowhere." The limits of the universe itself would have no more essential reality than the simple thought that produced them.

Brahma, as Creator, begins his creative work from the heart of every atom, of every particle of light. In its outward expansion, everything is manifested in the three universes.

This expansive understanding of Brahma's four heads may be described as a Dwapara Yuga view of cosmic creation. Such a view is natural especially to this ascending Age of Energy. For only with the awakening awareness of energy as the essential reality of matter can this deeper secret of creativity and of the appearance of life in its manifested state be seen as the outward function of Infinity itself.

The four heads of Brahma contain, then, the key to cosmic manifestation.

To recognize this truth is not to reject tradition, for even though one cannot reasonably claim that the universe was founded on a set of scriptures written by human hand, it was most surely founded on *truth,* which is the basis not only of the Vedas, but of all true scriptures. On the other hand, that truth is not limited to scriptural expression; indeed, it expresses itself ever anew. Brahma's creativity is active in every breath we take, in every ocean wave, in every flower that unfolds its beauty on a mountainside.

The number four indicates that this symbol for Brahma is fundamental to the "four-square" world of reality as we know it. In fact, however, it is known that universal reality corresponds rather to the principles of spherical geometry than, as people formerly thought, to the straight lines and flat planes of Euclidean geometry. The simple message of Brahma's heads, then, is not merely four-directional, but *omni-directional*. He is shown facing a flat world of only four compass points because the limitations of sculpture, of artistic convention, and of Kali Yuga mentality constrained artists to depict him that way.

Someday, artists will, I imagine, awaken to a new freedom of expression, which will enable them to create images of the universal, intelligent creative force, without taxing anyone's powers of recognition. Those images will be fluid in conception. Viewers will be able not only to appreciate them, but to love them.

Chapter Fourteen

The Garden Door

Entrance to the garden of paradise is blocked by a heavy door. The door's keyhole lacks a key. If after a long search you find one that will fit the keyhole, will you go on searching for more keys? or will you simply unlock the door and pass through into the garden? It seems obvious that the key has no other purpose than to open the door. It is not a collector's item. The pedant might see matters differently, but the sincere seeker says, "I've been waiting too long already!"

In the symbolism of Brahma we've found a key to universal revelation. It is a key that needs no polishing, for it slips smoothly into the lock, having been spared many of the storms of human interpolation—rained on, as it were, and rusted by time. The fact that Brahma is less popular than Vishnu and Shiva has spared us the objections of those people who, knowing countless stories about these other two, might quibble, "Oh, but what about this other story, and that one? Will those stories fit the same lock?"

Of course they will, if they are based on revelation rather than on human invention.

If our quest is for spiritual awakening, the door to it is the same for all: that of human nature itself, and of all natural creation. It is the doorway of life, the entrance by which all things made their appearance on the stage of cosmic manifestation, and by which they must withdraw again into their source in infinity. In man, this entrance and exit is the spine. Probably a similar passageway exists for all beings, anywhere, that are conscious enough to aspire toward enlightenment, whether they inhabit planet Earth or some planet at the farthest reaches of the universe.

To become an expression of Infinite Consciousness is to harbor some degree of awareness. Even rocks respond, however dimly, to human love or hatred. The greater that degree of awareness as it unfolds, budlike, during the wakening process of evolution, the greater also the consciousness of *personal* awareness. This consciousness of individual existence cannot but be separative at first, as an entity beholds itself as being distinct from every other individual expression in infinity. As this sense of separateness becomes intensified by feelings of attachment to that individuality, it becomes ego-consciousness. Thus, the ego was defined by Paramhansa Yogananda as *the soul attached to the body.* The seed of ego-consciousness sprouts in the astral, not the physical, body, and survives the death of the physical body.

The ego, then, is not the misfortune so many people consider it. It is a necessary stage in the evolution of manifested life toward divine Self-realization. Our ego-consciousness should be self-expansive, however, not self-contractive. It should reach out toward universal consciousness, and should not contract inward upon itself in fondness for its own separate identity. If the ego is expansive in the right sense, it will reach out to the universe in sympathy, and not merely in a spirit of intellectual questioning. For the essence of that Consciousness which produced us all is not only Intelligence, but Love: a sympathetic identity with all that exists. Love is as intrinsic to true wisdom as is the quality of intelligence. It is love, indeed, that brings clarity to the understanding.

To put it differently, if intelligence had no possibility of enjoying its own wisdom, it would not even be a living reality. Lacking that intuitive grasp which manifests itself as calm feeling—indeed, without love—the keenest Intelligence would be a mere mechanism, no more alive than a motor or a computer.

Contractive self-awareness withdraws its sympathies, and not only its intellectual focus of attention, from broader realities than its own, as it becomes increasingly absorbed in what it views as its own separate reality. Instead of being centered in calm intuition, then, its sympathies become agitated by their natural anxiety to protect the ego's sense of separateness. To promote its uniqueness, it sets itself in competition against other egos, perceived by it as alien realities. As the atheistic philosopher Jean Paul Sartre wrote, "To be conscious of another is to be conscious of what one is not."

The ego, in this state of immaturity, derives a certain pleasure (akin to the pleasure of scratching a mosquito bite!) from whipping itself up with emotions of jealousy, pride, bitterness, disappointment, anger, and other emotions, all of them unhealthy, but too familiar to most human beings to require further analysis.

Wherever a person travels on earth, wherever one might travel in the universe, and however varied the circumstances one might encounter, these basic truths must apply everywhere. The fairest Eden could hold no beauty for anyone whose consciousness was darkened by selfishness. And the darkest dungeon would be a scene of joy for anyone who, transcending ego-involvement, found his consciousness released to soar in inner freedom.

People who dream of someday living in an outer paradise—perhaps some Shangri-la—would do well to consider the unhappy lot of the people of Haiti. On that Caribbean island, the climate is ideal, the scenery, perfect, and the problems of self-maintenance, minimal. Ask the islanders themselves, however, how they feel about their self-perceived confinement there, and you'll learn that the commonest aspiration among them is escape from Haiti and the opportunity to live in the hustle, bustle, and noise of New York City.

People on the other hand who feel themselves constricted by their fancied dearth of opportunities might benefit from an episode in the life of Renaissance artist Benvenuto Cellini. The pope once had him incarcerated for insisting on being paid his back wages before he completed the pope's new commission. After his release from confinement, Cellini stated that, to know perfect joy, arrange to be thrown into a dark dungeon with no furnishings but a perpetually damp mattress, to be given no sustenance but dry bread and water, to have only rats for companions, and enough daylight to permit only an hour of reading every day. A further condition Cellini attached to this paradisaical state was simply this: Read the Bible for that one hour, and during the rest of your time, pray.

"The joy I experienced in that dungeon," Cellini wrote later, "I have never in my life known, before or since."

For mankind, as I said, the passage to awakening is the spine. In this sense, then, the spine itself is the "garden door" to which I alluded earlier. As a matter of fact, however, it would be more literally accurate to describe the spine as a corridor containing a succession of locked doors: *chakra*s, they are called in Sanskrit. To preserve the integrity of our analogy, it would be well to add that the same key fits all these doors. This key is the energy as it rises toward the brain through the spine, passing along the sushumna and stimulating the chakras, or nerve centers. The energy's passage through each of these "doors" awakens one to a new level of spiritual awareness and a heightened sense of well-being. It is as though, with its "awakening," each chakra dropped a veil that had been obscuring the ego's awareness. *Kosha*s, these veils are called: "sheaths," which surround and obscure the perfect clarity of the indwelling soul.

When electricity passes through a wire, it generates a magnetic field. This field is spiral in nature. The same thing happens when the energy moves through the body, particularly in its ascent up the sushumna in the spine. The magnetism generated is spiritual rather than physical, but this too is a manifestation of electro-magnetism, a phenomenon that is becoming increasingly recognized in physics, and that is also, in a subtle sense, spiral in movement.

Spiritual tradition likens this energy field to a coiled serpent, called in Sanskrit the *kundalini*. This kundalini has to be "awakened," or raised up to the brain. When the last veil of delusion over our consciousness has been removed, spiritual enlightenment ensues.

It would be absurd to imagine that divine enlightenment can be attained by mechanical means alone, any more than a telescope can reveal the rings of Saturn to someone who hasn't the interest to focus it. The energy of which we speak cannot unlock the "doors" of the spine, especially not that of the heart, until purification has been achieved of all selfish desires.

In images of Vishnu, a cobra is depicted coiled around the top of his head, or with hoods spread protectively above it. Vishnu's spiritual vision is symbolized by a half moon centered in his forehead to signify the spiritual eye.

Sometimes Vishnu, sometimes other masculine deities, are shown holding a snake in the fist. In this case, what is indicated is perfect control over the body's energies.

Shiva's trident conveys a similar message, stated somewhat differently. For human nature, although complex in its outer manifestations, is basically simple. The Bhagavad Gita hints at this contrast between outer complexity and inner simplicity in an opening stanza. The Pandava army, representing spiritual qualities, are described as "easy to count," for they are few, but strong. The qualities of the ego, on the other hand, represented by the Kauravas, are "difficult to count" for they are numerous and clamor loudly for our attention. Individually, however, they are weak compared to the forces of the soul.

The message of Sanatan Dharma is simple, though cosmic. The symbols through which it is expressed are correspondingly simple also.

Shiva's trident is set on a straight pole, symbolizing the spine. The three prongs of the trident signify, again, the junction of the three major currents at the base of the spine: the *ida, pingala,* and *sushumna.* Lest one wonder why the trident is not placed at the bottom of the pole to emphasize this meaning, the trident is also a weapon of destruction, cosmic in Shiva's case. Its placement at the top of the pole also emphasizes its paramount spiritual importance.

The ancient teachings of India are by no means alone in referring to these universal spiritual truths, though nowhere else, perhaps, do we find them referred to as simply and openly as in the Indian scriptures. My own familiarity is more with the Bible than with other scriptures, but from what exposure I have had to other scriptures, and from my own conviction that truth truly *is* universal, I cannot but invite the adherents of other faiths to conduct further investigations into this universality.

In the visions of the prophet Ezekiel, Chapter 28, we read: "Thou hast been in Eden the garden of God. . . . Thou wast upon the holy mountain of God; thou hast

walked up and down in the midst of the stones of fire."
Is it not clear that these "stones of fire" refer to the
blazing energy in the chakras, and the concept of walking up and down "in the midst of" them, to the energy
moving up and down the spine?

In the book of Zechariah, Chapter 4, we read, "I
have looked, and behold a candlestick [the spine] all of
gold, with a bowl upon the top of it [the brain] and his
seven lamps thereon [the seven chakras]. . . . And two
olive trees by it, one upon the right side of the bowl,
and the other upon the left side thereof [the iḍa and
pingala]."

In the Book of Revelation we find similar passages.
In Chapter 22: "And he shewed me a pure river of
water of life [the spine], clear as crystal, proceeding out
of the throne of God. . . . In the midst of the street of
it, and on either side of the river was there the tree of
life [the iḍa and pingala] which bare twelve manner of
fruits. . . . [There are six chakras in the spine, and one,
the *sahasrara,* at the top of the head. The six chakras
become twelve by polarity, a point I've described at
length in my book, *Your Sun Sign as a Spiritual
Guide.*] Blessed are they that do his commandments,
that they may have right to the tree of life, and may
enter in through the gates into the city."

Earlier in Revelation, Chapter 1, we read again of
these truths, but in a way that would require more
explanation than seems suitable for the purposes of
this book.

In the book of Numbers, Chapter 21, God tells
Moses, "Make thee a fiery serpent [Kundalini], and set

it upon a pole [the spine]: and it shall come to pass, that everyone that is bitten [by delusion], when he looketh upon it, shall live. And Moses made a serpent of brass [shining, in other words], and put it upon a pole." I once asked my Guru if Moses was a Self-realized master. "Oh, yes," he replied. "He had 'lifted up the serpent in the wilderness.'"

Psalm 81 states, "Thou calledst in trouble, and I delivered thee: I answered thee in the secret place of thunder [a clear reference to AUM]."

Proverbs Chapter 8 states, "Blessed is the man that heareth me, watching daily at my gates." Are these gates not strongly suggestive of the chakras?

Isaiah Chapter 40 refers to "the voice of him that crieth in the wilderness, Prepare ye the way of the Lord, make straight in the desert a highway for our God." The "desert" is the inner silence; the "highway for our God," the spine; the admonishment to "make" it "straight" is important for right meditation. As it says next in this passage, "And the glory of the Lord shall be revealed."

Ezekiel Chapter 43 begins with the words: "Afterward he brought me to the gate, even the gate that looketh toward the east. And, behold, the glory of the God of Israel came from the way of the east: and his voice was like a noise of many waters: and the earth shined with his glory." "East" signifies the forehead; the gate is the door of the sixth chakra, the "spiritual eye." The "noise of many waters" is, as we saw in an earlier chapter, the sound of AUM.

There are many other passages in the Bible that express these and similar truths. One would expect them to, for the truths are universal; they can hardly fail to appear in any scripture that is based on revelation.

The great Christian saint, Teresa of Avila, who lived in the Sixteenth Century in Spain, stated that when the soul enters the ecstatic state it "shoots upward like a bullet out of a gun." She also spoke of the soul as being centered at the top of the head, even as yogis claim.

The inner spiritual experiences I've described are available to anyone willing to undergo the necessary mental and spiritual preparation, which includes calming the mind and offering the heart's love up to the Infinite for purification. For these truths are as universal as the principles of mathematics.

The symbols of Vishnu and Shiva complement what we have seen already in the case of Brahma, with only the shift of emphasis that one would expect of the aspects of God as Preserver of the universe and as its Destroyer.

Vishnu is generally thought of as benign—naturally so, from the human point of view. His discus, like Shiva's trident, is for use as a weapon, but only in order to destroy evil and reinstate virtue. Vishnu's skin is depicted as blue, this "sky" color suggestive of infinite consciousness.

Shiva the "destroyer" is an ascetic—appropriately enough, for one who cares not for the lures of the world. He is usually shown seated in a meditative posture of calm withdrawal from worldly concerns. In keeping with a practice common among Indian holy men, his hair is matted to show his indifference to mere appearances. Scantily clad, his body—like those of many *sadhus*, or holy men—is smeared with ashes as a protection against the cold. His abode is the high Himalayas. His normal state is one of solitary absorption in communion with the Infinite.

Like Brahma and Vishnu, Shiva, though a renunciate, has a "consort," Parvati. I will not enter into the hidden meaning here except to reiterate what I said before, that Parvati signifies the inwardly balancing energy to the masculine god's outward attention. Shiva's consort inspires us to turn within in meditation, and to transform our identity with the body and ego into the realization of our infinite, divine Self.

In human relationships, similarly, the man needs to balance his outwardly flowing energy with inward inspiration; and the woman needs to balance her naturally inward flow of energy with the outer clarity that is usually experienced through self-expansion.

In fact, the ramifications of inwardly and outwardly directed attention are so many, and so varied, that it would be simplistic to refer to them categorically as only feminine or masculine. I have emphasized that these two energies exist to varying degrees in every individual. A person's sex, moreover, is not always the deciding factor in whether one of these energies is predominant over the other, though obviously one's sex hormones have a strong influence both physically and psychologically. The ideal human being expresses in himself a perfect balance of both energies. Nevertheless it is generally speaking true that, in women, the feminine energy predominates, and, in men, the masculine energy. It is better in any case to describe these energies as "masculine" and "feminine," rather than "male" and "female," since the latter terms refer more specifically to a person's sex.

Consider, then, an interesting difference between the masculine and the feminine view of things. It is not unusual, when a man and a woman walk downtown together, for the woman to make some such remark as, "How did you like those green shoes?"

"What green shoes?" asks the man.

"The shoes displayed in that store window," she replies.

"What window?" he asks again. They'd passed several windows, and he hadn't paid much attention to any of them. The woman, on the other hand, had formed an instant impression of them all, and had been particularly taken by those shoes.

"It was in the last block," she replies, reminding herself resignedly that men never notice *anything*.

The man, on the other hand, may be thinking, "This isn't the right part of town to be selling shoes. Too many cars; not enough pedestrians."

I once happened to notice that the altar cloth in a monastery chapel had been placed inside out. My first thought was that no nun in a convent would have made such a mistake.

Women end up telling each other, "Men just aren't practical." And men shake their heads in wonder with the exclamation, "When it comes to reality, women just don't have their feet on the ground." Both, of course, are right. And both are wrong.

Masculine energy, though more naturally outward, tends to think in terms of generalities. Feminine energy, when outwardly focused, concentrates more on the details of things. Both points of view are needed, if perfection is to be attained. In this context, then, a narrower focus on details is the sign of feminine "inwardness," and a broader attention to generalities the sign of masculine "outwardness."

To proceed any farther down this road, however, in the name of logical consistency would so labor the point that it would cease to be useful. Analogies can never be perfect. The American philosopher Ralph Waldo Emerson put it well: "A foolish consistency is the hobgoblin of little minds."

In the field of religion, however—and that is why I raised this subject in the first place—the inward activity of meditation may, unless it is deep, require stimulation and clarity by outward activity, especially by activity of a serviceful nature. For serviceful activity is self-expansive, in the sense of offering the ego into a larger reality.

Self-expansion that is not based on self-offering may only inflate the ego. Even if it increases one's awareness and understanding, it can do so only up to a certain point—like pushing mounds of earth outward to clear a flat space, only to find at last that one has created a huge self-enclosing wall. There are, then, two kinds of self-expansion: self-liberating, and self-confining.

Contraction also is of two kinds, spiritually: liberating, and suffocating. The liberating kind is when the ego detaches itself from outwardness and offers itself to the calm Self within. The suffocating kind is when the ego refers every outer experience back to itself and takes notice only of those things which seem to it to promote its own interests.

The self-liberating kind of contractiveness is achieved by prayer and meditation. Self-liberating expansiveness is achieved, as I said, by service to God, to God in others, and by the sincere practice of religious rituals. Each needs the other. Meditation gives meaning and inspiration to service and ritual. Selfless service of all kinds gives greater clarity to meditation—until, indeed, the mind has been lifted in meditation to a superconscious state.

Even the most spiritually expansive activity has no meaning if not animated from within by soul-inspiration. Unfortunately, the tendency of human nature is to view all things as "circumference everywhere, center nowhere." When the mind's attention is focused too much outside itself, it becomes superficial. This happens when religious symbols and rituals are given too much importance. Their inner spirit is then lost and forgotten.

Few people take into account, for example, the deeper meaning of the well-known image of Shiva as "Nataraj." Nataraj is a statue that depicts Shiva dancing. In fact, this statue is displayed on the cover of the present book. His dance depicts the vibration of *pralaya,* cosmic dissolution. *Pralaya* is the fiery end of all creation. That occurrence is not expected soon, however. To consider Nataraj as being relevant only to an event in the distant future is to overlook that Nataraj is perennially significant. Far more than the end of a Day of Brahma, Shiva's dance depicts also our present realities: *here, today,* in a sort of inward spiral to the present moment.

Curving inward from the eventual end of the universe, what Nataraj describes is also the end of every cycle of time—not always in flames, as depicted by the statue, but often drastically all the same: the end of a yuga, or great age of time; the death of a planet; the karmically inscribed "finish" for a country or a people; the ending to any specific historic period; the close to some dramatic story in the life of a family, or of an individual.

All things are permitted to endure for a time only. When their allotted time ends, the Cosmic Will is that they step aside to make way for new scenes in the cosmic drama, for new episodes in the divine dream. Whether they exit gracefully or weeping with a sense of tragic loss depends on how well developed they are in non-attachment: how willing they are to accept Shiva's energy, too, in their lives, as they accepted with gratitude Brahma's and Vishnu's energies.

How long every story lasts, moreover, depends on the amount, and also on the quality, of Brahma-like energy that went into their inception, and on the amount and quality of Vishnu-like energy that has sustained that activity. Shiva must, however, have his day eventually, too. As Nataraj, his significance is not only cosmic, but pressingly immediate for every one of us.

Nataraj signifies, finally, the dissolution of our own delusions, and our ultimate freedom in Infinite Consciousness. This deeply personal and inward understanding is lost, and is our greatest loss, when we think of that symbol as representing only an event billions of years in the future. Nataraj becomes for us then, instead, an attractive art object, displayed in our living rooms and treated as a conversation piece.

Another good example of how symbols come to be viewed as mere curiosities, once their inward meaning is forgotten, and worshiped in merely clamorous rituals (as if by noise to compensate for the lack of inner comprehension!) is the Shiva *lingam*.

The Shiva *lingam* has been mistakenly interpreted by Westerner scholars to represent the *phallus*. In fact, the lingam has a deeply inward and spiritual meaning; it has nothing to do with phallic fantasies, stimulated by Freudian symbolism. The lingam, considered as a symbol of spiritual inwardness, represents—again—the spine. And it is more than a symbol. Indeed, I was astonished one day during meditation to find my own spine and brain suddenly assuming the form, to my subjective awareness, of a Shiva lingam.

To argue against the Western explanation for the lingam would be to give it more dignity, even as a misconception, than it deserves. No devout Hindu thinks of it in that way, even if—one suspects—few Hindus really understand what the lingam means. One might point out, however—to show the absurdity of the

Western explanation—that if the lingam were really a symbol of fertility as is claimed, it ought more properly to have been assigned to almost any other deity than Shiva, the god of destruction.

This is not to say that there is no correspondence whatever between the phallus and the spine. The phenomena they represent are simply opposites to each other. The phallus draws the energy outward, toward physical creativity, The spine, by contrast, draws the energy *inward,* toward the renunciation of physical desire, and indeed of all material desires. The Shiva lingam, then, represents an alternative to physical pro-creation: energy rising inwardly up the spine, and an accompanying mental withdrawal from egoic entanglements.

The Shiva lingam represents what religion most needs: an inward focus, and rising energy in the spine. For until the attainment of superconsciousness, an inward focus, if it is not accompanied by rising energy, can bring the energy *down* the spine, toward subconsciousness and a spiritual sleep state.*

The garden door is the spine. Once the spine is entered, one finds a passageway before one, and not immediate entry into the hidden garden. Along this passageway one encounters a succession of gates, each of which must be unlocked and opened before the garden can be no longer glimpsed through a lattice, as it were, but entered into fully and enjoyed. The key to these gates is the same as to the door of the spine:

---

*As an aside, it is interesting to note that when woman is portrayed as sultry, she is always shown looking sleepy.

devotional aspiration, and energy applied upward with will power, but not forcefully; rather, with ever deeper relaxation and offering of the little self to the Divine Self of all.

Chapter Fifteen

The Importance of *Satsanga* (Good Company)

The soul is solitary. It comes into the body alone at birth. It leaves it solitarily at death. During its earthly existence it appears as if surrounded by others, but in fact in its essence it is ever apart from them, and alone.

And yet there is duality in the very fact of manifestation, with the appearance of separate existence from the Supreme Spirit. There is, first, the illusion of duality between Soul and Spirit. Next, there is the duality of the manifestation itself, which provides for every soul its complement: one, solar, the other, lunar; one, masculine, the other, feminine, with all the dual ramifications of meaning that we discussed in the last chapter.

Every soul, moreover, as it enters the realm of duality, assumes a certain duality in its own nature, for it contains in itself a polar opposition, positive and negative, masculine and feminine, active and receptive. In the human body, the positive pole is at the top of the head; the negative, at the base of the spine.

The Hindu scriptures pay little heed to the concept of soul mates, though Paramhansa Yogananda did state at least once that this is a true concept. Perhaps the ancient rishis feared that people might go seeking a soul mate on every street corner, instead of seeking, within, the one true Partner of their souls: the Infinite Spirit.

Nevertheless, outward relationships are important to earthly existence. They help us to project outwardly, where we can see and understand them clearly, the interplay of our own thoughts and desires, which need to be dealt with if we seek entry into the inner "garden" of divine consciousness.

For this reason also, most myths of the gods show them as having consorts, many of them as having offspring, and they are shown in constant interaction with one another. A strictly unilateral teaching that stresses only the "flight of the alone to the alone" might be philosophically correct, yet it would lack the vital aspect of immediacy that human realities demand. It would be like a marble statue, well formed but lifeless.

Recently I was invited to give a talk in Milan, Italy, in honor of the fiftieth anniversary of India's independence and Mahatma Gandhi's death. In my talk I suggested that what Gandhian *ahimsa* (non-violence) really stood for was not passive resistance, merely, but the dignity of personal freedom coupled with complete respect for others' right to the same freedom. Gandhi, in his campaign for Indian independence from British rule, captured the imagination of his countrymen by appealing to the one quality that, above all others, best expresses India's national consciousness.

Inner freedom, and respect for the right to the same freedom for everyone, is the ideal of *ahimsa*. It is also the ideal of true *satsanga,* good company, or right companionship with others. The tales of Indian mythology can never be rightly understood without a grounding in this fundamental attitude.

The reason why religion has never been really organized in that country, and certainly not with the ordered efficiency of the West, is that Indian culture is deeply committed to a sharing in inner freedom, to a commitment based on a dignified understanding that the true spirit of religion springs from inner awakening, not from outer affiliations. At the same time, India has shown the sophistication not to fall into the rational trap of "either/or" alternatives. It recognizes the importance of outer stimuli, too, through rituals of various kinds. And it recognizes the value of outer company to inner development. Rituals in themselves have power primarily only to the extent that we *give* them power, whereas other people influence us to the extent that they themselves *give us* energy.

"Environment," Paramhansa Yogananda used to say, "is stronger than will power." By environment he meant, above all, good company. This truth applies universally, at least up to the time when one has developed the inner strength to remain untouched by all outer circumstances.

Just how "good" should one's company be? Obviously, if it is composed of people as much in need of *satsanga* as oneself, it will be like two people hobbling along on three stilts instead of in the usual manner of each one balancing on his own pair. With three stilts, if either person loses his balance both will tumble down together. The company we seek, then, should not make us partners in misery. We should mix with people from whom we can draw inspiration. In any true relationship, moreover, there should be reciprocity. If we can give something, at least, in return, our relationship will be kept mutually creative and uplifting. For one person to give and the other only to draw, like a sponge soaking up water, results in loss for the one and no lasting benefit for the other.

Inspiration is of many kinds, and can be experienced in every walk of life. An aspiring artist would do well to study under someone with experience in that field. An aspiring businessman would do well to study under someone of business experience. An aspiring mountain climber would be flirting with death if he refused to learn from an experienced mountain climber.

Inspiration is far more than a process of receiving instruction in proper techniques. Every year, thousands of students graduate from art school, where they learned more techniques, perhaps, than any single artist in the past ever knew. Few of these graduates, however, go on to become even reasonably competent artists.

Again and again one hears successful people say, "What really got me started in my career was someone who really loved that work, and who took a personal interest in me. It was his or her deep feeling for the subject, more than anything else, that fired me with the desire for excellence."

In the spiritual field even more so, what brings life to it is not lifeless theology nor the pedantry of religious scholars, but the company of people who *live* the spiritual life. It isn't even competent instruction by people skilled in explaining principles and techniques that brings life to a subject—whatever the subject concerned. Life is breathed into the spiritual search as often as not by someone who may even be illiterate or quite lacking in eloquence. The inspiration may come from someone like an old sadhu I met years ago near Calcutta whose conversation as nearly as I could ever tell was only the blissful utterance, "Guru, guru!" I learned years later that this same sadhu had been sometimes observed levitating.

Inspiration depends not on words and explanations, but on *spiritual presence.*

For each of us individually, inspiration is what we feel *within* ourselves. If another person feels it more strongly within himself, however, that inspiration may be sufficiently magnetic for us to feel it also.

The teachings of India explain that inspiration is stimulated by the energy rising up the spine, particularly—this point can now be made—when that rising energy is dynamic enough to unlock the "gate" of the *anahat chakra,* or heart center, opposite the physical heart in the spine. Even when this heart center is only stimulated—opened ajar, so to speak—enthusiasm develops for one's subject whatever it may be. Without enthusiasm, outstanding success in any field is impossible.

The secret of intuitive understanding lies, as I have said, in attuning oneself from one's own heart center to the heart, or core, of one's subject. The secret of inspiration is similar. To draw the most inspiration from another person, attune yourself, at your heart center, to his or her heart. It is of course also possible to generate inspiration on your own and only imagine it to be coming from the other person. You may awaken this inspiration on your own by your affection for him, or simply by expecting to experience inspiration in his company. This kind of inspiration wanes gradually, however, for it lacks true power to survive the storms of doubt, discouragement, and negativity that from time to time assail the mind; nor can it pacify the raging waves of emotion like Jesus Christ commanding the storm on the sea of Galilee: "Peace. Be still."

There is a truth that was anciently known in India, but that is only beginning to be recognized in the West owing to the discoveries of modern science. It concerns the magnetic interchange that takes place between human beings. People have known about magnetism for centuries, of course, in a vague way. They've cognized it, perhaps, as a feeling of well-being in the company of some people, or perhaps, though undesirably, in emanations from them of moods of depression. Electro-magnetism, a relatively new scientific discovery, is becoming increasingly recognized as affecting even human intercourse.

The stronger a person's energy, the stronger his magnetic field. People with weak will power have low energy. People with strong will power, conversely, have high energy. "The greater the will," Paramhansa Yogananda used to say, "the greater the flow of energy." The greater the flow of energy, again, the stronger the magnetic field it generates. We are constantly affected, far more than most of us realize, by the magnetism that is generated by other people's thoughts, feelings, and, consequently, the energy they project into the atmosphere around them.

Thus we see that the insistence in the Indian scriptures on the importance of good company is based on far more than a suggestion to surround oneself with good examples. A person who is merely "goody-goody" may act a good example, in the sense at least that he doesn't misbehave himself, but his goody-goody-ness may be only the consequence of not having the courage to be naughty. We have seen that there is also danger from bad company, and this danger lies not only in the bad example it sets, but in the negative magnetism it generates. For although one person of negative magnetism may not have the power to exert much influence on others, joined to the company of others of similar interest the resulting vibratory exchange will result in stronger magnetism.

It happens sometimes, for instance, that an otherwise well-meaning person finds himself caught up in the frenzy of a throng of people screaming for someone's death. He is stunned, later, to realize how inflamed his emotions became. "I can't imagine," he exclaims, "what insanity possessed me!"

Good company, unlike bad company, is never hypnotic. For its influence is not exciting, but calming. In calmness, people never act against their higher principles. The waves of emotion are calmed not by suppressing them, but by *inspiring* stillness in the mind and heart—in the heart especially, for when the heart's feelings are like a flawless lens, intuition unfolds like a blossom and brings clarity to all one's perceptions of reality, revealing things as they truly are and not as delusive desires may have painted them.

There are many types of magnetism. Good company may be taken to mean association with anyone who is strong in that sort of magnetism which one hopes to develop. To acquire artistic magnetism, seek the company of people—and better still, of one person—with well-developed artistic magnetism. To acquire business magnetism, mix with those possessed of strong business magnetism. Success in any field depends more on magnetism, actually, than on knowledge. For magnetism *attracts* success, whereas knowledge merely tells you how success has been achieved by others.

Spiritual magnetism is what is primarily meant, of course, by the scriptural term, *satsanga*. Spiritual seekers should court the company of those above all who are strongly *and magnetically* spiritual.

There is a further caveat here, however: an important one. For just as there are many kinds of human magnetism, in the general sense of artistic, businesslike, scientific, amatory, and so on, so there are many kinds of each of these types of magnetism. An aspiring impressionist, for example, would do well to study under a good impressionist painter, and not under one who specializes in scenes of stark realism.

The same is true in every field. And it is also true in the field of spirituality.

Not every person of strong spiritual magnetism has a spirituality compatible with one's own. It is important to consult your heart's feelings. Ask yourself what resonates with your own inner being, with your own nature.

To shun all outward influences, however, in the name of preserving your own integrity would be to overlook the fact that all of us are intrinsic parts of one universal reality, and necessarily, therefore, interdependent. We are not as we appear to ourselves. We are products of the ceaseless interactions we've developed with the world around us. This conditioning process continues until we accept into the depths of our being the clarity of divine wisdom.

A mixture of diverse influences—even good ones—added to the mixture we already contain within ourselves, may prove confusing. People who, in the name of broad-mindedness, go to many teachers, study many spiritual teachings, and never commit themselves to any spiritual path because, as they quite rightly say, "All good paths lead to the same ultimate truth," forget that one can enter a building by only one door at a time. Hence the danger of syncretism, as opposed to what we might call *essentialism*, in religion. Syncretism tries to combine different spiritual teachings selectively, to show their over-all similarity. The result of such "cutting and pasting" is often a hodgepodge. Essentialism, a little-known word which I've deliberately given a new but more universal meaning, concentrates on the essential aspect of religion—that is to say, on inner awakening—and makes less of an issue of the fact that the inner sanctum has many entrances. The study of those entrances the serious seeker leaves to intellectuals and to bookish scholars.

The view of the fanatic, on the other hand—"My way alone is true. All others are false"—is proof of spiritual immaturity. The fanatic is one who has not yet learned to relate to other realities than his own. The view, however, that "all ways are good, so let's be equally open to all of them," is the way of the spiritual dilettante. It is usually not so much a reaction against fanaticism as a declaration of indifference to religion in general.

The road to wisdom lies between every pair of extremes: It lies not in spurning the fanatic's single-minded devotion, but in claiming, as Gandhi did, the dignity of personal choice combined with respect for the freedom of others to make their own choices. In personal choice, the Indian scriptures have always insisted, there should be singleness of both purpose and personal commitment.

The sincere aspirant, aware that he is anyway beset on all sides with multitudinous influences, most of them detrimental to singleness of purpose, begins by trying to find a teaching that most appeals to him, personally. He cannot afford, at first, to be too choosy. On the other hand, he knows he must find some one way to reach his goal; it is not enough merely to contemplate that goal from afar, which is to say, intellectually. Better dry cheese sandwiches than a merely poetic description of a feast. Better a few truths he can actually practice in his life than the most exalted sounding account of divine ecstasy. He seeks where he can, therefore, reads what he can, and does his best personally to live what he learns.

Gradually, the increasing magnetism he generates by the very act of seeking sincerely, and by the energy he devotes to the process, acts subtly to attract the interest of others who are dedicated also to the divine quest. Satsanga, in other words, comes naturally to him even if he doesn't seek it actively. It will of course come sooner if he recognizes the need for it, and seeks it actively.

Many dream of the hermit's life as an alternative to worldly company. Solitude, however, is not for the spiritual neophyte. The shadows of too many fears, false hopes, and unfulfilled desires lurk in the subconscious, ready to assume monster shapes and sizes. They can overwhelm him if he doesn't, at first, dilute their power over him by distracting his mind somewhat by outward activity, and by good company, until he is strong enough in himself to confront those subconscious shadows openly with the blaze of superconscious awareness.

The mere company of other devotees, however, as earnestly seeking but as fumbling in the dark as himself, ceases to give him satisfaction once he realizes that their excitement of "discovery" never seems to lead to the expected diamond mines. More often than not, in fact, they prove to be fruitless distractions from his own quest. Indeed, even the counsel of those more experienced on the path than himself may have proved more confusing than enlightening, and to have taken him only in circles.

Gradually, if he is sensitive, he may encounter an even subtler problem. Different guides, though each one perhaps good in himself, have different qualities of magnetism. A mixture even of good qualities may have the effect, on a magnetic level, of trying to thread a needle with loose strands instead of drawing them all to a point. That magnetism which attracts success is always generated by a strong flow of some particular quality of energy. The comparison with a flow of electricity breaks down at this point, for what we are describing is a subtle energy that is generated by particular states of consciousness, of which there are an infinite number. Different spiritual attitudes—that of servant for example, or of child, of friend or beloved of God, and even such impersonal attitudes as calmness and dispassion, oneness with all life, and formless self-expansion—all are beautiful, and are valid paths to God. They take one nowhere, however, if the devotee skips back and forth irresolutely from one to another.

Even this explanation is simplistic. Not only are there numerous subtle differences within each of these categories, but in the finest sense the categories themselves can never be adequately defined. They are too subtle for intellectual formulation. Their essence can only be experienced by intuition.

It is important at this point to underscore two truths: One, that magnetism is the single basic need for success in any field; and two, that many contradictory flows of energy, owing to the confusion of unfulfilled desires in the subconscious and conscious minds, prevent the clear flow that alone generates magnetism of any kind. There remains one further truth to be emphasized here: None of us *is* his desires, and none of us, therefore, is what he thinks of as his personality. As personalities, each of us is only a mixture of desires and reactions that we've developed over eons of time in our interactions with the world around us. Each of us in essence is unique; but that uniqueness is not our personality.

To develop a kind of magnetism that is compatible with this essential nature is the greatest need on the spiritual path. It is not as though this essential nature could ever be lost, for that *is*, since the beginning of time, what one *is*. Everyone, in all eternity, is unique. Our first need, however, is to strip away the false self-definitions in which we have encased ourselves.

Since worldly kinds of magnetism—artistic, business, animal, etc.—merely take us away from our soul-essence, what must concern us here is the development of our natural spiritual magnetism. Other kinds are helpful only to the extent that they help us to work out superficial patterns of desire in the mind. Once our natural spiritual magnetism, born of clear *and true* inner purpose, develops to a certain degree, we attract to ourselves those influences which help to reinforce it: spiritual companions, especially, and those who are able to share with us the higher ways of truth. Even though a profusion of such teachings may prevent us from developing that crystal clear direction which leads to the highest success, it separates us from the pack, so to speak, and helps us to understand that, out of a myriad of possible directions in life, one of them is the right one for us to follow.

Even if, out of many possible choices, we select a teacher who for various reasons appeals to us the most, we can develop only so much magnetism as he himself projects. His help may be deeply beneficial to us, and may take us to greater spiritual heights than we ever dreamed possible for ourselves, and even so it may be insufficient to take us to union with Spirit. How can we decide whom to follow? The decision at this point, fortunately, is not ours to make. Nor was it ever really ours. As our magnetism develops, we attract our own natural ray. It's that simple. In our very anxiety to find the best way we may miss it altogether. Perhaps we seek a broad highway when our own way would have taken us off the road onto a narrow and seldom trod path. The divine consciousness, operating through each of us, makes the decision. Our job is not to search with anxious hearts, but to make ourselves ever more receptive. The Indian scriptures put it perfectly: "When the disciple is ready, the guru appears." Meanwhile, be grateful for anything God gives you. Eliminate the spirit of criticism and fault-finding from your heart. Few saints, even, are perfect, though even with human imperfections they still have much to give. As Sri Krishna puts it in the Bhagavad Gita, "To you, Arjuna, who have overcome the carping spirit, I reveal these deeper truths." Gratitude is the surest way of developing the magnetism that attracts spiritual abundance into our lives.

A few sentences ago I introduced the word "guru," belatedly. Guru is the most sacred word in the spiritual lexicon. It deserves to be uttered with supreme reverence, with utter devotion, and with deepest, heartfelt love. Instead, it has been sullied by suggestions, and even by examples, of ruthless manipulation, personal ambition, power, and control. It has been debased to mean anyone who sets himself up presumptuously as being more knowledgeable than other people in any field. There are "investment gurus," "sports gurus," "horse racing gurus," "fashion industry gurus." The very word "guru" becomes an embarrassment, when mouthed by fools.

In fact, no one is fit to be called a guru in the true sense until he has realized oneness with God—until he is, in the highest sense, Self-realized. A guru in the lower sense of the term is one who is competent to teach in any given field. To use the word in this way would be no insult to the high and true meaning, the *satguru* who initiates the seeker into the supreme wisdom, were it not that this sublime concept is diminished if people are encouraged to dismiss the very possibility that *sat,* or divine truth, gurus exist. *SAT,* you will recall, is that aspect of the Supreme Spirit which is beyond creation itself. A *satguru* is one who has realized oneness with that highest aspect of Truth.

How to find and recognize such a *satguru?* Not by the size of his following. Not by the miracles he performs, which may indicate spiritual power but are not in themselves proof of Self-realization. Partly, a great guru can be known by the caliber of his disciples. To a great extent also he can be recognized by the regard shown for him by other reputable teachers. Even a true guru in the highest sense, however, may not be the right one for you, personally. The only real answer, then, is, Have faith in God. Whatever good way you follow will develop in you the magnetism to attract what is right for you. If, after a certain point, you realize that one way is no longer right for you, you will find yourself drawn naturally to what *is* right.

Don't be fickle. Don't look about restlessly for alternatives. One-pointed loyalty is the highest virtue. Remember also that it is a great sin to try to weaken another person's faith in his own way. It is also a sin to brood angrily on the defects of one's own way. God, finally, is the only Guru. He works through many human instruments, a few of which are perfect, but most of which are still imperfect. But if your devotion is above all to God, He will guide you rightly on your path to Him.

The point to remember here is something Paramhansa Yogananda said to his first disciple in America, Dr. M. W. Lewis, when they first met. Dr. Lewis was the president of the local chapter of another spiritual society, and believed in loyalty. But when he met Yogananda he recognized him as the right guru for him. Yogananda resolved his inner conflict by telling him simply, "Don't let sentiment rule you."

The highest divine magnetism has nothing to do with personality. Yogananda himself confessed it had been disconcerting at first to find that his guru, Swami Sri Yukteswar, spoke in terms of "cold spiritual mathematics." His guru was a *gyani*, or saint of wisdom, whereas Yogananda's nature was primarily devotional. Yet, as he wrote in *Autobiography of a Yogi*, "As I tuned myself to his nature, I discovered no diminution but rather increase in my devotional approach to God."

Another more trivial but still illustrative example may be seen from singing lessons that I took from an old lady when I was eighteen. Her aim was to help me learn how to place my voice. As I developed this ability, I was able to use my own natural baritone voice more clearly. It wasn't that I acquired her soprano tonal qualities.

What a true teacher can do for you is help you to develop *your own* magnetism. He will not impose on you his own.

There is a deeper aspect, however, to this magnetic exchange with a true guru. Yogananda often quoted the scriptural statement, "All of Krishna's soldiers were like Krishna." There is something too subtle to be defined, and much deeper than any personality trait, that the disciple does indeed take on by attuning himself to a guru. I have likened this special gift of the guru to a ray of the divine light. The clearer this ray, and the less mingled with other rays, the stronger the magnetism conveyed, and received. It is like a strong river that draws into itself every sluggish eddy, making the entire flow of consciousness pure and powerful.

There are countless divine rays. No two of them are the same. The Lord, who makes every snowflake unique, is infinite in the variety of His gifts of grace. When a river finally meets the sea, its individual drops of water enter that vast body of water, but their individuality is never lost even though they also recognize the sea itself to be their reality. On the journey to the sea, however, once they enter the river's powerful flow they are swept quickly and easily past obstacles that might otherwise delay their seaward journey indefinitely.

Dr. Lewis felt sad on the occasion of Paramhansa Yogananda's departure for the West Coast from Dr. Lewis's home town near Boston. "Never mind what happens to me," the great guru told him. "Just don't forget God." He was not severing the inner link that bound them. He was simply saying, "If you keep God first in your life, we shall remain ever united in Him."

The relationship with a true guru is a relationship in God. It is not personal. Woe betide that false teacher who prides himself on even having disciples. Jesus Christ called such people "thieves and robbers," snatching to themselves the devotion due to God alone. A good spiritual teacher tries to awaken love in you for God, never for himself. "God," Yogananda used to say, "is the true Guru."

The right guru's path is a path to God. It is the superficial student who focuses on the guru's personality, and who, in trying to attune himself to the guru, imitates that personality. One occasionally encounters such devotees—Westerner disciples of an Indian guru, for example, who somewhat ludicrously adopt Indian accents and mannerisms. I don't mean to imply that their behavior is wrong; it may help some of them to keep their guru in mind. But imitation is superficial.

Love God first. In that love, attune yourself to the guru's divine love and consciousness.

My own guru's most advanced disciple never learned even how to pronounce his *paramguru*'s (the guru's guru's) name correctly. What of it, when he was blessed to be able to commune with him in his meditations?

Accept, then, that every divine ray is unique. It is the shallow disciple who thinks, "Because Truth is one, therefore all teachings are one. I bow equally to them all." If you are not divinely drawn to a supreme, or *sat*, guru, pray that you be drawn to a disciple of such a one. For the divine ray is passed from generation to generation.

Even today, 2,500 years after the life of Buddha, Buddhists bow first to him. Within that supreme devotion they seek to attune themselves to the ray of divine grace which flows from the Buddha *through* his representatives, or teachers of his line, whom they rightly consider the Buddha's instruments.

Because all things exist as vibrations, and because one of the primary manifestations of vibration is music, one of the best ways of attuning oneself to the guru's ray, or vibration, is through chanting and music. "Chanting," Yogananda used to say, "is half the battle."

God sometimes sends a broader-than-usual ray of the divine light to earth. This is a band of grace by ascending which millions are brought closer to God. These special descents are known as "special dispensations." I shall discuss this aspect of our subject in the next chapter.

Anyone who sincerely follows any ray of the Divine is likely to be urged by relatives and erstwhile companions, "Don't become fanatical." In reply, he might think to himself (though it might well be impolitic to say so out loud!), "Do you want me to be as spiritually wishy-washy as most of you?" To be a fanatic means to refuse to relate to any but one's own reality. To be single-minded has nothing to do with fanaticism if one doesn't seek to impose his dedication on others. What the sincere devotee practices is *ahimsa,* non-violence, as Mahatma Gandhi did. Centered in inner freedom, he gives respect to everyone else's right to the same freedom.

Chapter Sixteen

The Avatara: Revelation, or Return Voyage?

Avatara, a Sanskrit word, means the descent of Divinity into fleshly form. *Avatara* is the act of descent; "avatar," without the "a", is its specific manifestation: the one who descends. From an *advaitic* view of *Vedanta,*[*] the universe itself, as a manifestation of the Supreme Spirit, is itself that descent. Usually, however, the word applies to a specific manifestation.

Traditionally speaking, Iswara, the Supreme Spirit— by most Hindus visualized as Vishnu—incarnates from time to time as a human being for the spiritual benefit of humanity. Vishnu descends from *Vaikuntha,* or heaven, where, according to mythology, he is said to reside.

---

[*]*Vedanta* is one of three basic Ways of Awakening in Hinduism. Usually described as "philosophies," or "systems of thought," they are known as *Sankhya, Yoga,* and *Vedanta.* Paramhansa Yogananda epitomized these three Ways as follows:

Sankhya's main purpose is to convince man of his need to rise above attachment to *maya* and to attain a higher state of consciousness; *Vedanta*'s is to describe the nature of that high state of consciousness; and *Yoga*'s is to show people *how to reach* that consciousness.

The essence of Vedanta is *advaitic,* or non-dualistic. Its focus is on that state which transcends the vibratory opposites of duality.

These three "systems" have been described as mutually exclusive. In fact they are complementary aspects of a single whole.

Kali Yuga, obviously, has been at work here. Even in his supreme, unmanifested state Vishnu has been endowed with human form, and is visualized as living in some idealized locale in outer space. Fundamentalist Hindus even insist that Krishna was himself an incarnation of that deity, and that, like Vishnu, he had blue skin; and that Vishnu, like Krishna, plays a flute. They believe the heaven where Vishnu lives is a place of scenic beauty, where his devotees dance around him eternally.

There is nothing wrong with such devotional images, as I've said repeatedly, if they inspire devotion. But there is no way to justify these fantasies rationally. Popular notions of Vaikuntha are comparable to Christian ones of eternity in heaven amid pastoral surroundings, with perhaps wisps of mist on the ground to make the scene ethereal. All those who have made it there play harps. . . . Well, better this, perhaps, than heaven as it has been visualized in many works of art: a royal court, with God and Jesus eternally ensconced (*trapped* might be a better word) on thrones of gold and the elect standing in reverent poses before them. These tableaux, when suggested seriously as our fate for having been good, provide sufficient incentive for the skeptic to cast about for more interesting alternatives!

The symbolism implicit, on the other hand, in the concept of spirit descending is based on fact. This isn't to say that God descends to earth from outer space, but only that, in order to incarnate in human form at all, His consciousness must descend in the way every soul does on entering the human form: from the medulla oblongata and brain down the spine, out into the nervous system, and thence to the rest of the body. The divine descent, then, is into human *consciousness,* and not only into human form. An avatar does not suddenly materialize himself, as he might when manifesting himself to a devotee ephemerally, and as he does in visions. Nor does his descent imply sublime aloofness from his human role—as if his appearance were only an act.

An avatar is popularly considered a manifestation of God Himself, rather than the re-appearance on earth of a liberated soul. He is thought of as never having been touched by the play of *maya* in which he condescends to participate.

Paramhansa Yogananda, in his written commentaries on the Holy Bible, discussed a comparable belief that is held by Christians. Jesus Christ, whom they consider the Son of God, is believed never at any time to have been subject to human imperfection. Yogananda stated emphatically that this belief is erroneous. God, he declared, would never try to help humanity by showing Himself as if human without really being human. Far from maintaining an aura of divine aloofness, He would identify Himself as much as possible with human life. Nor would His assumption of our human state be a mere show, acted throughout with a benign smile but without the slightest personal involvement.

"What sort of lesson would that be for humanity?" the guru demanded. "God wouldn't simply *pretend* to be going through the hardship and pain that, from the human point of view, are so real. He wouldn't have given us Jesus Christ as a sort of divine puppet. Jesus was a soul that had been liberated in previous incarnations. He had attained God-consciousness by undergoing the same hard struggles, and learning the same hard lessons, we all must face as human beings. He was born not to show us how great *he* was, but to give us hope that the state of consciousness he had attained, we too can attain."

Jesus, then, accepted actual suffering as a human being to show what it takes to find God: complete and utter dedication of the little self to the infinite, true Self, the Supreme Spirit.

As Jesus Christ himself put it, "By gaining his life [that is to say, by remaining attached to human existence] a man will lose it; by losing his life for my sake [in other words, by offering his life up to God] he will gain it" (Matthew 10:39).

In the Book of Revelation, Jesus also speaks of having "overcome": "To him that overcometh will I grant to sit with me in my throne, *even as I also overcame,* and am set down with my Father in his throne" (Revelation 3:21). For "throne" read, "state of consciousness." It was the fact that Jesus, too, had struggled and had "overcome" delusion that gives us hope that we ourselves may achieve the same victory. There would be little meaning for us in our own spiritual labors if the message of a divine incarnation were one of perfection effortlessly attained.

The meaning of avatara, Yogananda stated, is not that Divine Consciousness, which has never known imperfection, appears in human form to show us a reality completely alien to our own. Krishna, Jesus Christ, and all other avatars are not only *manifestations* of Spirit. They are descents also in the sense of knowing, from experience, what it is to be human beings who attained oneness with the Divine. *Their example shows us our own divine potential.*

Jesus Christ himself emphasized this message, declaring that we could all be like him. "Verily, verily," he said, "He that believeth on me, the works that I do shall he do also; and greater works than these shall he do; because I go unto my Father" (John 14:12).

And Krishna, considered by many to be Vishnu's avatar, and indeed his *"purna,"* or full, avatar, states in the Bhagavad Gita, "You and I, Arjuna, have passed through many births. I know them all, even if you do not" (4:5).

Many orthodox Hindus pass quickly over such passages, as do their Christian counterparts,* from a firm conviction that these divine incarnations could *never* have lived on earth as imperfect human beings. The scriptures themselves, however, do not endorse this pious conviction. Krishna's statement in the Bhagavad Gita: "Though unborn and immortal, . . . I manifest Myself on earth as a human being" (4:6), in no way means that he never had to face tests as a human being in order to reach that divine state of consciousness. His purpose in incarnating would have been betrayed had

---

*In the Bible the hints are more oblique, but they are there.

there been an absolute distinction between himself and the rest of humanity. God *identified* Himself with us to show us *our own* divine potential.

The soul, after it attains Self-realization, knows that it never lived in delusion at all, for everything it experienced during all its incarnations was a dream. Thus, every awakened master is in the same position Krishna was to state: "I am birthless and eternal; never have I lived in human form." What such a master means is simply the same truth Sri Krishna himself uttered in the Bhagavad Gita, "The soul [everyone's soul, in other words] is never born; nor does it die."

Yogananda told the story about a devotee offering flowers on the altar. All of a sudden he entered cosmic consciousness. "Oh!" he cried, "I have been worshiping another's image, and now I see that I, untouched by the body, am the Sustainer of the universe: I bow to myself!" And he began throwing the flowers on his own head. He wasn't being arrogant. Nor was he denying that he had ever been a devotee. He was simply recognizing that, although for incarnations he had been sleeping in delusion, he had now awakened to his true Self. That Self, for all of us, is the Supreme Spirit.

I have known saints to declare, "I have never incarnated," yet on other occasions tell certain persons, "We have been together in other lives." They were not contradicting themselves. Their meaning was determined by their point of view at the moment. A master has reached that state of realization in which the soul perceives that everything is only a dream.

Avatars have lived before, *as dreamers themselves in the cosmic dream.* An avatar, as distinct from an ascended master, or one who has attained perfect freedom in this lifetime, is born already free and perfect. He is like a graduate returning to the university where he once studied, to offer help, guidance, and encouragement from his own experience. He is not some Divine Prodigy who, omniscient from birth, has no need to study at all, but passes every exam effortlessly and with top honors. Such a "beyond genius" might fill us with awe and amazement, but his example would hardly encourage us in our own efforts to become good students. It is the ex-student who, having graduated, fills us with hope that we, too, may succeed in graduating. He is in a position to say to us, "I did it, and so therefore can you." His example is useful to us, not abstract. An avatar descends for no other purpose than to help souls that are in bondage to attain the freedom he himself has attained.

What, then, is the difference between an avatar and an ascended master? An ascended master, in the fact that his life has been spent *reaching up* toward liberation, carries in his consciousness the thought of total renunciation and withdrawal from worldly entanglements. He is not interested, usually, in roaming among the masses, uplifting them spiritually. Trailing behind him, like a vapor, is the memory of limitations finally transcended. And, like a soldier victorious after a long war, he isn't much interested in joining others in *their* wars.

Usually, once a master has attained liberation, his primary concern is for his disciples, not for masses of people at all different levels of spiritual maturity. His primary thought is to shake the dust of *maya* from his feet and leave this manifested existence behind him forever.

Only a very few masters, after attaining liberation, retain the pure and non-delusion-involving desire to help all humanity to attain the same goal. Such masters, if they willingly accept rebirth for the good of all, are born with great spiritual power. An ascended master is capable of liberating a few others, but an avatar is born with the divine power to liberate as many as tune in to his consciousness. The Bible states this truth, referring to Jesus Christ: "As many as received him, to them gave he power to become the sons of God."

Sri Krishna, speaking from a state of infinite consciousness and as an avatara of that consciousness, said, "Uniting yourself to Me, thus shalt thou come to Me" (Bhagavad Gita 9:34).

In *Autobiography of a Yogi,* the great guru Lahiri Mahasaya made this prediction concerning Paramhansa Yogananda when the latter was still a babe in his mother's arms: "Little mother, thy son will be a yogi. As a spiritual engine, he will carry many souls to God's kingdom." Indeed, Yogananda, like a mighty locomotive, was destined to pull a long train-load of bliss-seekers to their longed-for land of divine fulfillment.

240

It is said that when a soul attains final liberation, his relatives for seven generations in either direction are raised to spiritual freedom. This does not mean they are lifted to his own supreme level. Their degree of attainment depends on their purity of heart, and on the strength of their spiritual bond with their exalted family member. Dr. M. W. Lewis once asked Paramhansa Yogananda, in this context, "What about the disciples?"

"Oh," the master assured him, "they come first!"

An avatar, having emerged into the infinite light from what may be described as the long tunnel of spiritual evolution, delays indefinitely his own complete enjoyment of that light to return and help others find their own way out of the darkness. The tunnel is very long. We don't escape the limitations of human life after one lifetime only. Indeed, the soul's eternity of existence is not only from the time of its birth in human form, but from the beginning of time itself—indeed, from even before time's beginning. The soul is eternal, as God is eternal. As an ancient Hermetic teaching states it, "Thou art from old, O son of man, yea, thou art from everlasting." In the next chapter we'll discuss certain aspects of this long journey.

Meanwhile, a question remains to be asked: Has the avatara any special meaning for us personally, apart from the obvious benefit we receive from God's descent through His awakened sons for our salvation? That of course should be benefit enough! But what I mean is, is there some way that *we ourselves* can participate in this drama of divine descent?

In the last chapter I described the vibrational magnetism that emanates from a Self-realized master. I described also the importance of attuning ourselves to that magnetism, and of not scattering our attunement by running after every spiritual wonder that comes to town. Rather, I said, we should one-pointedly develop the particular quality of divine magnetism to which our souls are most strongly attracted.

In India they speak of the *ishta devata,* or chosen spiritual ideal. One's guru can be that ideal. It is well also, however, to hold a broader concept in mind lest we limit our concept of the guru to his human form, and overlook that that body and personality are only windows, so to speak, onto Infinite Consciousness.

A disciple once asked Paramhansa Yogananda, "Should I pray to you, Master, or to the Divine Mother?"

"To the Divine Mother," the guru replied.

He didn't mean *not* to pray to the guru as a manifestation of God. He himself often prayed to Sri Yukteswar or to one of his paramgurus, or to other saints. His meaning, then, was that the disciple should see the guru as a manifestation of the infinite Spirit, and not try mentally to separate him, or her, from that supreme reality.

Another disciple once said to him, "When I look at you, I see only the Divine Mother."

The guru didn't remonstrate against what some people might have thought required a protestation of humility. He simply replied quietly, "Then behave accordingly."

To worship an avatar as a man is to attune oneself to his human manifestation while overlooking the truth that, behind that form, his consciousness of oneness with God expands outward to infinity.

It is always wise, therefore, to concentrate on the Infinite, of which the outer manifestation is a minute expression. Otherwise, the tendency arises in human nature to identify the outer form with God. And that is the beginning of fanaticism.

Not many people are blessed to be drawn to an enlightened guru. Still fewer are blessed to come personally under the grace and protection of an avatar. Everyone, however, can come under that protection by faith, devotion, and inner soul-attunement. By means of an avatar's blessing, whether or not the avatar is still alive in the body, one may find himself drawn to someone who can personally give him the touch of the divine ray that every soul needs, for enlightenment.

It is extremely helpful, in any case, to bring the avatar out of the pages of history, or out of that divine form which one may actually behold before him, and into oneself, into one's own personal consciousness. The divine descent into human form will not be complete, where you yourself are concerned, until he can descend into your own body and mind.

Think of him in meditation, then, as the human being he is, or was. Concentrate on that one special avatar, among many, for whom your heart feels a particular affinity. If you have a guru, you may think of him thus, also. Visualize that spirit descending through your medulla, brain, and spine and out into your

243

nervous system, filling your entire body. Feel that he has, in some mysterious but exalted sense, become you. And feel divine devotion toward him, especially in your heart. *You* are that divine consciousness which now dwells in your body! Pray that it fill you, and purify you of every human imperfection. Uplift the attunement you feel in your heart, and offer it up to God. Pray that the avatara make you one with itself, with the Infinite Spirit.

In this meditation there is no presumption. Rather, it helps the divine avatar to fulfill his purpose in descending into human form at all: to give *you,* yourself, the grace to attain all that he himself has attained.

Chapter Seventeen

The Avatara and Human Evolution

God, through AUM, is forever active in creation. The very universe is an avatara in the sense of being Spirit's "descent" into manifestation. This is not, of course, the usual meaning ascribed to the word. Nevertheless, it sets the stage for the broader interpretation that follows.

According to legend, the Supreme Being as Vishnu incarnated* first as a fish, then a tortoise, a boar, and a man-lion before assuming human form as a dwarf, then perfect proportions as Rama and then Krishna. His progressive incarnations through lower forms suggest the stages of earthly evolution.

The Indian teachings focus primarily on evolution as a manifestation of developing consciousness. Even those more rudimentary stages are presented as progressive manifestations of the divine. The rishis described a gradual awakening from inorganic to organic matter, from plant life to the animal kingdom, thence upward to the human race. "God sleeps in the rocks, dreams in the plants, stirs toward wakefulness in the animals, and in mankind awakens to self-awareness."

---

*Scholars claim that the incarnations were originally Brahma's.

245

Evolution doesn't end at the human level. In self-awareness, indeed, it has only reached its beginning. Moreover, since the creation of mankind no more advanced form has been required, for the human nervous system is already capable of resonating with the highest states of consciousness. That capacity needs, however, to be developed. The average person uses only a small fraction of his brain potential. Human evolution, then, consists in developing that potential to its fullest. One lifetime is not sufficient for that development. Still less is it adequate for evolutionary progress at lower levels.

God is not simply amusing Himself. He created life that it might participate consciously in a great adventure. Most science-educated people assume a pseudo-vedantic stance in these matters: Accepting a general evolutionary move upward, they reject the idea that *individual* awareness evolves also. They see the forms, but not what lies behind those forms. Like a theater audience, they observe actors coming out onto the stage, then leaving it again, but know nothing of what happens backstage. Even if they accept the idea of an infinite consciousness, and the possibility that life is a manifestation of that consciousness, they aver that, once the stage appearance is over, what remains is infinite consciousness once again.

They are deluded by appearances. For, backstage, the actors live on. Donning new costumes, they appear again and again in different guises.

The soul, once the body that housed it dies, is not able to merge back into the ocean of Spirit for the reason that it is also encased in an astral energy-form. This astral form, in turn, is a shell housing the even-subtler causal body of ideas.

At this point, the wave analogy we offered earlier ceases to state the case clearly. Paramhansa Yogananda refined that analogy, therefore, with another one. Imagine a bottle, he said, floating on the surface of the sea. This bottle represents the physical body. Enclosed within it is another bottle, representing the astral body. Within that second bottle is still another, representing the causal body. The water represented by the wave in our former analogy is now contained in that innermost bottle. It cannot merge back in the ocean until its last remaining "bottle," the causal body, is broken.

Freedom to merge in God comes only after the soul transcends every vestige of attachment even to the causal body. Attachment is, forever, the impediment to divine union. Shedding the thought of separateness from the infinite ocean, the soul achieves omnipres-ence—that state for which, in the depths of its being, it longed eternally.

At lower levels of material manifestation, conscious-ness, though actively present, is indistinct. A wave at its inception lacks definition, and swells only slightly as if uncertain of what it intended. The *energy* that goes to produce the wave, however, is already there, ready to generate its upward thrust. And the *idea behind* that energy has already given it direction. Even low levels of manifestation, such as rocks, contain a hidden force, and behind that, a consciousness that remain unaffected when that manifestation is dispersed, as, for example, when a rock is smashed to pieces.

The importance of the material universe is that it brings cosmic thought and energy to a focus. We ourselves experience a need to "materialize" our ideas, in the sense of expressing them clearly. School teachers often remark that to explain a concept to their students helps to clarify their own understanding of it. And an artist's vision is never so clear to himself as when he puts the finishing touches to his painting of it. In any creative labor, the main beneficiary is the creator himself.

The material universe wrote the natural *"fini"* to cosmic creation. The very devas consider man fortunate, so it is said, in possessing a human body, for only on the physical plane can the basic spiritual lessons be learned, their deep insights brought to a clear focus, and inner victories won that lead to high spiritual realization.

The process of spiritual development begins far back in time.

A portion of the divine consciousness first manifested itself in the form of ideas. These ideas were formed primarily of broad principles and general directions. Because consciousness at that stage of manifestation was so closely attuned to the Supreme Spirit, its power was, virtually, limitless. Specificity, however, would have limited that power. Yogananda described the ideas on the causal plane as "blueprints" for the continuance of cosmic creation. God's way, it should be understood, is not man's way. An architect must plan his blueprint carefully, step by step, working out specific measurements for every wall, window, and door. The cosmic "blueprint," by contrast, is relatively free-flowing and spontaneous. The details work themselves out naturally with the "work's" progress, because the medium employed—that is to say, energy—is itself conscious. Beginning at the center of everything created, consciousness and energy expand effortlessly outward into further manifestation. Divine consciousness takes the fundamental ideas it projected and clothes them in energy; then, as energy, it gives those ideas shape, color, and substance.

Thus, the creative impulse crystalizes energy into material forms. We who behold these physical forms think of them as self-defined. As Gertrude Stein, the poetess, wrote, "A rose is a rose is a rose." But the truth is that material forms only temporarily manifest the energy and consciousness that went into producing them.

At the astral energy level, countless different vibrations are brought into manifestation by Brahma, the creative force, from the formative center of ideas. The natural expansiveness of that energy is kept centered by its feminine "consort": the consciousness of individuality. This is, in part, why souls are described as feminine in relation to the Supreme Spirit, the Masculine Principle. For the feminine principle centers outward awareness in itself, whereas absorption in the masculine principle expands self-consciousness to infinity. The consciousness of individuality, with which the heart of every atom is imbued, defines itself, as it matures, as ego-consciousness. Only on turning within to its Infinite Source does that sense of selfhood break the limitations of ego and become infinite also. As long as its attention is directed outward through the senses, nourishing "Brahma's" outward creativity, the ego is not yet ready to fulfill its divine destiny.

At the lower stages of manifestation, the creative force impels the first vague sense of individuality toward upward evolution. Self-awareness, because it is still indistinct, has no *desire* yet to progress. Individuality exists, and continues after the dissolution of each successive material form it inhabits, but its self-motivation is minimal. When that physical vehicle is destroyed, its individual vibration of energy is simply impelled outward again into matter. It is the infinite creative impulse, not material desire, that pushes it toward the experience of greater clarity in its expression of awareness. Life evolves not so much because of a Darwinian struggle for survival as because there is an impulse at the center of all manifestation to reclaim its own innate, superconscious state.

Evolution at the Human Level

Once evolution reaches the human level, the impulse toward self-development ceases to be wholly blind. For human awareness has enough clarity to define its goals, which it views as personal and, increasingly, imperative. Not for mankind, the patience of the sea shell that, moving slowly back and forth for fifteen long years, succeeds at last in wearing a hole deep enough in hard rock to enable it to nestle down comfortably. Awareness at the human level becomes *self*-awareness; it becomes clearly defined as ego. The ego's needs, too, are more or less clearly defined. It declares, "This is what I want, and I want it *now!* If in getting it I deprive others, that is their problem, not mine!" The French philosopher Jean Paul Sartre—one of what I would call philosophy's "intelligent idiots"—said it well for this primitive type of humanity: "To be conscious of another is to be conscious of what one is not."

Mankind, at the initial stages of his evolutional journey, is selfish in a way that the lower animals haven't the clarity to be. We see many human traits and foibles also in animals, but they are "practice runs," so to speak; animals haven't mankind's conscious commitment to self-protection, self-aggrandizement, and self-promotion. Their consciousness, being relatively dim, cannot produce strong ego-bonds.

When individual evolution reaches the human level, it doesn't all of a sudden become intelligent. Still less does it become wise. Unaccustomed, rather, to reasoning at all, its first impulse is to go on living more or less as it did before, by animal urges. To expect a newly incarnated human being to take intelligent responsibility for his actions is unrealistic. Spiritual development warrants encouragement, but it ought never to be forced on anyone, any more than one tries to force an infant to study calculus. To ask a "new soul" to think deeply would be to ignore its real level of development. Maturity comes not with physical adulthood, but with spiritual development. To achieve wisdom, more than one lifetime is needed. The ego takes as many incarnations as it wants to discover its true nature: a spark of the mighty blaze of infinite consciousness.

The Castes

Spiritual development at the human level was delineated in ancient times as a progressive series of what were called *varna*s, or castes. This progression became institutionalized, and gradually hardened into what was, in effect, a system of socially sanctioned injustice. Originally, however, it was based on an enlightened understanding of human nature; its purpose was to encourage people to develop towards their own divine fulfillment. The *varna*s were not so much a system as a teaching, based on inner revelation and on the self-understanding of great rishis.

As it became systematized, however—especially under the consciousness-crystalizing influence of Kali Yuga—it became an instrument of suppression.

In the American south before the Civil War, similar conditions prevailed: the institution of slavery. Plantation owners opposed the idea of freeing their slaves, who they insisted were treated like family, loved, befriended, and cared for solicitously. Even in cases—there must have been some—where this was true, and the slaves received a measure of security they would not have had if they'd been forced to fend for themselves, the injustice to them was profound in a deeper, spiritual sense. For they were denied the right to develop the quality a human being most needs for his own spiritual evolution: personal initiative.

In India, too, the people of low caste were often—though, again, not always—sincerely loved and cared for by people in higher castes. In that country, too, however, the initiative of the lower classes was suppressed.

The worst aspect of slave mentality, which the caste system also produced, is that in many cases it was the suppressed people themselves who welcomed it. In modern times, the choice has been offered to whole nations: security, under a state-controlled system, or freedom, under a system of free enterprise. And people have repeatedly opted for personal security, even if it deprived them of their freedom and initiative.

Institutionalized religion provides another example of this slave mentality. For it defines faith, not in terms of courageous affirmation, but of security. It demands conformity to an institutional norm, rather than giving individuals the freedom to live by their conscience. Strange to say, perhaps, this definition has been widely accepted as right and just, providing as it does a sense of security against the danger of divine displeasure. Thus, persecutions have even been committed to protect that "faith," with people glancing hopefully over their shoulders for clerical, or divine, approval. Initiative, which results in the exercise of personal conscience, has been suppressed with assurances of an eternal reward in heaven for the "faithful," who have accepted the arrangement as "the will of God."

People fortunately are beginning to see more and more clearly that, lacking the consent of free will, there can be no true conscience, and that lacking conscience there can be no true faith. Therefore, they are beginning to reject the restrictions imposed upon them by religious institutions.

The problem lies not so much with institutions, as such, as with the entrenched self-interest of the people running them, and with the lack of initiative, on the other hand, in those whom they control. Nevertheless, institutions are, in fact, needed in this world; they help to give a necessary direction to human behavior. Problems arise only when those directions become *directives,* and when people willingly submit to being chained.

For the odd thing is, they do submit, even when there is no one to force them into bondage. Countless numbers prefer not to bear the burden of personal responsibility: not to have to worry, for example, about security in their work, or about where their food and lodging come from, even if accepting guarantees of security results in their never attaining to full dignity as free human beings. They vote for politicians who will promise them security, even if those persons have been known to break all their promises. At least, those voters think, the politicians have had the "compassion" to *make* those promises!

Simple logic makes it clear that the promises cannot but be lies. For no government can create wealth: It can only spend it. Pouring out largesse to people as a means of buying votes saps their initiative, and at the same time deprives those of their earnings who alone produce the nation's wealth. The only way a government itself can create money is by printing it, in the process inflating the currency, and, consequently, debasing it.

Providing too much unearned security to the "underprivileged" deprives them of the challenge to develop their own initiative. At the same time, it weakens initiative in the providers. A slave owner—to use our first example—discovers that his very responsibility keeps him from being free, himself. For it prevents him from taking the risk of testing new ways of doing things. He imagines himself to be in control, but in fact the system he runs is like a wheel, and he must turn with it as surely as everyone else, even though he doesn't consider himself bound to it.

Any system that presumes to provide for others, but doesn't let them reciprocate honorably, paralyzes both those who are controlled and those who do the controlling.

Aristocracy, too, is a system that paralyzes initiative. The paralysis begins with the tendency of "nobles" to disparage initiative in those beneath them, socially. Their presumption of superiority is based merely on inherited wealth and prestige. These advantages breed false notions of nobility, however, based on so-called "gracious living." They discredit that which alone is truly noble: nobility of character. Aristocracy produces, finally, an effete outlook on life which deadens initiative as surely in the rulers as it does in those whom they rule.

The caste system in India, compared to class distinctions elsewhere in the world, was relatively benign. At least it actively promoted kindness and respect, and a calm acceptance of deficiencies in the lower classes, rather than leaving these attitudes wholly to the will (not always so "sweet") of the controlling individual. That system, too, however, paralyzed initiative at every level of society. And because India's civilization is so old, its castes long ago became ossified as a supposed reflection of the divine order.

It is easy to criticize. Critics of that system would do well to remember that people everywhere live in glass houses. No one can afford to throw bricks.

Fortunately, human nature *is,* gradually, growing more refined. A sign of this improvement may be seen in the simple fact that people cry out more and more frequently against suppression of any kind. Another sign is that people are demanding the right to *exercise* their initiative. The process is slow, but there is ample reason to hope. The water pressure behind a dam may build to the point where the dam bursts suddenly. Perhaps even some global catastrophe will force the needed shift in consciousness.

Originally, the caste system was based not on birth, but on a person's own natural inclinations. As a later scripture declared, "One who is born a brahmin is not for that mere reason a brahmin. To be a brahmin, he must have the character and consciousness of a brahmin."

Caste, as it was originally understood, recognized evolution as the refinement of consciousness. It was not a democratic institution, in the modern sense. For social governance today, nothing better than or even as good as democracy has been proposed. Even so, it is always well to remember that people thrive when they honor truth, but lose heavily in the end when their motives are clouded by self-interest.

In ancient India the norm was not mass rule, but rule by the few who, setting personal interest aside, had demonstrated a sincere concern for the general well-being. At the same time, the masses were free to speak out, and were listened to. A king ruled by the consent of the people. In the normal course of events, that consent could be counted on without the modern rush of campaigns and speeches to solicit it. The system worked better in those times than modern-day democracy would have, for though people weren't asked to express their opinions, when they didn't really have any; urged to speak, when they weren't particularly eager to do so; and encouraged to decide what they wanted, personally, rather than accept what was generally best for everyone: yet they were given a voice whenever they wanted to speak out, and their reactions were invited whenever there was an important decision to be made. Such a system of governance was, perhaps, more feasible in small countries. I am not suggesting it as a model for today's "super-powers."

Human consciousness, at its lowest level of refinement, is unwilling to reason deeply. It virtually never thinks unselfishly. And it is overwhelmed by any challenge to think creatively. If what physics tells us is true, that Nature abhors a vacuum, it is equally true that a mental vacuum abhors having worthwhile ideas thrust into it.

Those in ancient India whose nature demonstrated this inchoate ego-awareness were designated as *shudra*s. They were on the bottom rung of humanity's evolutional ladder. The scriptural statement quoted above might be adapted to them: "A person born into the shudra caste is not for that mere reason a shudra. To be a shudra he must have a shudra's deficiencies of character, and his relatively unrefined degree of awareness."

It would have been simplistic to assign shudras to a formal place in society, since birth might have placed them at any social level. By defining the level of evolution at which they lived, however, it was possible to encourage them to follow their own natural direction of development. Shudras, rightly perceived, are "kindergarten" students in the school of human evolution. They sink naturally, therefore, to those levels of activity which require a minimum of creative initiative.

The epitome of this "kindergarten class" is what people the world over regard as peasant mentality. Actually, a particular peasant may be bright and intelligent, and not a true *shudra* at all. There is a type of human being, however, found at every level of society, whom the term "peasant" aptly describes. His manner, regardless of upbringing, is coarse; he thinks first in terms of satisfying his physical appetites; only rarely does he show himself capable of initiative, except in his readiness to accept favors from others. His lack of creativity is a travesty of his divine potential, for he needs continual supervision in everything he does, lest he break things or misplace them.

The caste system was not meant to be an instrument of suppression. It wasn't even a system, really, so much as the simple recognition that men simply are not all created equal, except in their divine potential. No one was told what his position in life had to be. People were encouraged, rather, at every level of evolution to grow at their own natural pace. What the teaching did was help to clarify what constituted, for each of them, his next stage of natural growth.

For the shudra, a recommendation for further growth was that he work under people who were more developed, spiritually, than himself. Indeed, the custom of having servants, though nowadays deplored, was actually beneficial to the servants themselves as long as the service they gave was voluntary, and as long as the system fostered mutual respect. It was spiritually beneficial also to their employers, provided they saw themselves not as commanding or condescending, but as helping those they employed.

As the developing ego begins to awaken to the advantages of having a human intelligence, it stops relying on strength alone to get what it wants, and begins using its intelligence. Gradually, what it develops is the sort of shrewd cunning that is found typically in merchants.

This, then, is the second stage of human evolution. It was called the *vaishya,* or merchant, caste. For the merchant must use his intelligence to get ahead in life. Typically, moreover, he defines "getting ahead" as accumulating wealth. At higher levels of evolution, a vaishya sees himself as providing society with its practical needs. Where, first, he concentrated on fulfilling his selfish desires, at higher levels of development the vaishya caste produces musicians and artists. It leaves to a later stage, however, those attitudes of which the pure aim is, through the arts, to help people spiritually.

A shudra typically perceives himself as more acted upon than acting. Still typically, therefore, he resents having others tell him what to do, even when he has the need to be told. Often, in this democratic age of ours, such a person will demand heavily of others, "Say, who do you think you are?" By contrast, the question a typical vaishya asks is, "What's in it for me?"

There are many merchants, of course, who derive great satisfaction from giving generously to others. In such persons, the bonds of selfishness have already begun to loosen. For them, to live only for the advantages they can squeeze out of others is no longer attractive; they have more expansive uses for their creativity.

The purpose of the caste system, then, was to inspire expansion beyond ego-centeredness, until self-interest included the well-being of others; and then to refine that consciousness further until at last one perceived his true self as the infinite, divine Self. Rightly understood, this teaching discouraged the merchant, for example, from thinking that his true duty in life was to exercise his cunning toward selfish ends, even though this attitude was accepted as natural to him at his own stage of development. He was shown a further road to be traveled in his development, in other words. What the caste system provided him with may be described as a road map.

The ego, as it achieves progressive refinement, no longer wants to attract wealth to itself; it begins to give generously to others. For it understands that there is far greater satisfaction in giving than in taking. People at this stage of maturity develop executive qualities— not so much as a liking for telling others what to do, but as a desire to help them to fulfill their own natures. *Kshatriya* was the name assigned to this level of human evolution. In contrast to the vaishya's typical question, "What's in it for me?" the kshatriya's natural question is, "What's in it for everyone?" His nature is epitomized by the selfless ruler, or by the warrior hero who willingly sacrifices his life for the good of others.

Obviously, not all kshatriyas, recognized as such by society, are noble by nature. Equally obviously, no society is so simply organized as to consist only of peasants, merchants, warriors, and—the fourth caste, as we shall see in a moment—priests. What the caste system described originally was a loose social system that allowed people to gravitate to positions for which their own natures fitted them.

The kshatriya mentality, as it becomes gradually refined, reaches the point where it realizes that the universal well-being of which it has dreamed is an abstraction. Indeed, the executive mind grows naturally toward a more abstract understanding of life. It employs not only its intelligence, but its will power, in directing others. As the will develops, its normal inclination is toward intellectual refinement, for will and intellect are both centered in the frontal lobe of the brain, at the point between the eyebrows. We see this direction of development among successful executives everywhere in the world. The popular imagination sees them mistakenly in gross caricature: the avaricious tycoon, the "wind-bag" of a politician, the ruthless military general. In fact, many people in these positions have become connoisseurs of fine art, music, and literature, and sponsors of the advancement of religion. If their interest lies in serving others' well-being, and not only in managing them, they come finally to realize that what helps people most of all is not material prosperity, but a deepening spiritual awareness. Love of God, service to Him in all, and wisdom—these, the refined kshatriya comes to realize, are treasures more precious than gold or rubies.

Once the ego attains this level of refinement, it becomes by nature scholarly, or philosophical, or priestly, and loses its penchant for directing other people's activities. If priestly in its inclinations, it feels called upon to dedicate itself to the spiritual welfare of all.

Such, then, is the true brahmin, or spiritual guide, the teacher of others in the ways of truth. The brahmin typically is a priest, or serves in some comparable role of spiritual service to society. His typical question of life is, "What is true? And what, in everything, is the divine will?"

As human consciousness, centuries ago, lost its clarity during the descent of civilization into lower ages, people's spiritual ideals were obscured. Most of them could no longer imagine a greater good for society than that it be run competently. The kshatriya then came to be accepted as the ideal human being. For brahmins lost their former prestige; their role came to resemble rather that of the grandfather in a family. During higher ages, people gave the highest respect to wisdom. With civilization's decline, however, respect shifted and became respect for power. No longer were brahmins looked up to, and indeed, no longer, generally, were they wise.

Above and below the officially recognized castes were persons who, for either meritorious or egregious reasons, belonged to none of them. The misfits were those who set themselves in rebellion against, or who refused to accept, the social norms. The over-qualified were the Self-realized saints, whose cosmic vision lifted them above ego-consciousness altogether. Since all human beings have the same divine potential, innately, it was recognized, and with approval, that a few of them might be inspired to shortcut through the entire system and go straight to God. The Bhagavad Gita states, "Even the worst of sinners, by steadfast meditation, speedily comes to Me."

Originally, as I said, no one was *born* into a caste. He was what his own nature declared him, regardless of his parentage. With civilization's decline, however, brahmins began to want their children to be respected as they themselves were. They began, therefore, to teach that it was heredity that made them brahmins. Their descendants, diminishingly true to that brahminical nature, ceased to be looked up to as spiritual guides.

When brahmins lost their rightful place in society, kshatriyas, as I said, came into pre-eminence. Typically, the respect that executive types feel for those of priestly or philosophical bent is always somewhat thin. Their supercilious attitude derives from the fact that they feel drawn in that direction inwardly, themselves; it is their own natural next level of refinement. For what people criticize in others always indicates qualities from which they hide, because unwilling as yet to face them, in themselves. The executive mentality feels a special respect for ordered efficiency, and tends to look condescendingly on those who seem to have their "heads in the clouds." Thus, the kshatriya's respect for brahmins has always required boosting by a strong tradition. With the increase of materialism, that respect descended to the level of mere lip service.

Bereft, then, of true spiritual guidance, the kshatriyas began to want social power and prestige. Taking their cue from the brahmins, they proclaimed their own offspring to be kshatriyas like themselves, and began to concentrate on siring royal, or aristocratic, dynasties.

The vaishyas, of course, beholding their own desire for self-aggrandizement justified by their social superiors, threw modesty to the winds and began to glory shamelessly in their wealth.* At the same time, they

---

*Marwaris, a wealthy merchant community, used to enlarge their girth as a means of flaunting their prosperity. When banqueting, a marwari would tie a string about his waist and eat until the string broke. So fat were many of them that, when walking, their stomachs protruded before them like steamer trunks.

began trying to influence the ruling classes to accept proposals for their mutual aggrandizement.

The shudras, finally, having learned to view wealth as the summum bonum of existence, applauded anyone who would promise them money and security without their having to earn it.

And thus society tumbled into Kali Yuga—a shambles from which it is only now struggling to emerge.

As the caste system came to be practiced in its later, diseased, form, it contributed to the general spiritual degeneration. For it encouraged selfish gain, not selfless service. It encouraged egoism, not the gradual loosening of egoic bonds. What resulted finally was, in Yogananda's term, "misery-making karma."

The Law of Karma

Karma is a law that determines a person's natural level of evolutional development, and also his actual position in society. Karma is a universal law, and the companion to the law of reincarnation. Karma is not, and is wrongly understood to be, a teaching of divine punishment for the wrongs one commits. It is, rather, simply the law of cause and effect on levels far subtler than that on which the laws of physics operate, though it includes these laws also. Karma embraces every action, every thought, every feeling in the universe. Karma attracts to us whatever vibrations of energy we ourselves project.

Modern physics has made us aware of karmic principles as they apply to the material level: that like attracts like, for instance, and that every action attracts an equal and opposite reaction. Karma is also the magnetism generated by whatever type of energy we entertain.

Because our every deed and desire is tied to ego-consciousness, the energy they generate rotates, like a vortex, around the thought, "I am: I want; I am the doer; I am the owner; I'm the one who is affected." This vortex of energy settles in the spine at its own level of "specific gravity," according to whether it is grossly materialistic, or generous, or spiritually elevating. As the opportunity arises for fulfilling a desire, or for the boomerang completion of a deed, the energy in that vortex is released, and attracts to the ego its own natural consequences.

People don't "work out" their karma, as many imagine, by mere activity. The shopkeeper who tries to excuse his lack of spiritual focus with the explanation, "I'm a karma yogi" (a seeker of enlightenment by the path of selfless service) is only deluding himself. What he really is, simply, is a "karmi" (one who is immersed in ego-motivated activity). Karma is worked out by *right* action, and even better by offering the impulses buried in the subconscious up to the liberating influence of superconsciousness. While most people cannot accomplish this end deliberately, since they know nothing of their own subconscious impulses, it can be accomplished by generating a flow of energy and devotion up the spine to the brain, and by asking for, and receiving, the downward flow of grace from above.

Christian critics accuse the Hindu religion of not recognizing the saving power of divine grace. (Again, as quite frequently, they confuse Hinduism with Buddhism.) They are mistaken. Indeed, *kripa,* the Sanskrit word for grace, is greatly over-used in India, where masters have always discouraged, as Buddha himself did, this pleasant hope of "something for nothing": "I'm willing to repeat a few prayers, Lord, but *You* please do the hard work for me!" Therefore they stress the importance, just as Jesus did,* of *personal* effort. What that effort does, however, is open curtains, so to speak, in the mind, that the sunlight of divine grace may enter in.† This teaching is equally a part of the teachings of Buddha, for only in the superconscious state can salvation, in the form of *nirvana,* be attained.

Karma determines a person's circumstances in life. According to the energy generated by his way of life in the past, he attracts good or bad "luck," as he may choose to call it: squalor or riches, good or ill health, disruptive or harmonious surroundings. Karmic attraction may cause him to be born into a lowly peasant's hovel, or into the mansion of a moneyed but selfish merchant, or into the palace of a benign ruler, or into the simple residence of sincere spiritual aspirants. He himself has ordained these outer circumstances. But the process is by no means simple and clear. Birth into the merchant's home, for instance, may be due to a shared love of peaceful surroundings, and not to the fact that he himself is mercantile by nature.

---

* "Why do you keep saying, 'Lord, Lord,' and never do what I tell you?" (Luke 6:46)

† "Behold, I stand at the door, and knock: if any man hear my voice, and open the door, I will come in to him, and will sup with him, and he with me" (Revelation 3:20).

We ourselves, whatever our birth in this life, determine to some extent what we shall make of this life. The young peasant may, by hard work, become a farmer. If karma—his own and others'—permits, he may even become a ruler, or a saint and yogi. But if past karma clouds his will, he may feel no desire even to rise to that first level of farmer.

Mankind, alone among earth's inhabitants, has the free will to rise spiritually by self-effort. This is the reason why the Hindu teachings give paramount importance to personal initiative. The caste system was meant to encourage initiative, and to inspire its development in the right direction: toward soul-liberation.

Free Will—a Sacred Trust

Free will, however, is a sacred responsibility. It is not given to man to be abused. For as a man can rise, so can he also fall. The subconscious memory of past sense-indulgence may call to him during moments of laziness or spiritual indifference, and suggest to him the comfort of old sense gratifications. The closer a soul comes to escaping the web of *maya*, moreover, the more *maya* itself, the satanic force, offers conscious resistance to this seeming presumption. To win final release, the soul must prove *to itself* that the ego plays no part at all in its expanded consciousness.

Not all shudras by nature are "new souls," freshly arrived on the scene of human evolution. Many of them are "old timers," tired of the seemingly endless struggle, and willing to doze in ignorance again at least for a time. Many people at all stages of development are there as back-sliders, and not as spiritual mountain climbers.

It is even possible for the ego to slide back to lower-than-human levels of evolution again, though Paramhansa Yogananda stated that, except in cases of repeated and virtually incorrigible depravity, such animal interludes endure for one incarnation only.

The spiritual path has been called a razor's edge, for the way to enlightenment is straight, and very narrow. To deviate from it is to find, repeatedly, that there is simply no alternative to the one which the saints and sages in all religions have indicated.

We should therefore heed the teaching on which the caste system was founded, and apply it faithfully in our own lives. Many people in India concentrate on the duties, prerogatives, and restrictions of caste. Everyone's real duty, however, is to his own spiritual development. His prerogatives are none, really, except to love God. And his restrictions are all self-imposed, by the feebleness of his will and by his lack of courage to renounce the ego and reach out to infinity.

The Races of Man

Paramhansa Yogananda said that the four castes describe the true "races" of mankind. These distinctions alone divide human beings into natural categories. The members of these four "races" feel a natural affinity for others of the same "race," and may feel none for others of their own skin coloring and nationality. A genuine vaishya, for example, will feel more comfortable in the company of other vaishyas than in that of his own family members, if they don't share his sense of caste identity. A shudra feels most at home with other shudras. An aristocrat feels at home with other aristocrats. And a monk feels happiest in the company of other monks.

The beauty of the caste system, rightly understood, is that it fixes no one in a permanent mold, but encourages all according to their own natural line of spiritual development. Moreover, it gives to everyone a clear directive in those attitudes which lead to final liberation. The ultimate purpose of reincarnation is to refine the ego's understanding until the ego perceives itself as a thin veil, merely, through which the infinite light of Spirit shines. Tearing asunder that veil, the soul emerges at last into absolute, eternal bliss.

Few liberated masters there are, as I remarked in the last chapter, who return to earth to continue the work of helping struggling humanity. Those who do so are the avatars. As Paramhansa Yogananda put it in his beautiful poem, "God's Boatman":

> I want to ply my boat, many times,
> Across the gulf-after-death,
> And return to earth's shores
> From my home in heaven.
> I want to load my boat
> With those waiting, thirsty ones
> Who are left behind. . . .
> Oh! I will come again and again!
> Crossing a million crags of suffering,

With bleeding feet, I will come—
If need be, a trillion times—
As long as I know
One stray brother is left behind.

Chapter Eighteen

Symbolism in the Bhagavad Gita

The crown jewel of the spiritual teachings of India is the Bhagavad Gita. Not only is it beautifully and inspiringly written, but it encapsulates all that is highest, noblest, and best in the Hindu Way of Awakening. It contains the very essence of the Upanishads, which in turn contain the essence of the spiritual teachings of the Vedas. Finally, unlike those more ancient works, the language of the Bhagavad Gita is comprehensible to anyone well versed in Sanskrit.

The Bhagavad Gita recounts a conversation between Arjuna, who represents the aspiring devotee, and Krishna, representing the soul, or God. Hence the title of Paramhansa Yogananda's voluminous and in-depth commentary on the book, *God Talks with Arjuna.** I got to read that book first in its manuscript form in 1950, and was held in complete awe. It was by far the deepest and most consciousness-expanding work I had ever read, or have ever read since. I mention having read it then, nearly fifty years ago, because it has molded my thinking all these years, and has given me a lifetime of teaching to ponder and digest, besides having influenced my own spiritual growth.

One way to judge a work's greatness is by the breadth of its effect on other disciplines. Einstein's

*Self-Realization Fellowship, Los Angeles, California, 1997.

Theory of Relativity, though its mathematics to most people is incomprehensible, has had a seminal influence not only on every scientific discipline, but also on the humanities: philosophy, sociology, psychology, religion, and others. Relativity comes up frequently even in everyday conversation.

The same may be said of Darwin's Theory of Evolution. Whatever history's final judgment on either of those theories (and solid proof of Darwin's, at least, remains still elusive; Einstein's, with recent talk about a holographic universe, is showing a few cracks), both theories have had an impact far wider than the audiences to whom they were directed. I doubt that very many people have even read them in the original. Of Einstein's theory it used to be said that only ten people in the world could understand it. Fortunately, they were the right ten: scientists highly regarded in their field. Fortunately also for both theories, the world was ready to receive them.

In the same way, I venture to assert that even if *God Talks to Arjuna* is never read by the masses (and it is deep reading), its impact will be far-reaching. For the book, like the works of Einstein and Darwin, is seminal in its power to influence people in every field of interest. Writers and teachers, perusing it with insight, will encapsulate its message for broader audiences. And the book will satisfy an increasingly urgent need for insight into life's basic predicament: who we are, where we are headed, how to get there. At the same time, the truths it teaches are simple, as truth always is. *God Talks with Arjuna* speaks directly to our own age, and to the quest for understanding of spiritual seekers in every age.

I was privileged to be present during part of the time that Yogananda was dictating his book. Although many commentaries on the Bhagavad Gita have been written over the centuries, Yogananda's work was a response to none of them. After it was over, he told me, "I understand now why my guru told me not to read other people's commentaries. He wanted me to concentrate on the Gita itself, and not to be influenced by any other thoughts."

In fact, the entire work came to him in superconsciousness. He would turn his eyes up to the spiritual eye and pause briefly, fixing his concentration in the state (which was normal to him) known as *nirbikalpa samadhi,** and then he'd begin dictating. After finishing the book, he explained, "I tuned in to Byasa [the author], and asked him to speak through me." Ecstatically, then, he exclaimed: "A new scripture has been born!" And so I myself deeply believe.

The Bhagavad Gita itself is short. The ancient rishis' style of writing, as I've said already, was terse, suggesting volumes of meaning in single sentences. The Bhagavad Gita contains teaching for every level of spiritual

---

*Sri Ramakrishna called this state *sahaja* (easy, or natural) *samadhi.* Paramhansa Yogananda described it as that state of total immersion in God when the sage, or yogi, can descend into sensory awareness and carry out his normal duties without losing inner contact with infinite consciousness.

I myself had occasion a number of times to observe in him what could only have been a vastly expanded consciousness. Sometimes he would correct me for something I had said, or even thought, when distant from him. I don't think he'd been concentrating on me, particularly. He was — simply, but amazingly — aware. Once I expressed astonishment at his knowing. He replied, "I know *every thought* you think!"

development. Like a divine mirror, it reflects back to the reader his own present state of consciousness, and his potential for further growth.

A certain Indian novelist, self-condemned by the shallowness of his writing, described the book recently as banal and affected. Great sages, on the other hand, have pronounced a very different verdict. Swami Sri Yukteswar, Yogananda's guru and a great *gyani,* or master of wisdom, was asked the question by the famous sage Dabru Ballav, "Do you know the Bhagavad Gita?" Sri Yukteswar replied, "No, sir, not really; though my eyes and mind have run through its pages many times."

Modern commentators have declared that the teaching of the "Gita," as Hindus fondly call it, relates specifically to one or another of the basic paths of yoga: karma yoga, the yoga of action; bhakti yoga, the yoga of devotion; gyana yoga, the yoga of knowledge and discrimination—literally, of wisdom. Each one sees in it what he himself is predisposed to understand. But the Gita rises transcendent above them all, a teaching for everyone, at every level of spiritual development, and somehow beyond all teaching itself. It conveys to the reader an aura of the highest revelation.

Christian missionaries, finding that many statements in the Gita resonate with the teachings of Jesus Christ, argued that its author must have lived after Jesus, and that he had simply paraphrased the words of Christ. Granting that what Jesus said was the truth, the truth he uttered could hardly be considered his own property. It was universal, and therefore open for discovery by anyone.

The fact that Alfred Russel Wallace made the same discoveries as Charles Darwin, though his book, unfortunately for him, was published a week later than Darwin's, only corroborates that what both men had written were in fact discoveries, and not merely inventions. Whether the first of those two scriptures, then, was the Gita or the Gospels of Jesus Christ is irrelevant. That the two should agree on fundamental truths is testimony to the truths themselves, and to the revelation on which both those teachings were based.

On the other hand, there is ample testimony in Indian history, and in the Bhagavad Gita itself, to date it centuries before Christ—indeed, even before the life of Buddha, who lived five centuries earlier than Jesus. For though Krishna refers in the Bhagavad Gita to a number of spiritual teachings, he is silent on the best known one of all: Buddhism. Again, although Krishna uses the word *nirvana,* which Buddha later made well known, he does so only twice in the Gita, and in a different sense from that used by Buddha, or at any rate by Buddha's spiritual descendants.

And, again, what does it even matter? Truth is eternal. It is as much alive in the noise of a modern airport as it was in the peaceful forest hermitages of ancient India. Paramhansa Yogananda once remarked to a group of us that he'd written his poem "Samadhi"— one of the greatest mystical poems, I am convinced, of all time—while riding the subway in New York City, one of the least spiritually uplifting environments, surely, in the world!

The setting of the Bhagavad Gita is a battlefield; the time: the eve of a great war. Krishna has kindly agreed to act as Arjuna's charioteer, and Arjuna asks him to drive between the two opposing armies that he may survey them. In that setting, the famous discourse takes place. Arjuna poses spiritual questions: Krishna answers them. Most of the discourse is taken up with those answers, but also important are the questions themselves, for Arjuna asks them on behalf of every spiritual seeker.

His first question is concerned with the very necessity for this war. "Those who oppose us," he laments, "are my own kinsmen. Surely it would be sinful to kill them. I would rather relinquish all our rights in this cause than be guilty of slaying my own relations!"

And so we come to a dilemma that immediately reveals the multi-layered nature of this scripture. For, to many people, the dilemma is literal; it concerns actual warfare. Krishna's reply is valid for that layer of understanding, but he then takes the subject deeper, and then deeper still.

The first hint that the struggle is in fact psychological and spiritual, rather than military, is given in the very first sentence of the Bhagavad Gita. Dhritarashtra, the blind king, and father of the hundred warriors who oppose Arjuna and his brothers on the battlefield, addresses Sanjaya, who has the gift of spiritual vision to see the battlefield from afar. Dhritarashtra asks Sanjaya: "On the holy plain of Kurukshetra, where my sons and those of Pandu were gathered together, eager for battle, what did they?"

Few commentators, if any, have noticed the hint given here. Paramhansa Yogananda points out that, in the story's context, Sanjaya is observing the conflict *as it is taking place*. In this stanza, however, the question is phrased *in the past tense*.

For it is only *after* a test in life that we introspect, asking ourselves, "How did I fare? Which side was the victor?" During the heat of combat, we haven't time or energy for such reflection.

Sanjaya, representing the quality of introspection, is not asked, "How are my sons faring? Which side appears to have the upper hand?"—a natural question for Dhritarashtra to ask, considering Sanjaya's gift of distant vision. Nowadays, if a person is interested in a game between two outstanding teams, he turns on his television set to see the live action, if possible. He wants to know what is happening while the game is progressing; he doesn't want to see the outcome merely on the news, later on.

Yet Dhritarashtra's question, supposedly uttered at the start of the action, is, "What *did* they?"

Dhritarashtra represents the mind. He is blind because the mind can perceive only through the senses. Sanjaya's gift of distant vision suggests intuitive, rather than reasoned, introspection. For intuition alone gives true self-perception.

Other hints are given also in the Gita. Chapter Thirteen begins, not with a hint, but with the clear statement: "*This body* is the battlefield."

Many readers of this present book—indeed, probably most of them—are already familiar with the Bhagavad Gita. Others can read it easily, for it is quite short, and is available in bookstores everywhere. A beautiful poetic translation that I highly recommend also is Sir Edwin Arnold's *The Song Celestial*. I should warn those of exacting disposition, however, that Edwin Arnold often paraphrases instead of giving us a literal rendition, for the sake of poetic beauty.

The Bhagavad Gita describes the opposing armies as representing the forces of good and evil. The reader is free to interpret this confrontation on whatever level he himself considers helpful. If his thoughts run to social causes, he may take the struggle as representing the forces of righteous patriotism against unlawful seizure and oppression. If his thoughts run to religious freedom, he may take it as representing the right to be guided by one's own conscience rather than allow that conscience to be suppressed by the dictates of an established institution.

In fact, because good and evil are fundamental issues in life, this story could be, and has been, applied to every conceivable situation. So universal is it, in fact, that some people may wonder what makes this war itself so particularly special. Countless struggles throughout history have been viewed as pitting good against evil. Is the attraction of this story, then, only that the conflict takes place in the romantic mists of an ancient world? Would it have had less impact, for example, had it been set in a cowboy town in the American "Far West," with the brave sheriff striding up Main Street to shoot it out with the town's leading bad man, that the good townsfolk might be liberated from the yoke of oppression?

It's an interesting question. What makes certain works great, and so many others mere pastimes for an idle weekend? One might say that the merest "dust-up" between a schoolboy and the local bully symbolizes the eternal struggle between good and evil. Of course it does, as even the tiniest atom symbolizes the solar system, a galaxy, the very universe. Size, antiquity, and relative historic importance don't account satisfyingly for the greatness of one story, and the utter commonplaceness of another.

There is a vibration, however, in every written work that conveys, in a few of them, a sense of deep relevance, and in the vast majority a sense of inconsequence and triviality. It depends on the consciousness with which their composition was infused. A book written with superficial understanding remains superficial no matter how portentously its author declaims his thoughts. Emerson wrote, "What you are speaks so loudly that I cannot hear what you say." The very rhythm of an author's sentences, the words he or she chooses to use, the sentiments expressed: All these speak volumes to the aware reader even before he turns the first page. Nor do these factors alone tell the whole story; the process is not a mechanism. No system could ever be created to ensure something so subtle as a book's vibrational impact. Ultimately, it comes down to the energy and consciousness that radiates from its pages.

Marpa, the guru of Tibet's great yogi Milarepa, ordered his disciple, then newly arrived for training, to remove his books on black magic from the bookshelf. A brief glance had sufficed Guru Marpa to realize that their subject matter was offensive.

Even the vibrations of rocks reveal a certain energy and consciousness. How much more so, the vibrations of great scripture. These have the power of superconsciousness, a power which impregnates every word and brings it to life. Such is the glory of the Bhagavad Gita, and of the longer epic, the *Mahabharata,* of which the Gita is an excerpt. It is a power beyond words, beyond the teaching itself, and far beyond the vast hoard of information that the scripture and epic contain. Even as history, their enormous appeal lies not only in the description of life in ancient times, but in their incisive description of our own times as well—indeed, of all historic time. Their message is as over-arching as eternity.

The warriors in what is known as the battle of Kurukshetra represent all our mental characteristics. To the lover of English poetry, they suggest the first line of a poem by Sir Edward Dyer: "My mind to me a kingdom is." For in the *Mahabharata* the mind is portrayed as a kingdom. Our mental characteristics are its citizens, each with its own distinct personality. The country is in a state of internal warfare. On the good side are the qualities that can help us, spiritually; on the other side are our evil tendencies: the grumblers and complainers, the ambitious and unscrupulous, the well-fed and over-comfortable—those "citizens" whose sole interest lies in preserving their material luxuries, regardless of the ethics involved.

Krishna points out, in answer to Arjuna's lament, that death cannot destroy the essence of who we really are, any more than removing an overcoat can destroy us. The seeming end to life is an illusion. When the body dies, its ego-essence simply leaves it, and goes elsewhere.

Taken literally, this teaching is itself important. Krishna's meaning, however, goes much deeper. It relates not so much to the body's mortality as to life as we are living it here and now. Negative traits, which pull the mind downward, have no reality in themselves. They represent only a commitment of energy: vortices whirling around a center of ego-consciousness. We think that if we renounce our sense-habits we'll abandon the very source of our happiness; we may actually fear that our capacity for enjoyment will atrophy. And so we lament, with Arjuna, "How can I kill this part—this *very dear* part!—of my own self?"

Krishna replies: "You are grieving needlessly, O Arjuna. The very energy you have directed toward sense-pleasures will simply be transmuted into higher manifestations of that same energy." With transmutation, what one discovers actually is *greater* happiness, and a greater capacity for enjoyment. The transmutation of sexual desire, for instance, fills one with intense *inner* pleasure, and bestows also great mental clarity. The enjoyment of good food—how inspiring I found this particular statement of my guru's!—can reappear as a thousand delicious tastes all crushed into one!

Every sense pleasure, once the desire for it has been overcome, is transformed into a subtler kind of delight a thousandfold greater than before; it is experienced also *in the physical body.* The longer and more deeply we meditate, the more our senses become purified. Colors, then, seem more intense, music more beautiful, fresh scents more delectable.

The Bhagavad Gita in which the inner psychological struggle is described is a brief episode in the longest epic ever written, the *Mahabharata.* This epic is based on events in actual history. Like many stories in the Old Testament, however, it weaves about those events a pattern of allegory. The entire epic is, in fact, an allegory. Even its historic characters, of whom there are several, symbolize human characteristics, good and evil.

Most of those historic characters are mentioned also in the Bhagavad Gita: Krishna, Arjuna, Sahadeva, Nakula, Bhima, Yudhisthira, Draupadi, Drona: Each of them, in the story, represents a particular psychological trait. As for the invented names, their Sanskrit roots reveal a variety of specific mental qualities. The good and the bad range themselves into opposing armies: on the one side, the spiritually elevating; on the other, those which debase human consciousness.

Psychology, as a science, is relatively new. Its best-known contribution to modern knowledge is the discovery that people are motivated more than they realize by their subconscious desires and impulses. Psychologists warn against the harm that can result from suppressing our subconscious urges. The Bhagavad

Gita agrees with them. It poses the question, rhetorically, "What can mere suppression accomplish?" It gives, however, a resounding "Yes!" to transmutation. For inner peace cannot come by permissive acceptance of our weaknesses. To attain peace of mind, we must first acknowledge that the subconscious and superconscious are in fact at war, and that they pull us in opposite directions. There has to be final victory in the struggle—victory, moreover, with honor. Until then, there can be no lasting peace. It is essential, therefore, that we side with our higher nature, and recognize in that downward pull the determined foe of our happiness and well-being. The downward pull is all the stronger for not being recognized. To see it in true perspective, however—that is to say, in its relation to the truth—is possible only in a state of superconsciousness.

Good habits also have their roots in the subconscious. In other words, it is not the subconscious itself that opposes our spiritual endeavors. Usually, however, habit sides with our downward inclinations, not with the aspirations that would take us upward. For the first requirement for spiritual progress is that we develop initiative, and not rely on the support we receive, rather more passively, from past habit. Drona symbolizes the power of habit. He is described in the *Mahabharata* as the teacher of both families of warriors. On the battlefield, however, he fights on the side of material desire.

The oft-expressed modern advice is, "Go with the flow. Accept your lower nature as a part of who you really are." Such advice has a pleasant ring to it! (Who, after all, wouldn't rather be spared having to fight at all?) But the "peace" gained by acquiescence is not true peace at all; it merely skirts the issues while resolving none of them. It is the peace craved by a slave mentality, for it sacrifices initiative to the false—because fleeting—security of submission. Self-justifyingly it demands: "What else could I have done?" This kind of "peace" is purchased at the cost of personal dignity and of one's own sense of self-worth, the natural concomitants of a clear conscience.

No decision based on an attitude of psychological laissez faire can bring about enduring peace, any more than truce resolves the issues in a war. Methods that don't inspire us to self-transcendence only create fresh ego-vortices in the mind. Affirmations, though helpful if directed toward superconsciousness, are self-defeating, in the end, if their aim is simply to help the ego settle down comfortably into itself. What psychological self-help methods affirm, usually, is self-acceptance, not radical self-transformation.

I am reminded here of a woman who was praising a self-help seminar she'd enrolled in. She'd wanted to stop smoking, and to lose weight. "So," inquired a friend, "did it help you?" The woman was holding a lighted cigarette in her hand, and seemed more than ever inclined to a gentle suggestion of *embonpoint*. "Oh, yes!" she replied. "Perhaps not the way I expected, but, . . ." She hesitated, then went on brightly, "I've learned to accept myself as I am!"

"Self-help" methods of this sort are not directed toward self-conquest. They are more like modern medicine in the sense that they address the problem but don't seek positive solutions. They bring you back to normal: They don't pretend to make you *better* than normal. They don't help people, for example, to find lasting joy. They don't stress ego-transcending attitudes such as self-forgetfulness and joyful service of others. These alone lead to true inner happiness. But what those methods say instead is, essentially, "Tend to your own investments." The general result of this kind of advice is increasing self-preoccupation, and self-centeredness.

It is interesting to see how very opposite was the view of life held in ancient India. Modern psychology began with a study of mental aberrations. It continued on to projecting those aberrations onto normal mentality. The natural conclusion drawn from this projection has been that none of us is completely normal, or even wholly sane; and this, of course, is more or less true.

There is, however, a disadvantage to such a view: It doesn't lead anywhere. It suggests that all of us live in a cave, in a manner of speaking. It accepts that it would be nice to find a way out of the cave, but it can't really tell us whether such a way exists. Still less does it suggest what we might find, if we ever did get out. The "realities" psychology addresses pertain to life in the cave itself. A psychologist would—and, of course, with perfect justification—put it this way: "Our concern is with people's *present* predicament. This, to them, is what is most pressing and immediate."

Fair enough. There is also, however, a need for long-term solutions. These are the Gita's concern.

The premise in modern civilization is that the realities of human nature begin at the bottom: that self-understanding must be approached through our lower nature, not through our higher. To Darwin, evolution is consequent upon the survival of the fittest, by a process of natural selection. In his scheme of things, the *will* to evolve was not even a factor. He might indeed have discovered this will even in an animal's choice of a habitat suitable for its survival, but this explanation would have offended against his mechanistic bias.

Arnold Toynbee, the British historian, saw the rise of civilizations as a response to challenges, but again, not as being motivated by any aspiration deeper than the mere will to survive.

And human nature itself, since Adam and Eve, has been viewed as inherently sinful. It was no great leap, from that view, for Darwin to attribute our very appearance on the stage of evolution to the monkeys.

That whole scheme of life is a view upward from below, not downward from above. Darwin actually explained man's sense of humor as a sublimation of the ancient urge to kill. To him, there could be no reaching up in light-hearted gaiety toward a joy we all intuit in our souls. The mechanistic view of life is objectionable if only because it is so unrelentingly drab.

The ancient Hindu view of life, by sharp contrast, was downward from the heights. It saw life's deepest motivation as a reaching out toward our true origins in infinity, and not as a blind instinct to avoid being slain, rended, and gobbled up. The rishis gave us a vision *of where we are headed* on our long evolutional journey. Accepting the cave as a metaphor, and our need to find a way to escape from that cave, the Hindu Way of Awakening would say, "Here is the exit, and this is the scenery you'll feast your gaze on when you emerge from your darkness."

The Bhagavad Gita urges us to banish the hypnosis we live under: the fallacy that our weaknesses define us as we are. It gives a clarion call to victory on the part of the highest and best that is in us.

In the *Mahabharata,* even the historical characters are to some extent fictionalized. There is, for instance, an account for which I know no parallel in Indian history: Draupadi, a beautiful maiden, marries all the Pandava brothers together. There have been cases of polygamy in India, but none of polyandry that I know of, common though the practice was in Tibet. In the *Mahabharata,* Arjuna, the principal hero, wins Draupadi in an archery contest. On his return home with her and his brothers, and before they enter the house, he calls out, "Mother, I have brought home a prize."

Their mother, unaware of the nature of this "prize," calls back, "In that case, my son, be sure to share it equally with your brothers." Since their mother's word could not be falsified, the brothers all had to marry the same girl!

288

There is a deep meaning in this story. The Pandava brothers represent the five *chakra*s, or energy-centers in the spine, and the spiritual qualities that manifest in the mind once their energy is directed toward the brain. Draupadi, their "wife," represents the coiled "feminine" energy, *kundalini,* at the base of the spine. When kundalini is raised up the spine, she passes through the chakras, uniting herself with each one of them in turn. In this awakening of inner energy lies the secret of our eventual enlightenment. There is significance even in the fact that it was Arjuna who won Draupadi. But this is a subtlety of the yoga science that it would take too long, here, to explain.

Draupadi's husbands, the Pandavas, represent the primary qualities we need, to find God. The lowest two chakras, known as *muladhara* and *swadisthan,* are located respectively at the base of the spine and an inch or two higher up, and are symbolized by the brothers Sahadeva and Nakula. These men are half-brothers to the other three, having had a different mother. The reason for this semi-relationship is that the qualities represented by Sahadeva and Nakula are developed more by affirmative will of the ego than by soul-inspiration.

Sahadeva represents *yama,* which means control, the first necessity on the spiritual path. Essentially, *yama* means the avoidance of attitudes that prevent one from attaining inner peace. These attitudes are five in number: the desire to inflict harm; unwillingness to face the truth; the desire to possess what is not rightfully one's own; attachment to what *is* rightfully one's own (including one's own body);* and the incontinent expenditure of energy, especially sexual.

Nakula, Sahadeva's twin, represents *niyama*, or "non-control," which means adherence to attitudes that conduce to inner peace. These, too, are five in number: cleanliness (of heart as well as of body); contentment (an attitude described by Yudhisthira as the "supreme virtue"); austerity (the meaning of which, essentially, is to live centered in the Self, especially in the spine); introspection (the word in Sanskrit is *swadhyaya*, meaning, literally, "self-study"); and devotion to God and to one's own spiritual search.

The third chakra, called *manipur*, is situated in the lumbar region of the spine, opposite the navel. This chakra is symbolized by Arjuna. When the *manipur* is awakened, there manifests in the mind the soul-born quality of fiery self-control. Arjuna is the brave hero of the *Mahabharata*—despite his brief moment of weakness, which is recounted at the beginning of the Bhagavad Gita.

Next up the spine is the *anahat chakra*, the heart or dorsal center, opposite the physical heart. This center is represented by Bhima. The *anahat chakra*, as I said earlier, is located pivotally in the spine. The awakening of intense feeling there can either draw our consciousness upward in devotion, or take it downward again into the emotions. Ultimately, intense devotion in the

---

*The literal translation of this *yama* is "non-acceptance." Patanjali states in his *Yoga Sutras* that perfection in non-acceptance bestows the power of remembering one's past incarnations. Such distant memory comes, however, only after one achieves complete non-attachment to the present life. Hence, non-acceptance means not to accept *anything* as truly one's own — not even one's own body.

heart is what makes us ready for enlightenment. Awakening of the heart's feelings, however, produces an inner storm that can be weathered only by deep calmness. Bhima, in the *Mahabharata,* represents this feeling quality. He is vigorous in all that he does, whether in a righteous cause or in error.

The topmost center in the spine itself is situated in the cervical region, opposite the throat. It is called the *vishuddha chakra,* and is represented by Yudhisthira, the oldest of the Pandavas. As the rising kundalini awakens this center, it produces in the mind a deep sense of calmness and expansion. Yudhisthira, in the *Mahabharata,* is the calm arbitrator, ever seeking to promote *dharma,* or righteousness. He is also, for that reason, given the epithet, *Dharmaraj,* or "King of Righteousness."

The center of ego in the body is the medulla oblongata, at the base of the brain. Evidence of this fact may be seen in egotists. Their pride causes tension in the upper neck just below the skull, drawing the head backward. Proud people, therefore, are described as "looking down their noses" at the world. To bow before others—the universal gesture of humility—is symbolically to release tension in the upper neck.

The medulla's positive pole is the spiritual eye, which appears spontaneously within the forehead during deep meditation. The spiritual eye is the doorway to soul-consciousness, and is represented in the *Mahabharata* by Krishna.

So long as the ego has not been transcended in soul-consciousness, but retains its center in the medulla, one is not safe yet from *maya*'s snares. Unfortunately, the mind, when in a "Yudhisthira mode"—that is to say, when feeling calm and uplifted—may consider itself safe from temptation, and end up being tricked again into a long descent.

The drama of the *Mahabharata* (after preliminary, and allegorically important, genealogies and family histories) actually begins with a challenge to Yudhisthira by Duryodhana, who represents the ego and material desire. The challenge offered is a gambling match. Yudhisthira has a weakness for gambling. The mind, similarly, after it attains inner peace, may toy with the thought, "Why not one last fling, just for old times' sake? Surely I can't be affected now!"

Shakuni, Yudhisthira's opponent in the match, is dishonest. As Jesus Christ said, with reference to Satan, "He is a liar and the father of lies" (John 8:44). The dice are loaded. Yudhisthira ends up losing everything: his freedom, his brothers' freedom, their wife, the entire kingdom.

Thus the soul, even on the threshold of enlightenment, must stand firm in its determination to merge in God. As my guru once told me, "Remember, you are not safe until you attain *nirbikalpa samadhi*." Even the temporary divine union known as *sabikalpa samadhi* is experienced only during perfect stillness. It cannot be maintained after leaving one's meditation.

What the *Mahabharata* is really describing, however, is how the ego fell in the first place, eons ago. By the time kundalini has risen to the vishuddha chakra, one ought to be fairly familiar with the dangers of descent.

We find here then, in fact, an Indian version of the old allegory of Adam and Eve. It is painful to reflect that we might ever fall again into former errors, but that likelihood is greatly diminished by the fact that we have already been schooled by that sternest of all tutors, Experience.

The symbolism, both in the long epic and in the Bhagavad Gita, is exhaustive. The chariot; Krishna's holding of the reins; his taking Arjuna between the two armies; the names of the opposing warriors; the significance of Bhishma, the grandfatherly figure in the story; the blast he blows on his great conch shell to encourage the forces of material desire; the relatively small army on the side of right compared to the great size of the opposing host; the blindness of Dhritarashtra, the old king; Duryodhana, "King Material Desire"; Arjuna's standard, the monkey emblem; the reasons for Arjuna's despondency; Arjuna's bow, Gandhiva—what it means, why he picks it up, and why he lets it slip from his grasp: These details and many more, even in the first chapter of the Bhagavad Gita, are deeply allegorical, and might easily make the subject of an entire book. They are explained at length in Paramhansa Yogananda's opus.

The subject of this present book, however, is specific, and cannot afford a detour. Its message concerns the panoramic sweep of India's ancient teachings, and the universality they reveal of truth itself. That revelation is the Hindu Way of Awakening. It forms the heart not only of Hinduism, but of every true religion in the world.

Chapter Nineteen

Tantra—the Way of Confrontation

The banishment of Yudhisthira and his family from their kingdom; the fall of man, represented allegorically by the expulsion of Adam and Eve from the Garden of Eden; the oft-heard warning to spiritual seekers not to "tempt" Satan: All these things are spelled out memorably in the Bhagavad Gita, where, in Chapter Two, Krishna explains how devotees fall.

"If one ponders on sense objects, there springs up attraction to them. From attraction grows desire. Desire, impatient for fulfillment, flames to anger. From anger there arises infatuation (the delusion that one object alone is worth clinging to, to the exclusion of all others). From infatuation ensues forgetfulness of the higher Self. From forgetfulness of the Self follows degeneration of the discriminative faculty. And when discrimination is lost, there follows the annihilation of one's spiritual life."

The process begins with the simple act of "pondering on sense objects." This is the gambling match to which Yudhisthira was challenged. This is the "fruit" in the garden of Eden that was forbidden to Adam and Eve. The "dice" in the match played by Yudhisthira were loaded. The "serpent" in Eden was too "subtle" to be bested by reason. In the very act of "pondering" objects of the senses, the energy flows toward them, and with energy, feeling. Once feeling becomes involved, the difficulty of extricating oneself becomes ever greater, for with that involvement comes ego-commitment.

The important thing, obviously, is to extricate oneself as early as possible from this process, before ego-commitment becomes entrenched. At whatever stage one finds oneself on that downward slide, he should remember the encouraging words of Paramhansa Yogananda: "A saint is a sinner who never gave up."

How, then, to extricate oneself? At the start of the descent it is easy to say, Concentrate on God, on infinity, on devotion, on raising your consciousness—all those things, in short, which we have already identified as vital to the Way of Awakening.

What to do, however, once an attraction has already "sprung up"? What to do when, from that first tiny seed of attraction, the weeds of desire have already grown? What to do, when the desire becomes importunate, and cries loudly for fulfillment, flaming to anger when thwarted rather than subsiding with a mumbled apology? What to do, when the mind insists, further, "I must have *that object,* and no other!" What to do, in short, to prevent oneself from reaching the point where one forgets he even *has* a higher Self, and a nobler destiny to fulfill?

Swami Sri Yukteswar, in *Autobiography of a Yogi,* is quoted as giving this advice: "Even when the flesh is weak, *the mind should be constantly resistant.*" Herein lies the key to an important, but widely misunderstood and also widely abused teaching of India: tantra.

Tantra has been written about, taught, and one might even say promoted extensively in recent years. Many see it as an outstanding example—attractive to some; repellent to others—of what they consider the "exotic" nature of Hinduism.

Tantra is misunderstood also in India. Indeed, it lends itself to misunderstanding. At the same time, it fills a spiritual gap that, for most people, represents a real problem in their spiritual lives. Tantra's popular image is that it offers a way to enlightenment through, instead of by avoiding, sensual pleasures, and particularly through the enjoyment of sex.

What has given this interpretation a patina of respect is that in modern times there exists a belief among psychologists that self-expression can help one to achieve release from suppressed desires and emotions.

Many years ago in California I participated in a "workshop," where the instructor urged us to work out our suppressed rage by hurling fistfuls of mud in anger at a wooden board. I wondered, What if I can't feel any anger? Shall I try to whip it up in my heart? Shall I try to pretend an emotion just in order to get rid of it? I was reminded of a little verse by A.A. Milne in a book of poems for children. The verse was about someone called Sir Brian, "bold as a lion," who cried, "Take that! and that! and that!"

Well, I failed to work myself up into any semblance of rage. Apart from my own difficulty in that attempt, I felt growingly convinced, as I glanced around at others in the class, that the practice itself was, for all of them, entirely wrong.

What if I'd actually been able to feel release from some pent-up anger? Would throwing mud angrily have accomplished any lasting good for me? With time, that first sensation of release would have passed—perhaps minutes later, perhaps after an hour, perhaps even after a whole afternoon. And then what? My anger would have returned, *reinforced,* now, by the fact that I'd affirmed it. Release through giving vent to one's feelings is temporary, never permanent. To affirm anger is, in the long run, to be more inclined than ever to be angry.

One may defend such practices logically, or rail against them equally logically; a good theoretical case can generally be made for almost any contention. The validity of a theory, however, must finally be tested by its concrete results; there is no need to theorize in such matters. Frankly, I have yet to see anyone with eyes shining and an appearance of conviction that he's found real freedom through emotional release.

The test of concrete results should be applied to every vaunted method for attaining inner freedom.

A certain group of people (most of them Westerners), following what a revolutionary "guru" from India had assured them was an authentic spiritual practice, made it a practice to indulge frequently and promiscuously in sex, persuaded that the "joy" they derived from it was a sort of divine "ecstasy." They would gather together in group sessions for greater emotional release, shout "chaotically" as they affirmed other kinds of release as well. Pent-up frustrations would be screamed agonizingly into the room: "I hate my mother! I hate my father! I wish I could kill them both!"

Spiritual practice normally produces certain recognizable signs: a radiance in the eyes, a smile rising from inner calmness. Apart from the fact that most of those people displayed an absurd sense of pride, and utter disrespect for their fellowman, their eyes were dull, their expressions lacking in all spiritual vitality. Everyone I encountered from that group seemed to me—to borrow a colorful expression of Jesus Christ's—"dead." The teaching they'd embraced was, as nearly as I could gather, "Do whatever you like, and just call it spiritual. Calling it so will make it so. You may then consider yourself a saint." Whatever the theoretical merits of this "system," in concrete results it was a disaster.

What they were practicing was not tantra, though it was touted as such. Tantra addresses itself, rather, to a real need on the spiritual path. For the fact that a path is even needed at all presupposes that there is yet some goal to be reached. It presupposes, indeed, that some people may still be far short of that goal.

Assuming, then, that one finds himself still caught in the web of *maya:* How is he to extricate himself? Oh, yes, of course—by devotion, meditation, uplifted thoughts, non-violence, truthfulness, self-control, and all the other teachings we've written about already. But what is one to do when a particular delusion is too strong for him to set it resolutely aside? What to do, in fact, when it seizes and shakes him like a rag doll?

"Don't indulge," would be the correct spiritual advice. But what if, despite every good intention, you find yourself indulging anyway? In that case, should you give up? Should you rage against yourself? hate yourself? accuse yourself of inexcusable weakness and, consequently, define yourself in the very terms of that weakness? Will you skulk down darkened alleys for the rest of your days (or, perhaps, nights), wrapped in a cloak of guilt and shame? Some people actually imagine that shame is their expiation for guilt. What it becomes for them instead, however, is an easy excuse to persevere in their errors.

To burden oneself impotently with the assumption of blame is like a drowning man asking someone to hand him a heavy stone.

When the ego is facing weakness in itself, it has certain eminently predictable ways of—as it imagines—getting out of its predicament. Shame is one way, and the plea, "Well, at least I'm sorry for what I did!" (Okay, be sorry—but to keep on *affirming* your sorrow? Once, surely, is enough! Why keep on mentally repeating the deed, establishing formal residence, so to speak, in the recollection of it?)

Another of the ego's reactions to its weaknesses is to protest—as the members of that group did that I just mentioned—"What do you mean, telling me I shouldn't be like that? God made sense-indulgence pleasurable, didn't He? Doesn't this mean indulgence is a good thing? Obviously, He *wants* us to enjoy ourselves!" Here, in fact, we find an example of the anger Krishna described as one of the stages of descent. The ego, when confronted with a fault, won't even permit people to discuss it. The person becomes irascible as soon as the subject is raised. A pathetic, but common, case in point is the anger alcoholics so often display in defense of their habit of drinking.

Other people try to protect themselves with the declaration, "Well, after all, it's all *maya,* isn't it? Just a delusion, so the scriptures tell us. So what does it matter what pleasures I indulge in? They're all a dream anyway!" This pleasant-seeming self-justification demonstrates a complete misunderstanding of the vedanta teachings. In fact, the consequence of wrong living is that God's dream itself becomes, for the individual dreamer, a nightmare. To one who is still asleep, that nightmare can seem very real!

Others, again, cry, "Oh, but what I'm doing isn't *indulging!* All I'm really doing is working out my karma." Well of course, what they are really doing is *working themselves more deeply into* their karma. Certainly they aren't working their way out of it!

Still others may say—do say, all too often—"Everyone does it, so what's wrong with doing it?" Their belief seems to be that truth can somehow be voted into existence. Divine law, however, doesn't operate according to democratic principles. Mankind cannot decide by popular vote, for example, to repeal the law of gravity!

Well, even so, what's wrong with the argument: "Do it because everyone does it"? After all, we're talking about *people,* not the laws of physics. Unfortunately for this argument, Cosmic Law rules just as inexorably in the lives of human beings. Look again, I say, at the concrete results.

Look at the life of that "everyone" who "does it." Has that "everyone" found the happiness he dreamed of? Look about you in society: See all the smiling faces. Then follow those smilers back to their own homes. Behold them when they are no longer playing to a crowd, like comedians. Behold them in the privacy of their own kitchens and bedrooms. Behold them interacting with their own families. Behind their public masks you'll find so many lonely drifters, often desperately unhappy. They wend their way through dim corridors of existence with only guttering candles of faint energy to light their way.

Essential for every person—for every ego, before it can redirect its energies upward—is the simple self-admission, "I'm on a downward spiral, but I refuse to descend any further. I repent. I choose to retrace my steps to my true home in God." There is no way honestly to deny that one has erred. Nor, unfortunately, is there a way suddenly to soar back on eagle wings to that long-ago abandoned Eden. One must do one's best to fly, yes—on wings, if possible, of prayer, meditation, devotion, and all good spiritual practices. But one must also confront, as best one can, one's inner darkness. One should not bemoan it, however, nor give it a reality it needn't have for anyone. *There is a right way to confront it.*

And here lies the need for tantra.

Paramhansa Yogananda used to say, "You can't banish darkness from a room by beating at it with a stick. But turn on the light, and the darkness—yes, even of a thousand years—will vanish as though it had never been." His solution has all the simplicity of divine wisdom. For only by the "light" of superconsciousness can the darkness of delusion be dispelled forever.

And yet—and yet: A question arises in the mind. What if, engulfed in all that darkness, we can't locate the light switch? Suppose, while searching for it, we bark our shins on the furniture, or stumble over hassocks, or trip on the edge of a carpet? In these cases we naturally tell ourselves to walk more slowly and carefully. If we bumped heavily into anything, we wouldn't flee in the opposite direction: We might only crash into something else. What we do, therefore, is back off carefully, and just as carefully experiment with other directions.

A man I once knew had been an alcoholic. He'd conceived a deep desire to know God, but his habit mocked at him, and so did his companions in error. "Come on, Joe, that isn't *you!* How can you pretend to be something you so obviously aren't?"

My friend's desire was strong, and he answered his own self-doubt and the doubts of his friends, "I can't help my bad habit, but at least I can also do something good with my life."

And so he sat daily in prayer and meditation: his prayer beads in one hand, a glass of whiskey in the other. The day arrived when he realized he was feeling so much joy in daily communion with God that the whiskey no longer held any allure for him. Years later—which was when I came to know him—he had a job working in a factory. He told me with a smile, "I hear AUM so loudly, it drowns out the noise of the machinery!"

This, then, is tantra: to accept what is, but replace it gradually with something better, until a new fulfillment overwhelms the falsity of the other, and robs it of its very lure to fulfillment. As Yogananda put it, "Once you taste good cheese, the stale kind you've enjoyed will lose all attraction for you."

Tantra also means detaching the mind from whatever one is doing. Even while drinking, for example, detach yourself mentally. This means looking squarely at the act, rather than glancing sidelong at it with the pretense that it isn't there, and isn't really tempting anyway. Accept it honestly, in other words, but at the same time try to diminish the appeal it holds for you. Affirm mentally, instead, "I *am not* this weakness. I observe the action in myself, but that is not who I am."

It is all right to hate sin, but don't hate the sinner. This means one shouldn't hate oneself, either. Hate the weakness, but never condemn yourself for being weak. Self-hatred only gives strength to weakness. The way to freedom lies through a mountain pass of calm impartiality.

One step in this direction is to accept the enjoyment itself as a fact. It doesn't help to pretend that the enjoyment doesn't exist. People who try to overcome sexual temptation, for example, only create problems for themselves, and for their partners, if in their attempt at spiritual zeal they hate themselves, and by extension their partners, and try to persuade themselves that they hate the act itself. They should offer the enjoyment up, rather, to a higher joy. Spiritualize it. See it, if possible, as an expression of higher and more refined feelings. View sexual desire, for instance, increasingly as a manifestation of divine love. To view pleasure impartially does not mean to view it without feeling, but rather to offer the feeling up to the spiritual eye; to *experience* it there, and hold it at that point rather than dwell on the feeling in the lower chakras.

Thus, by "repenting," or withdrawing from the spiral descent Krishna described, one gradually loses the very desire for sensory enjoyment. God becomes, ever-increasingly, one's only reality. With the diminishment of desire comes a diminishment also of attraction. And as attraction diminishes, one no longer—as Krishna puts it—ponders on it.

Tantra is essentially not so much a path as an attitude of mind. This "mental resistance," counseled by Sri Yukteswar, becomes necessary when confronting experiences that are inevitable. In such cases, what is needed, instead of an abrupt break with temptation, is gradual mental disengagement from it.

There is another attitude to hold in these matters, more difficult to practice but important—indeed, even essential, once a certain degree of calmness has been attained. For every physical pleasure is only an echo of soul-joy. If the pleasure you feel in anything can be turned inward, and used to remind you of the joy of your own being, it can actually nourish that inner joy, and thereby increase it.

It is here, however, that the tantric teachings become fraught with peril. And it is for this reason that the wise warn against them so sternly, when viewed as a practice to be actively pursued rather than reluctantly accepted. For if a person tries to increase his inner joy by deliberate outer stimulation, he usually falls into Yudhisthira's error in his acceptance of the challenge to a game of delusion.

I once knew a master of tantra—one of only three or four in all of India, or so I was told. Even from birth he had been a highly advanced yogi; otherwise he could not have embraced those practices without endangering his spiritual life. Even he, however, warned people never to attempt this aspect of tantra.

It is only from a high state of superconsciousness that one can afford to look *maya* fully in the face, and draw from her those inner benefits which are, in fact, her secret gift. Even my mention of this practice, then, is to some degree forced out of me rather than freely offered. I offer it because so much has been written on the subject, and so enthusiastically, urging poor innocents to play with fire the danger of which they know nothing.

Tantra, then, in this last aspect, should be utterly shunned. As an attitude, on the other hand, to hold in mind when unavoidably confronted by delusion, a tantric attitude is necessary and helpful. The best counsel always is one many Christian mystics have given: "Flee the occasions of sin." If fleeing becomes out of the question, however, then remember Krishna's warning, and Sri Yukteswar's advice: Even if your body embraces sin, try mentally to hold yourself somewhat separate. Pray for increasing inwardness in your confrontations with delusion.

I have described previously the ascending and descending currents in the spine, known as *iḍa* and *pingala*. These currents are related, I said, to our emotional reactive process: our likes and dislikes, our attractions and aversions. Thus, when anything pleases us, we experience—whether consciously or not—an automatic upward movement of energy in the spine. This ascent takes place through the *iḍa* nerve channel. The subtle currents in the spine are also reflected in the physical breath. Thus, simultaneously with that ascending energy, and as an automatic corollary to it, our inhalations become stronger.

Again, when anything displeases us, there is an automatic descent of energy through the *pingala* nerve channel. And again, simultaneously, our exhalations become stronger; often, indeed, with the downward movement we sigh.

This too, then, is tantra: to discriminate between outer excitement and its accompanying *inner* ascent of energy in the spine. Concentrate on that rising energy, rather than on the outer pleasure itself. Pleasure is, in fact, only a reflection of the positive welcome we extend to it in our minds. Be aware at the same time of your increasingly strong inhalations at such times, and relate them, too, to the spinal energy.

The process begins with mental reaction, which draws the energy upward through *ida,* which then excites the breath and causes a strong inhalation, which then projects the energy outward. The way to disengagement is to reverse this process: First, calm the breath by deep, controlled breathing. Second, balance the upward flow in the spine with a downward flow. Finally, calm the mind, focusing your concentration at the point between the eyebrows.

Again, look beyond any *outward-seeming* cause of depression or disappointment, and realize that its real cause is your inner *reaction* to outer circumstances. This reaction is accompanied by a descending flow of energy in the spine. Notice the increased strength of your exhalation, and relate it, as well, to the spinal energy. Concentrate on that downward flow as a feeling, first, of emotional withdrawal, and then of calm interiorization into the inner Self.

In these ways, your reactive process will become neutralized, and you will learn to achieve calmness under all circumstances. In inner calmness comes the attainment of true happiness and joy.

By Kriya Yoga, which is the central teaching mentioned in *Autobiography of a Yogi,* one learns control of these spinal currents, and thereby gains control of the entire reactive process. Gradually, in this way, one becomes released from dependency on any outer circumstance.

The awakening of the five chakras in the spine brings to each of them a deep calmness, as the deeper spinal energy passes through them on its way to the brain. Stimulation of the chakras, on the other hand, in response to outer stimuli, induces a sense of excitement, even of nervousness. This sensation is centered in the chakras themselves, similar to the way an earthquake radiates out from its epicenter. Most people, however, are conscious only of the peripheral excitement of the senses themselves. This excitement, in any case, can be calmed by directing the energy upward from the related chakra, or chakras, to the brain. The energy must then be held firmly at the point between the eyebrows, until the feeling becomes calm. To chant AUM mentally up and down the spine at the chakras, while concentrating simultaneously at the Christ center, is an excellent method for transmuting the energy in each chakra into spiritual awareness.

Thus, it may be seen that the basic purpose of tantra is transmutation, not, as many people ignorantly claim, mere enjoyment. When tantra is embraced as a path, however, rather than as a necessary attitude to be held during times of unavoidable confrontation with *maya,* it steps into the domain of legendary dragons who, in their shadow-role, devour all intruders. Though tantra has been known to produce quick results, its usual consequence is an equally sudden fall. Tantra, therefore, should not be considered a path to God, as valid as any other. Use the attitudes it encourages, rather, when delusion-inducing circumstances cannot be avoided. Then devote your energies as much as possible to what is called "the right-hand path": devotion, meditation, and positive offering of the heart's love to God.

The more highly developed a person is, the more the tantric attitude of detachment becomes a direct confrontation with Satan himself. Again, this confrontation results not by inviting his appearance, but demands that one hold, even in confrontation with him, an attitude of unshakable calmness in the certainty that God alone exists.

Buddha, before he attained final enlightenment, was suddenly confronted with a vision of sensory and sensual attractions. He didn't avert his gaze fearfully from those temptations. Calmly, rather, he smote with his knuckles three times on the ground and declared firmly, "Mara [Satan], I have conquered thee!" Instantly the vision disappeared, and Buddha passed beyond them to the highest state of Self-realization.

It is well to meditate on his attitude on that occasion. He didn't "ponder on" those temptations, as in Krishna's warning. He looked on them, rather, with complete indifference, negating their very reality by his absorption in Ultimate Truth.

This is the attitude to which every devotee should cling. As long as there is fear, Yogananda said, one has not yet completely worked out the karma one fears. Fear itself is an indication of subconscious recognition that something still remains in the subconscious to be exorcised.

Inner indifference is the key—not coldness of heart, but calm detachment, coupled with openness of the heart to Supreme Love and Bliss.

To view dispassionately even that which would naturally seem repulsive or terrifying, and to know to the depths of one's heart that nothing can ever harm the inner Self—this is an aspect of tantra that advanced souls have been known to practice—though here again, only when they are firmly anchored in the Self. Otherwise, such a confrontation might well prove unsettling, not liberating.*

Certain tantric deities are actually portrayed, for this purpose, as ugly or ferocious. Such tantric practices may include meditating in crematory grounds, where the impermanence of life assumes a grim immediacy. All such practices have the goal of inspiring the meditator to rise above oppositional likes and dislikes. They are by no means intended to present ugliness or ferociousness to the mind as attractive images.

Such practices are self-defeating, however, for those who lack grounding in the sweetness of devotion. While they may increase the will power, and thereby help spiritually up to a certain point, they may also engender attitudes of egotism, and a fascination with

---

*On a somewhat comparable note, I recall trying years ago to practice *titiksha,* mental resistance — in this case, resistance to cold. It was the middle of winter. In an unheated bathroom, I took a cold shower. None of the luxury of preceding it with a hot shower! I soaped myself thoroughly in the cold water, then rinsed off all the soap. The whole process took time. My mind was unable to fend off that shivering reaction: "I'm freezing c-c-c-cold!" The result was that it took days for me to feel really warm again.

Extreme practices, in other words, are beneficial only as long as we can preserve an inner calmness.

"*siddhi*s," or spiritual powers. Both powers and egotism lead, eventually, to a spiritual fall.

Tantra, then, is a way of *necessary* confrontation, primarily, as it were under duress. As such, it is an important adjunct to every quest for enlightenment. Whatever you behold in life, view it impartially, not with personal involvement. To be enthusiastic is always good—the spiritual path is not for aspiring zombies!—but offer the enthusiasm itself up to God, to the higher Self. Don't shun the world. In short, don't be a coward! But don't embrace life the way most people do. Enjoy everything *inwardly,* in the Self.

Perhaps the best counsel in this respect is simply this: *Give* energy to others, and to life, but don't *draw* energy from anyone or anything. Recognize that the source of all your energy resides in the Self alone.

Chapter Twenty

The Divine Mother

I have tried in this book to bring divine truths down to a level of common human experience. For until that denouement in the divine drama when revelation brings to us a radically new awareness of reality, we can only reach out to the unknown from that which we know already. We must build our edifice of understanding gradually; we cannot construct the roof until we've erected the substructure to support it.

This is the difficulty with all human mentation: its slowness, its deliberation. But this is also its advantage. For only the foolish try to soar in lofty flights of understanding while they still lack the lifting power of intuition. They are impatient with the bricks and mortar of reasoning. But we shall never understand anything except on the basis of our own experience. Nor shall we be able to grasp the essence of truth, which is God, until we have understood the essence of our own selves.

Each one of us, as far as we ourselves are concerned, is the central reality of the universe. From that point alone can we reach out to others, to the world around us, to the very universe and to very God (to use a delightful, if archaic, expression from the earlier version of the Anglican *Book of Common Prayer*).

Paramhansa Yogananda defined divine vision as "center everywhere, circumference nowhere." When self-awareness is expanded into cosmic consciousness, the Self perceives itself as centrally present in everything.

To define God, then—not centrally, but peripherally only, as having an outer form separate from our own—is to cheat ourselves of really knowing Him at all. Had Sartre, the French existentialist, been a mystic instead of a nihilist, his dictum, "To be conscious of another is to be conscious of what one is not," would have been phrased very differently. He might have said, "To be truly conscious of another is to be conscious of one's own self in that form."

Truly to know oneself requires that one transcend personality and ego, likes and dislikes, ability and ineptitude, strength and weakness, all form, emotions, and thoughts: rising to that innermost part of one's being which, quite the opposite of unconscious, is the condensed essence of every level of consciousness we possess. This is the state known as superconsciousness. It is the divine within us. It is the state in which the soul knows completely, not by inference but by total recognition, that it is and always has been Truth itself: "knowing, knower, known, as one."* The ancient sage Patanjali described this recognition as *smriti*: divine remembrance.

In superconsciousness, our awareness flies into the unknown and recognizes it as, forever, our true

*From the poem "Samadhi," by Paramhansa Yogananda. This poem appears in its complete form in the first edition of *Autobiography of a Yogi,* reprinted by Crystal Clarity, Publishers, Nevada City, California.

homeland. Since that state is native to us, we intuit something of its reality even in our ordinary state of ego-awareness. When scripture, or when great saints, tell us that Love is the essence of eternal truth, there rises within us a feeling of glad recognition. "Yes!" we cry, "I know it to be true, because underneath all my restlessness I sense that I, too, am that!"

On the other hand, if anyone were to declare, "Total indifference is the essence of truth," or "boredom," or "meaninglessness," as a few self-styled philosophers have done, something within us would rise up in instinctive repudiation. Only by quelling this natural impulse, perhaps from a desire to be scrupulously fair, could we even consider such nonsense. Many intellectuals, pondering heavily on life's "verities," reach the point where they finally embrace the absurd; then they preen themselves on their aloofness to "mere" feeling. But what even they were really seeking was intuitive recognition. Intuition, though it sometimes defies reason, is never irrational. The truth is always simple. Pride is what sends philosophers down labyrinthine byways in frowning cogitation.

The recognition that Love is truth has nothing to do with sentimentality. It is not like telling oneself, "God must be love, because I *want* to be loved." It is those who have the clearest insight, not those who are the most self-deluded, who have firmly declared from their own direct experience that God is Love. Every great saint in every great religion has declared the same truth. It is also a testimony to the veracity of those sources that their statement sparks a recognition in ourselves. Whether the scriptures also describe God in cosmic terms, as masculine, feminine, or both, or neither; whether they call God Mother, or Father, or Friend, or Beloved: All this really has meaning for us only to the extent that we ourselves resonate with the concepts.

Instead, then, of repeating the explanations I've already given in this book, which describe God in His cosmic aspects, let us accept simply that the divine consciousness is infinite, and, in that infinity, infinitely varied. The heart, however, wants something more. It needs a different kind of clarity, a clarity of feeling, not of intellect only.

Love uplifts feeling toward superconscious awareness. Emotion, on the other hand, produces waves on the surface of consciousness, and disturbs its clarity of perception. Emotion is reactive. Like the ocean waves, the higher the wave of positive reaction, the deeper its corresponding trough of negativity.

Another simile will be helpful also, in a different way: Emotion clouds our mental skies. When the cloud-covering is dense, we see things more dimly; the denser the clouds, the greater our spiritual darkness. Calm love, not excited emotion, is the key to wisdom, for love's rays radiate a warmth that, like summer sunshine, banishes our mental clouds.

Deep feeling, and not an absence of feeling, is the key to even intellectual clarity. To suppress feeling altogether, as a means of keeping our skies uncluttered, is to deaden our very desire to look up. We must refine our feelings, not destroy them.

Only the ignorant—especially nowadays, when every child knows something of the vastness of the cosmos—can seriously imagine God as possessing human emotions: jealousy and wrath, or as holding partiality to any one group of worshipers over all others. Let us then leave aside projections of such mere aberrations of human nature, and pay God the compliment of imagining Him as at least somewhat better than we are. Let us imagine God, as I once suggested to an atheist that he do, as the highest potential we can imagine for ourselves: a potential of feeling as well as of superior intelligence.

Is jealousy such a potential? Surely not! Jealousy prevents us from even aspiring to the heights. Is anger, then? Again, certainly not. Anger, as most people know it, is emotion run riot. From such emotion there rises an almost visible vapor which, even though invisible, obscures our ability to perceive *anything* as it is.

Generosity is a loftier emotion than jealousy, and calm acceptance than anger. Kindness is nobler than cruelty; sympathy, than disdain; forgiveness, than an insatiable thirst for vengeance. Even the worst criminal, though steeped in negative motivations, cannot but sigh inwardly, sometimes, for peace of mind, for love, for beauty. Why these sentiments, which are so very different from his usual state of mind? Because all of us are made in the divine image. We suffer, if we desecrate that deepest secret of our own being, whether the desecration be done in complete ignorance, or by deliberate (though still ignorant) choice.

Let us, then, contemplate God as the fulfillment *of our own* deepest needs and highest aspirations.

There is something in all of us that reaches outward, and upward, in longing. Behind every desire lies the belief that, when our deepest longing is fulfilled, we'll know peace. At least peace. Dwelling further on this thought, we realize that we want our peace to be conscious, and not like the dim awareness of a clam. We also want our peace to be capable of calmly sustaining every shock, even that of death. We'd like our peace to be unmarred, and we'd like it to be ours forever.

On the other hand, we'd like it to remain interesting! We don't want our peace to become boring, nor to carry us drifting passively into subconsciousness.

Peace, when considered alone, *is* passive. As we contemplate it, however, we find ourselves thinking, Wouldn't it be wonderful, in our peace, to be able to let our hearts expand freely and serenely and embrace all others, and life itself, with love and joy; never again to feel the need to protect ourselves from the threat of enemies or of other opposition!

Peace is the basic condition for every positive state of mind: love, and joy, and blissful awareness of life's beauty and perfection. Without peace, these transcendent states are unimaginable. But with peace, all good things seem possible.

And so—we dream not of peace only, but of other, deeper fulfillments. We dream of love, and radiant joy.

The person of undeveloped consciousness, however, is not easily inspired by abstractions. And so that criminal, even while thinking of love, visualizes it not as the cosmic force that holds the atoms together, but as he would like, at least, to see it manifested in his family. Perhaps, then, he thinks ruefully, "My God, if only that woman would stop nagging me for just twenty-four hours! And if only those kids weren't such insolent brats!" And so, the soft sentiment passes.

But supposing, instead, he thinks of his mother. In this reflection, are not his sentiments more likely to remain tender? There are unloving mothers aplenty in the world, but somehow the mental association of tenderness and unconditional love is stronger with the mother image than with any other. Women, too, may feel equivocal sometimes about their husbands, and exasperated occasionally by their children, but they are likely to think of their mothers with unalloyed tenderness—if only when Mother is far away, or perhaps safely dead!

Let me intrude a little personal recollection. When I was only nine years old, the doctor recommended that I be sent away to school in Switzerland for my health. Our family lived in Romania—a universe away, it seemed to me. I had grown up speaking English, German, and Romanian, but no French, which was the language of my new environment. I was homesick, and desperately unhappy.

And then, after several months, Mother came to visit me. I first saw her walking up the street from the train station, her very stride demonstrating her eagerness to be again with me. Oh, what joy I felt! Even today, that flash of memory brings tears to my eyes.

There is something in the image of the mother, especially if removed from the specific nature of an individual, that inspires everyone. Although we owe our physical existence first to our fathers, even as the universe owes its creation to the transcendent Spirit, it was our mothers who carried us, who nurtured us, who suffered for us in giving us birth.

There are many kinds of love, but love for the mother, inspired initially by the mother's love for us, is very special.

I don't mean to imply that the mother aspect of love stands alone, nor that it is, necessarily, the most satisfying for everyone. It is simply very special.

But there is other beauty also, for example in an ideal relationship between a man and a woman. Many people in India pray to God as their Divine Beloved. In that other great Indian epic, the *Ramayana,* its central characters, Rama and Sita, portray for all time the Hindu ideal of a perfect marriage, deeply rooted in mutual love and respect, in shared loyalty, service, and self-giving. Rama's and Sita's was a love calm, noble, and dignified, ever centered in the inner Self. From such love, however, unless the heart is as pure as clear crystal, it is very difficult to keep one's mental skies free of the clouds of emotion. Rama's and Sita's love was divine; for ordinary human beings, it was almost impossibly perfect. To Hindu husbands who want their wives to behave like Sita, I say, "In that case you, first, be like Rama!"

It is difficult even for mothers to expand to others the love they feel for their own children. It is not so difficult, however, to create an abstraction of love for one's own mother, and refine it to such a degree that one visualizes motherly love as smiling at one from Nature herself—from every hillside, from every flower.

Usually, human beings need some sort of human image to inspire them: the brave hero, rather than the abstraction, courage; the noble public servant, not that abstraction, service; the kindly healer, not that indefinite quality, kindness; the wise elder counselor, not the vague abstraction, wisdom; the living person who expresses joy in adversity, not simply "joy-in-adversity"; the serenely humble monk or nun, not the somewhat nebulous virtue, humility.

We need to think of God, too, as our own nearest and dearest, and not as the cosmic abstraction, only: Love. With this clearer focus on the Divine, we can relax into that calm acceptance which is the foundation of true devotion. God, as an even more abstract concept than Love, appeals still less instantly to the heart. We want to know that He, or She, is Love, but then we also want something we can love in more human terms.

Many people find supreme appeal in God's aspect of Father. Others, on the other hand, find that masculine image a bit distant. To them, it suggests justice, not love; the challenge to face life's tests "like a man," or "like a grown-up woman now, not a little girl," rather than a smile of tender approval and kindly encouragement.

Thus, the Divine Mother image can be, perhaps for most people, especially dear. Hindus find it particularly so. And the Roman Catholic missionaries discovered wherever they went in the East that they reached people more easily by expressing devotion to Mary, the mother of Jesus, than by praying only to Jesus. As Paramhansa Yogananda put it, "The Mother is closer than the Father."

In the world today there is an imbalance in favor of masculine energy. Too much logic, and too little love. Dependence on rules, but too little emphasis on mercy. Stress on aggressive power and worldly importance, but too little on service and humility (although these have greater, though subtle, power, for they can influence people to *want* to change, and are more important also in the eyes of God). Women instinctively feel the need for correcting this imbalance.

Alas, too many of them try to cast themselves in a masculine mold. They try to prove that they can be just as competent, intelligent, and able to win victory's laurels as any man. Well, why not? Of course they can! They already *are* quite as competent, and quite as intelligent—more so, indeed, in their own way. They are also quite as capable of winning their own laurels. Of what use then, to them, the laurels of a victory many of them don't even really want? They need only to approach life situations in their own way, rather than as men do. In the nature of things, most women are not likely ever to be as good at being men as men themselves are. In trying to be so, they miss their own calling. Far worse, society finds itself thrown into confusion.

A mere glance at the pages of popular fashion magazines shows the self-image a growing number of women are trying to project. Women? They look more like panthers! The inter-relationship between the sexes has become, all too often, not one of love or of mutual support and appreciation, but of ceaseless competition. Disharmony in the home has become almost the norm, and antagonism between men and women has increased to the point where it almost seems, sometimes, as though the world were divided into two hostile camps.

I know a number of men who, even well into middle age, have never had a girl friend—not because the idea of being married held no appeal for them, but because they felt intimidated by the hostility and aggression they felt from the other sex. And some women, for their part, loudly disclaim any interest in men, whom they perceive as aggressive and insensitive "hulks."

Unfortunately, both sides are right. Many men react with instinctive aggressiveness when confronted by what they perceive as a threat. Other men, when threatened, simply withdraw into themselves. Women, for their part, perceive masculine aggressiveness as intolerable bullying, and masculine withdrawal as a proof of insensitivity. Neither side properly understands the other, and in this gladiatorial arena I see no possibility that either side will emerge the victor. Both, rather, can only lose, for they destroy the very thing they themselves most want: loving harmony.

As long as women perceive themselves as persecuted victims of male aggression; as long as they feel themselves threatened and oppressed by "the system"; as long as they dwell on the thought that they are not getting a fair chance to fulfill themselves; they will attract the inevitable consequences of such attitudes: insecurity, and low self-esteem. The magnetism they project cannot but return to them with boomerang effect.

Women, far more so than men, have the potential to uplift humanity. For feeling, not reason, is that aspect of human consciousness which can inspire, purify, and transform. If, instead of developing with calmness and dignity, it grows like a wild hedge, twining its limbs about itself with untamed emotion, it creates only disorder. Women have a responsibility to society; first, however, they have a responsibility to themselves. And whatever else is said, women are unhappy with the present state of affairs. Mother Nature, through their discontentment, has given them a motivation to change.

The cure for a persecution complex is not reassurance from others, no matter how earnestly it is offered. The cure for personal insecurity, or for low self-esteem, is never arrogance or domination over others. Women will never be contented for long if men acquiesce, as many are trying to do, to their demand for equality on masculine terms. The cure for discontentment will come when women acknowledge their gifts as uniquely their own. Men, also, must accept that this gift is right and true, and absolutely necessary to the equilibrium of society as a whole. Mutual recognition will come, not from aggressive competition, but from shared respect and appreciation, and from an attitude of friendly cooperation, not of seizing from one another angrily.

Much of the problem today arises from the simple fact that people sense a new consciousness in the air. We have emerged from Kali Yuga—a male-dominated era when physical force seemed the only way of attaining one's objectives—and are already being swayed by the fresh spring breezes of Dwapara Yuga, the Age of Energy. There will be increasing awareness of the need for feminine inwardness as a balance to masculine outwardness; for inner inspiration as a balance to outward conquest; for feeling, as the very essence of consciousness itself. In the struggle to adapt to these changes, it will be increasingly necessary to distinguish between calm feeling, which is intuitive, and the disruptive feelings of raw emotion. There is a need—now, *today*—to recognize the importance of inner peace as the soil in which alone the plant of true happiness can flourish.

Will it take a global war to bring humanity to this recognition? One devoutly hopes not.

The role of the Divine Mother in Her *sattwic* aspect—as distinct from the restlessly *rajasic* and the inertly *tamasic* aspects of Nature—is, as I stated earlier in this book, to draw all Her children, all self-aware beings everywhere, back to oneness with God. Women, more naturally than men, can manifest this feminine aspect of Cosmic Nature, if they so choose.

Every human being has an obligation above all to himself to live according to high ideals. In society, people have a duty also to help one another, and to injure no one. None can offer more inspiration to others than he actually feels in himself. Everyone should strive always, therefore, if only for his own sake, to reach out toward that high potential. If there is a single need, greater than any other, on earth today, it is for love. And selfless rather than self-interested love is more easily and universally comprehensible when we identify it with mother-love than with any other form of love.

The Divine Mother, then, is a concept that can change the world, and in a way that is desperately needed. Worship of the Divine Mother—human-like in a sense, but also formless and infinite—can inspire sweetness once again in the human heart. It can bring humanity back to that vitally needed balance without which the world already invites its own destruction.

Women will have an important role to play in this transformation process. If a woman's self-image is one of uplifted inwardness and queenly serenity, rather than aggressive competitor, she blesses not only society as a whole, but her spouse, her children, and above all herself. Indeed, the success or failure of the human race has always depended far more on women than on men. The future will be determined, not by inventions and intellectual discoveries, but by love, kindness, fellow-feeling, and by turning within for our inspiration in everything we do.

Hindus fondly quote the refrain from a famous poem by Shankaracharya:

> Bad sons there are many,
> But never has there been a bad Mother.

Considering how little this statement jibes with the evidence, since many mothers show themselves to be uncaring, indifferent, and capable of mistreating and even, occasionally, murdering their own children, it says much for Indian womanhood that Hindus can even quote this statement sentimentally. Yet I've never heard it quoted except with heartfelt and quite touching conviction.

It must be added, nevertheless, that Shankaracharya's poem was not written in praise of human motherhood. He himself was nothing if not realistic; he saw human existence itself as an illusion. His poem, then, was in praise of the Divine Mother. And of Her he spoke truly: "Never has there been a bad Mother."

We should try always to refer present to cosmic realities. No human mother is perfect, unless indeed she has attained saintly perfection in God. All human mothers are, however, channels for the Divine Mother–consciousness. Some of them, it must be granted, are clearer channels than others. Some of them, conversely, are quite impure channels: Their selfishness muddies, or desiccates with sirocco winds of anger and hatred, the flow of pure love. It is women's responsibility to open their hearts to the love that is implanted in them by Nature, like a seed, through the miracle of birth. This gift is an irrefragable instinct. Human beings have—unfortunately, in this case—the free will to over-ride their own natural instincts. It helps, therefore, to study the instinctual ways of animals.

The Divine Mother is the source of the mother-instinct. We are Her own. As Yogananda prayed, "Divine Mother, naughty or good, I am Thy child. Thou *must* release me from this nightmare of delusion!" You can pray like that, with confidence, to the Divine Mother: scoldingly if you like; with pressing urgency if you like; demanding of Her in ways that you might not dare to address the Heavenly Father. We are Her own; She is forever ours. It is easier to establish a relation of mutual trust with the Divine Mother than with God in any other aspect.

Thus, the classic Hindu symbols for the Divine Mother: Durga, Uma, Tara, Parvati, Kali, Lakshmi, Saraswati, and others, while helpful insofar as they draw our attention to different aspects of the Infinite Being, are not the images necessarily to which feeling most instantly responds from its innermost being, as to an ancient memory. When it comes to giving our unconditional love to God as our Divine Mother, the most meaningful image will always be that which is *most meaningful, personally, to ourselves.* Whatever image we hold dearest in our hearts, then, we should accept as our own. We should then view that consciousness as loving us transcendently, unconditionally, as wanting nothing from us in return but our own true and highest good.

For incarnations, the Divine Mother has nurtured us through human mothers—in accordance with our own karma to receive. Always, transcendent above that lesser love, She has whispered to us in our souls, "Won't you look now to Me? I, alone, am eternally your own. Lo! others may disappoint you; they may forsake you; all of them will be snatched away from you at the fall of life's curtain in death. I alone have been, and ever shall be, yours through eternity!"

As the Divine Mother said once in a vision to Paramhansa Yogananda, when he was still the boy Mukunda: "Always have I loved thee! Ever shall I love thee." Saints who have beheld Her in vision speak of Her, not as those sometimes grotesque or fiercely challenging deities that are depicted in certain Hindu paintings, but as transcendently beautiful. She is different for every beholder, for She satisfies the deepest longing of every human being for motherly perfection.

I remember it as though it had been only yesterday, though it happened nearly fifty years ago: the Divine Mother appearing to my guru in ecstatic vision, and his crying out, "Oh! Mother, You are so *beautiful!*" His whole heart, I felt, was poured out in that single rapturous exclamation.

Hinduism doesn't tell us in what specific form to visualize the Divine Mother. Indeed, it tells us to go beyond images—to visualize Her with expanding love in the world around us: in the flowers, in the sunset, in everything that seems to us most touching, beautiful, and inspiring. Then, it tells us, intuit Her smile behind our every lofty sentiment; and finally, visualize Her as nirakara, "formless."

We attract to ourselves whatever attitudes we project. Hatred attracts hatred. Indifference attracts indifference. Remember, though human beings can always misunderstand our feelings for them—Kamsa, for example, hated Krishna, who was Love incarnate; Ravana hated Rama, the epitome of divine nobility and generosity; the Pharisees hated Jesus, whose compassion flowed out and embraced all—God never misunderstands us. He (She) responds unfailingly to whatever prayer we offer.

Make no mistake, however: Every attitude, every state of consciousness, every desire *is* a prayer. It is to our hearts that God listens, not to our words, no matter how finely we chisel them. God receives our love, and responds accordingly—not through other people, necessarily, but always, unfailingly, in our souls.

By loving God as our Divine Mother, we attract that motherly aspect of the Divine Consciousness, and develop in ourselves the complete trust that brings to us, in return, the most instant response.

Men can advance as easily as women in this form of devotion, though it is easier for women to manifest that motherly consciousness in their own lives, and thus to attune themselves to it in their behavior. For men, it helps to visualize women, also, as manifestations of the Divine Mother, however imperfectly some of them play that role. The ideal for the devotee, always, is to see the universal in the particular, and eternity in the moment.

Everything, when viewed with the eyes of wisdom, becomes a symbol of Infinity. It is a window onto the universe. And even though that window need cleaning, a glimpse of the Divine can almost always be caught, through it.

Ultimately, the symbols in Hinduism, like the symbols in every true religion, are meant to expand our consciousness, to remind us of universal truths within ourselves. No temple, no church, no synagogue, no mosque, no Buddhist vihara can monopolize truth. Outer forms can only remind us of who we are, within. In the highest and truest sense, the human body is the true shrine, for it is within ourselves, first and foremost, that we worship God wherever we sit, kneel, stand, or bow to the ground to pray. As we move about in the world, we are, consciously or unconsciously, on a pilgrimage. By treating life as sacred, for it is a manifestation of God, our own lives become sanctified.

The Divine Mother is that aspect of God which the planet most needs today. We need to bring love back again—unconditional, trusting, self-giving love, a love that asks nothing in return, but that gives of itself generously, freely, and forever. Such, surely, more than any other human feeling, is mother love.

Chapter Twenty-One

Unity in Diversity

When I was a baby and still learning to speak, my father pointed to something moving on the road and said, "That's a horse. Horse!" he repeated for emphasis.

Well, I'd already got the facts straight from our Romanian nurse. How, I thought, could my parent try to play such a low trick on me?

"*Nu!*" I cried indignantly. "*Cal!*"

Both of us were right, of course. Repeatedly in this book we've seen alternatives that were not mutually exclusive, though they appeared so at first. Aristotelian logic, on which Western reasoning is based, separates issues into alternatives wherever feasible: "either/or." Reality, however, is rarely so accommodating. Often, an issue is simply one of "both . . . and."

Many religious quarrels are like that problem I had with my father. Different words are used to describe the same thing: horse, cal, cheval, cavallo, Pferd, ghoda. Shakespeare might have put it this way: "A horse by any other name would smell as horsey"—though perhaps he'd have found some more suitable character than Juliet to voice the sentiment.* Underlying all

---

*An author cannot help worrying, sometimes, whether his light jests may have no meaning for certain people. The above is a paraphrase of a

linguistic differences there is, generally speaking, unanimity of desire, tendency, and observation.

In English we say, "I am hungry": the "I" is central to the thought; hunger modifies it. In French, the expression is, "*J'ai faim*—I have hunger." Here, the "I" is secondary; the abstraction *hunger* is central. In Italian, the expression is, "*ho fame*": similar to the French except that the pronoun "I" is not stated at all, but is only implied in the verb. In Bengali the expression is, "*Amar khide peyechhe*—My hunger has got," or "has arrived." In this case, the word *hunger,* though abstract also, is viewed in its relationship to the speaker; it describes a state of mind. These subtle distinctions reflect, and also influence, people's attitudes.

The English expression in this case, and in many cases like it, forces a certain emphasis on the ego—or, rather, perhaps one should say, on the importance of *personal clarity*. In this respect, English is more individualistic than many languages. This trait makes the English speaker less willing to abide by the rules of grammar, for it gives his language a certain flexibility in invention. Openness to innovation is often lacking in other languages. In Latin-based languages, for example, their relatively rigid structure makes them less welcoming in this respect.

Their emphasis on abstract nouns, moreover, forces a certain abstraction of thinking. Modern English defies even its grammarians, by avoiding wherever possible the indefinite pronoun "one," and substituting for it the personal pronouns "you" and "we." In

well-known line in the play, *Romeo and Juliet:* "A rose by any other name would smell as sweet."

French, by contrast, the word "*on* (one)" is used constantly. In Italian and Spanish, one doesn't even address a person directly in formal speech. Instead, one addresses him in the third person as if acknowledging his "aura": "*Lei,*" and "*Usted.*" Most English abstract words derive from the Latin, or from Latin-based languages.

In Bengali and Hindi, on the other hand, the emphasis is not so much on intellectual abstractions as on states of mind. Their very manner of expression causes Indians to think philosophically, yet at the same time in terms that are concretely related to human needs. "My hunger has. . . ." We've seen this Indian tendency to "earthy abstraction," as we might call it, repeatedly presented in this book.

English expressions such as "I am hungry," while they emphasize the first person singular, don't necessarily imply egoism, or selfishness, though of course they may do so. Often what they reveal is a tendency to want to anchor one's ideas, to get things clear according to one's own understanding. There is a great emphasis on specificity in the English language; vague generalities tend to expose themselves as the impostors they often are.

There are, of course, countless other influences at work in every language. From single examples it is difficult to generalize too many specific conclusions. Even so, it is fascinating to ponder them. For instance, the rigid structure of Latin-based languages places a certain limitation on spontaneity. A masculine adjective at the beginning of a sentence makes it impossible to change to a feminine noun later on, without starting the sentence all over. English, though less logically structured than French, is at least in this respect more intuitive. Its flow has always, to my mind, seemed to have something akin to the crystal clarity of a brook—in contrast to the unyielding firmness of a rock. English is, I think, an ideal medium of communication in this Dwapara Yuga, with its focus on energy and, consequently, on relative fluidity.

Another interesting point is that in languages of which the adjectives are either masculine or feminine, women are obliged to use feminine endings to describe themselves. This one simple fact makes them dwell on their own femininity in a way women needn't do in English. *"Sono lieta,"* says an Italian woman, meaning, "I'm delighted." An Italian male says, *"Sono lieto,"* with the adjective ending in "o." That feminine "a" becomes, for every woman, a constant affirmation of sexual distinction (as, of course, the masculine "o" becomes also for men). In English, "I'm delighted" is the same for both sexes, and produces far more than in Latin countries the tendency to equate equality of the sexes with a denial that sexual differences are anything more than biological and purely superficial.

Linguistic differences make a fascinating study. To capture the "mood" of a language through this kind of awareness carries one a long way toward mastering the language itself.

The same may be said of religion. The essential truth in all religions, like the central point of a circle, is one. The path inward to that center is the Way of Awakening in every religion. The Ways of Belief are like lines radiating outward from that center. No two of these lines are parallel; each one radiates out in a different direction. The longer these lines, moreover, the more widely separated they become from one another.

The circle is a necessary concept for understanding the universe. And there would be no circle, and no center, were there but one straight line.

"Unity in diversity": This is an expression one hears often in India. There is beauty in the fact that diversity exists. For everything in creation is unique. No two human beings are ever exactly alike. Were a thousand of them to live through similar incarnations as pirates, merchants, housewives, beggars, artists, farmers, danseuses, kings or queens, each would live those lives differently. Personality itself, developing in reaction to experience, would differ in each case depending on the seed-awareness of each soul. From the outset of the soul's manifestation in eternity, it is unique. This uniqueness is not a question of personality. Our essential individuality influences us, however, even on a personality level, for it helps to determine the nature and quality of our reactions. People's responses to life situations are never exactly alike.

Many differences in religion, too, are vital and worthwhile. Were we to stress *only* the unity of religion, insisting too much that the differences, because superficial, are unimportant, we'd be left with something reminiscent of those uniforms people used to wear in communist China. The idea, there, was to emphasize people's equality, but the result was that they all looked equally drab, and equally uninteresting.

In this respect, indeed, the comparison of religion with modern science, which I made earlier in this book for emphasis, needs to be colored in, so to speak. In science, definitive agreement is important. The Law of Gravity is the same everywhere, no matter what language expresses it. In religion, however, nuances of definition are subtle, and can never be understood in quite the same way even by two people who speak the same language, and belong to the same religious community. These differences do not, however, eliminate the need for emphasizing the underlying *oneness of purpose* in religion. Quite the opposite, they only increase that need.

Unity of purpose, as opposed to agreement on matters of definition, is more important in religion than in science. The farther religious definitions diverge, the greater the possibility for serious misunderstanding—unless there is a corresponding recognition of certain common intentions, and, better still, of common experience. Recognition of a common center not only makes the divergences acceptable, but creates a basis for meaningful communication between the different religions. Indeed, it also makes these divergences no longer threatening, but interesting and enjoyable.

Religious experience, in contradistinction to religious dogmas, cannot be reduced to any set formula. In mystical experience there is always a measure of individuality until such time as the ego itself merges in the Infinite. The important thing to realize is that differences of experience are not essential; they are superficial, relatively speaking, and they become increasingly so the more remote the experience is from the absoluteness of truth.

This book, then, is not a plea for sameness in religion. It is only a plea for recognition that, however differently the truth is expressed, *in essence* it is the same. Whether we call it God, Dieu, Dio, Jehovah, Yahweh, Allah, Brahma, or the eternally aware state of Nirvana—these are only words. The closer we come to our own center, the closer we are to true unity, a unity not constricted but eternally free from all restriction. Differences, in reference to that center, are peripheral. In divine union, they cease altogether.

From an acceptance of essential unity, even the differences between one religion and another assume a certain charm and beauty, because it is understood, then, that the same heart of truth vitalizes them. Without this vision of central unity, however, religion becomes gradually mummified into a system of lifeless rules and dogmas, which, for lack of a vitalizing life force, crackles with brittle intolerance. In linguistics— to return to my first example—awareness of different ways of expressing the same thoughts helps to produce mental flexibility.

An English friend of mine was asked by a Frenchman to help him with his English. At one point in her instruction she said, "The English expression in this case is, 'Take a photograph *from* the window.'"

"But that's not possible!" the man objected. "In French we say *'depuis* [after] *la fenêtre.'* You have to say *after* the window, not *from* it." English, she explained, is different in this respect. "But it just can't be!" he expostulated. Convinced that she simply didn't know her own language, he ceased studying with her.

Now, I submit that many differences in religion are similar to that simple prepositional conflict. Prepositions, often, are not completely logical in any language. Granted, religious differences are more deeply rooted, and have stronger emotional associations. Even so, compared to the central relation of the soul to its Maker, they *are* peripheral.

What I have suggested in this book is that our gaze be not only outward, away from the center of truth, but inward as well, to that point within us where all differences disappear. As long as only the differences are emphasized, rivalry and prejudice are bound to increase, and the very emphasis will only broaden the divergence. Movement in this outward direction will also be toward greater isolation, which is a characteristic of pride.

The broader our understanding of life, on the other hand, the more willingly we find ourselves embracing it in its very variety. A mark of greatness is always a tendency to seek unifying principles underlying superficial diversity. A great physicist looks for underlying relationships between divers natural laws. The wise politician seeks the general good of all, not only of a few. The deep thinker seeks truths that pertain equally to countless life situations. It is the petty-minded person who seeks to prove that his ways are the best, and his beliefs unique.

Already today, in religion, there is a growing recognition of the existence of a Way of Awakening. There is an increasing concentration on the eternal verities rather than on theological niceties. There is also a growing interest in religious *experience,* as opposed to religious beliefs. Meditation groups are appearing everywhere; many of them include the study of yoga and of Eastern mysticism. Their study is not pursued with a view to conversion, but to an enhanced understanding of their own spiritual traditions.

There is also, of course—inevitably—a reaction against this trend. There are people who, like King Canute, determine to stem the tide of change. The wise submit to change, if it is unavoidable, and see what good can be made of it. But narrow loyalties never *seek* understanding, even in such matters as how best to defend that which one believes. They are convinced that they understand already.

In silent communion with God there no longer remains Christianity, Judaism, Islam, or Hinduism, as such, for in soul-consciousness the mind ceases to think at all. There remains only what Paramhansa Yogananda described as "wistful yearning." With this recognition there dawns an *appreciation for* religious differences, not a wish to negate them. Instead of generating a desire to convert others to one's own ways and beliefs, it produces respect for every sincere form of worship, and, indeed, even a certain pleasure in the differences, as lending color and variety to the great tapestry of truth.

Does the vision of unity I've described demand, as its corollary, a hands-off policy of not sharing one's vision with others? By no means! Why should it?

Let me inject here another personal note. I was never able to feel at home in the Anglican church of my own upbringing. Despite exposure to it since my infancy, I never resonated with it inwardly. My mother, and most of my relatives, felt quite at home with it, and as far as I could tell thrived in it spiritually. As for me, I could only say that it was simply not my way.

Paramhansa Yogananda stated that many souls with long experience in India are now being reborn in the West. Many Westerners, on the other hand, with long experience in Europe and America, are being reborn in India. The purpose for this exchange is to encourage greater world unity. Many Indians today, I've noticed, look more like typical Wall Street stockbrokers than like Indians. The main difference is that they have brown skin. And many Westerners seem perfectly at home with Indian ways. For myself, I confess I have always had to affirm my Westernness. I'm happy to live in Western countries, particularly if I can be of service here, but I feel a deep-seated nostalgia for India: for her music, her manner of dressing, her kindliness to all forms of life, the sweetness of her devotion, her gentle acceptance of others, the subtlety of her sense of humor—above all, her longing for the eternal verities. These things inspire me as no other culture has ever done. Perhaps it is as well that I've been born into a Western body, for my longing for eternity lifts me in soul-aspiration above national boundaries, and deepens my desire to win release forever from the trammels of ego in the realization of oneness with Brahman.

Nevertheless, I see no virtue in not sharing with others that which I myself consider to be infinitely precious. I do not believe in conversion; that is to say, I do not believe in *imposing* my ideas on others. To share with them is generous: to convert them, however, would be a presumption. For truth must be recognized; it can never be driven down people's throats.

On the other hand, an awareness of other Ways of Awakening should enhance our own experience of the truth. Certainly it need not be a threat to it. For instance, studying how a Hindu understands certain passages in the Bible may help Jews and Christians to gain deeper insight into that scripture. By studying the Bhagavad Gita from a Western perspective, a Hindu's insight into that scripture may be enhanced similarly. In every religion there is a tendency to become settled in old and traditional ways of thought. New insights can be helpful in keeping one's thinking fresh.

Dogmatism, on the other hand, stifles mental elasticity. Eventually, it turns people into what Yogananda described as "psychological antiques."

Mutual respect; mutual appreciation. These attitudes are vitally important. Without them, the present age of instant communication and rapid travel might easily make people more judgmental of differences between countries, cultures, languages, and religions. Global awareness might only increase their intolerance, which formerly amounted only to indifference. In such a case, to emphasize the differences would only deepen already-existing animosities and prejudices.

If, however, we are predisposed to understand others, any knowledge we gain of them will foster good will. The French have a saying, "*Tous comprendre c'est tous pardoner*—To understand all is to forgive all": a necessary beginning, surely. At last there comes a realization, however, that there is indeed nothing to forgive. There develops effortlessly, instead, a respect and appreciation for all.

Fortunately, the trend toward understanding is already developing in the world. Broadening awareness of other countries and customs is already bringing an increased appreciation for their ways. They go against this growing trend who insist that their own ways are the best. Rather, many people are expressing a growing sympathy for others. They are finding, more and more, that they actually *enjoy* the variety.

Hinduism has been more tolerant of other ways than, perhaps, any other religion. In my own experience, when traveling in India, I have found Indian Catholic priests expressing an appreciation for the fact that I see myself as both a Hindu and a Christian. Whatever judgment I've encountered in that country has come from Western missionaries. This difference in attitude between Indian and Western Christians is a result, then, not of religious but of cultural conditioning.

A swami I knew was once invited to debate with a Roman Catholic priest. The priest, a monsignor, spoke first; the swami was then expected to try to rebut his arguments. Instead, when the swami's turn came he threw the traditions of debate out the window. All he said was, "I have no quarrel with anything the distinguished monsignor has said to us. I would like only to pose him one question. Reverend Father, you call your church 'catholic.' Why do you place 'Roman' before that word?" Since catholic means universal, the swami was asking, Can universality be limited?

With a sweet smile he concluded his account to me of that episode. "The monsignor paused; he'd been expecting so much more! Then he replied, 'You are perfectly right!'"

ABOUT THE AUTHOR

J. Donald Walters is widely considered one of the foremost living experts on spiritual practice.

An American born in Rumania and educated in England and America, Walters was raised as an Episcopalian. He studied at Haverford College and Brown University. Later, through his discipleship with the great Indian sage, Paramhansa Yogananda, Walters became steeped in the wisdom of India. He was eventually initiated into an Indian monastic order and took the spiritual name, Swami Kriyananda.

Walters' books and music have sold over 2.5 million copies worldwide and are translated into twenty-four languages. He has written more than 70 books and composed over 400 pieces of music. He is also the founder of Ananda, a network of spiritual communities with branches all over the world.

INDEX

Resources
A Selection of Other Crystal Clarity Books

Autobiography of a Yogi
by Paramhansa Yogananda
trade paperback

One of the great spiritual classics of this century. This is a verbatim reprinting of the original, 1946, edition. Although subsequent reprintings, reflecting revisions made after the author's death in 1952, have sold over a million copies and have been translated into more than nineteen languages, the few thousand of the original have long since disappeared into the hands of collectors. Now the 1946 edition is again available, with all its inherent power, just as the great master of yoga first presented it.

The Path—
One Man's Quest on the Only Path There Is
by J. Donald Walters (Swami Kriyananda)
trade paperback and hardcover

The Path is the moving story of Kriyananda's years with Paramhansa Yogananda, author of the spiritual classic *Autobiography of a Yogi. The Path* completes Yogananda's life story and includes more than 400 never-before-published stories about Yogananda, India's emissary to the West and the first yoga master to spend the greater part of his life in America.

The Promise of Immortality
The True Teaching of the Bible and Bhagavad Gita
by J. Donald Walters
trade paperback and hardcover

Many books have been written about meditation. But this new book is something more. There is a power to this work that will give you an entirely new understanding of your potential—to expand your consciousness beyond anything you can now imagine, to the state of superconsciousness. This is not a book based on theory alone. The author writes with a simple, compelling authority, born of actual experience of the truths he presents. Glimpse into the heart and soul of someone who has spent nearly fifty years exploring the innermost reaches of human consciousness, and who has dedicated his life to helping others on the sacred journey to self-transcendence.

The Art and Science of Raja Yoga
by J. Donald Walters
hardcover

The Art and Science of Raja Yoga contains fourteen lessons in which the original yoga science emerges in all its glory—a proven system for realizing one's spiritual destiny. Absolutely unique, this is the most comprehensive course available on yoga and meditation today.

Over 450 pages of text and photos give the reader a complete and detailed presentation of yoga postures, yoga philosophy, affirmations, meditation instruction, and breathing techniques. Also included are suggestions for daily yoga routines, information of proper diet, recipes, and alternative healing techniques. The Art and Science of Raja Yoga comes with an audio CD that contains: a guided yoga postures sessions, a guided meditation, and an inspiring talk on how the reader can use these techniques to solve many of the problems of daily life.

Awaken to Superconsciousness
Meditation for Inner Peace, Intuitive Guidance, and Greater Awareness
by J. Donald Walters
trade paperback and hardcover

Many people have experienced moments of raised consciousness and enlightenment—or superconsciousness—but do not know how to purposely enter such an exalted state.

Superconsciousness is the hidden mechanism at work behind intuition, spiritual and physical healing, successful problem solving, and finding deep, lasting joy. In Awaken to Superconsciousness, J. Donald Walters shares his knowledge of the ancient yoga tradition, explains how to apply yoga principles to daily life, describes how to attain inner peace, and provides inspiring meditative exercises.

Hope For A Better World!
by J. Donald Walters
trade paperback

In these turbulent times when wars, religious strife, stifling bureaucracy and urban decay threaten our very humanity, reducing us to social statistics, a fresh approach to the creation of a truly viable society is desperately needed.

In this intellectual tour de force J. Donald Walters analyzes with deep insight the views expressed by many of the great thinkers in the West, including Plato, Copernicus, Machiavelli, Malthus, Adam Smith, Charles Darwin, Karl Marx, and Sigmund Freud. He studies their conceptions and misconceptions about the individual's relation to himself and to society. He shows where their influence has proved adverse, then offers deeply considered, fresh alternatives. Walters urges the reader to resist the hypnosis of "intellectual authority." Seek the key to a happy and fulfilled life, he says, in personal integrity.

Ananda Yoga for Higher Awareness
by J. Donald Walters (Swami Kriyananda)
trade paperback

This unique book teaches hatha yoga as it was originally intended: as a way to uplift your consciousness and aid your spiritual development. Kriyananda's inspiring affirmations and clearly written instructions show you how to attune yourself to the consciousness of the poses, so that each posture becomes a doorway to life-affirming attitudes, clarity of understanding, and an increasingly centered and uplifted awareness. Excellent for beginning and advanced students. the ancient science of yoga.

How to Meditate
by John (Jyotish) Novak
trade paperback

This handbook on meditation is an aid to calmness, clarity of mind, and, ultimately, inner communion with God. *How to Meditate* offers clear instruction on the basic preparation for meditation, how to quiet the mind and senses, and breathing techniques. Much loved by readers for its clarity, *How to Meditate* is written by a disciple of Yogananda who has been teaching and practicing meditation for 28 years. An indispensable aid to the sincere meditator, and a glimpse into the ancient science of yoga.

The Essence of Self-Realization
The Wisdom of Paramhansa Yogananda
Edited and compiled by Kriyananda (J. Donald Walters)
trade paperback, hardcover, and book-on-tape

Here are jewels from a master of yoga. Yogananda's words of wisdom have been lovingly preserved and recorded by his disciple, Kriyananda. The scope of this book is vast. It offers as complete an explanation of life's true purpose, and the way to achieve that purpose, as may be found anywhere.

Meditation for Starters
by J. Donald Walters
book, cassette/CD (narration and music, 60 minutes)

This book gives both beginning and long-time meditators proven techniques and powerful visualizations for achieving inner peace. Written with simplicity and clarity, it also provides a way for readers to look at meditation as a "starting point" for everything they do. The companion audio is available separately on both CD and cassette, or can be purchased as a set with the book.

Audio Selections from Clarity Sound & Light

Autobiography of a Yogi
by Paramhansa Yogananda, read by J. Donald Walters
(Swami Kriyananda)
audio book, selected chapters, 10 hours

Now, the original, unedited 1946 edition of *Autobiography of a Yogi* is available, with all its inherent power, in audio book form. Read by Swami Kriyananda, a close, direct disciple who lived and studied with Paramhansa Yogananda. Followers of many religious traditions have come to recognize *Autobiography of a Yogi* as a masterpiece of spiritual literature.

Kriyananda Chants Yogananda
by Swami Kriyananda (J. Donald Walters)
cassette/CD, vocal chant, approx. 74 minutes

Kriyananda sings the spiritualized chants of his guru in a unique and deeply inward way. Throughout the ages, chanting has been a means to achieve deeper meditation. This music is powerfully uplifting.

Mantra of Eternity—AUM
by Swami Kriyananda (J. Donald Walters)
cassette/CD, vocal chant, 71 minutes

AUM is the vibration that underlies and sustains all of creation. Kriyananda chants AUM to the soothing accompaniment of tamboura. Chanting of Sanskrit mantras in India is often used for healing, calming the mind, and reducing stress.

Mantra
by Swami Kriyananda (J. Donald Walters)
cassette/CD, vocal chant, 70 minutes

For millennia, the *Gayatri Mantra* and the *Mahamrityunjaya Mantra* have echoed down the banks of the holy river Ganges. Allow the beauty of these sacred sounds to penetrate every

atom of your being, gently lifting you to a state of pure awareness. Chanted in Sanskrit by Kriyananda to a rich tamboura
accompaniment. "Ancient, unhurried majesty."

NAPRA ReView

Himalayan Nights
by Agni and Lewis Howard
cassette/CD, instrumental, 60 minutes

Seamless sitar, tabla, and tamboura on one continuous track—
a soothing tapestry of sound. Use *Himalayan Nights* as a relax-
ing musical background for any daily activity. ". . . will gently
refresh and purify the spirit." *Music Design in Review*

Raga Omar Khayyam—Himalayan Nights 2
performed by Agni and Lewis Howard
composed by J. Donald Walters (Swami Kriyananda)
cassette/CD, instrumental, 63 minutes

Inspired by Persia's classic love poem, this timeless music will
take you on a wondrous carpet ride of sound. The rhythm of
the tabla weaving around the subtle sitar melody speaks to the
soul, calms the mind, and uplifts the heart.

**For a free Crystal Clarity catalog,
or to place an order, please call:
800-424-1055, or 530-478-7600
Or visit our website at: www.crystalclarity.com**